Governor LeRoy Collins
of Florida

Governor LeRoy Collins, 1955–1961. (*Courtesy, Sue Evans*)

Governor LeRoy Collins of Florida

Spokesman of the New South

Tom Wagy

THE UNIVERSITY OF ALABAMA PRESS

Publication of this book was made possible, in part,
by financial assistance from the
Andrew W. Mellon Foundation and
the American Council of Learned Societies.

Library of Congress Cataloging in Publication Data

Wagy, Thomas R., 1946–
  Governor LeRoy Collins of Florida.

  Bibliography: p.
  Includes index.
  1. Collins, LeRoy.   2. Florida—Governors—Biography.
3. Southern States—Politics and government—1951–
4. Southern States—Race relations.   I. Title.
F316.23.C65W34   1985   975.9'063'0924 [B] 84-164
ISBN 0-8173-0222-0

To Pat and Angela

Contents

Photographs

Acknowledgments

Although any errors in this book are my responsibility, I would like to thank several persons for their assistance. Dr. Virgil H. Conner suggested the topic. Jay B. Dobkin and Paul E. Camp, special collections librarians at the University of South Florida library, guided my research in the Collins Papers. Ed Tribble, archivist at the State Archives of Florida, aided me in my work with the correspondence of Governor Collins.

Several students have written theses and dissertations on Collins's career. I have used some of these extensively and have acknowledged my indebtedness in the Notes. Dr. Jean G. Hales, of Florida State University, Dr. Bess Beatty, of Shorter College, and Dr. Dorothy Dodd, retired Florida state librarian, read the manuscript and offered sound advice. Patty Paul and Mary McRory, librarians at the State Library of Florida, also furnished assistance. Nancy Rogers, of Rome, Georgia, typed the manuscript and contributed suggestions on matters of style. The editors of the *Florida Historical Quarterly*, the *Arkansas Historical Quarterly*, and *Apalachee* have permitted me to use material that appeared previously, in different form, in their journals.

All persons who were interviewed made important contributions to this undertaking. Especially beneficial were the comments of Allen Morris and Malcolm B. Johnson, who shared with me their extraordinary knowledge of Florida politics. Governors Millard F. Caldwell and Orval E. Faubus, of Florida and Arkansas, respectively, also provided valuable information. Governor LeRoy Collins cooperated with every request I made. Throughout many hours of conversation, he was honest, introspective, and informative. His influence on me goes well beyond the material in this book.

Dr. William Warren Rogers, of Florida State University, not only guided this work from its inception as a master's thesis but also patiently initiated a novice into the art of historical research.

More importantly, he communicated to a skeptical Yankee his love for the South—its land, its people, and its history.

Also offering support were my parents, Lawrence N. and Bernadine G. Wagy, and my daughter Angela. Finally, I am indebted to my wife, Pat, for the inspiration and aid she provided.

Governor LeRoy Collins
of Florida

Introduction

Thomas LeRoy Collins was a "New South" politician who served as governor of Florida from 1955 to 1961. Scholars have pointed to the recurrent emergence of a New South as a major theme in the history of the region since the Civil War. They discovered that—during the 1880s, the 1920s, and the years following the Second World War—the convergent goals of leading politicians, businessmen, and publicists resulted in demands for governmental and economic reform. For the New South movements of the 1880s and 1920s, initial research focused on personalities. State studies followed. C. Vann Woodward (*Origins of the New South*) and George Brown Tindall (*Emergence of the New South*) then wrote regional syntheses. No general study of such stature has yet been written on the period since the Second World War. Instead, research has concentrated on the era's leading political personalities and on regional themes, such as changing racial customs. The purpose of this book is to contribute to an understanding of the postwar era by evaluating the gubernatorial administration of one of the New South's most distinguished spokesmen.

LeRoy Collins's philosophical precepts derived from his legacy as a native of the South. Born a shopkeeper's son in a small, class-conscious town, he subscribed to the principles and goals defined by his family's status. Allegiance to the church, to public education, and to free enterprise circumscribed a lifelong philo-

1

sophical creed. Politically, "business progressivism" in the 1920s impressed on Collins the potential for cooperation between government and free enterprise in stimulating prosperity. Franklin D. Roosevelt's forceful response to the hard times of the 1930s reinforced Collins's faith in governmental leadership for reform. As governor, he sought institutional and economic changes that would allow his state to enter the mainstream of urban, industrial America.

While championing a new Florida, Collins encountered ideologies and institutions that remained from the state's agrarian heritage. Despite repeated appeals, he failed to gain adherents for a revised view of states' rights and responsibilities. Further, he could not loosen the agrarian-conservatives' tenacious hold on the malapportioned legislature. Most importantly, he, as well as other New South advocates, confronted anachronistic racial traditions. Twentieth-century nationalism, forged in part by the communications revolution, made the South's legalized system of racial discrimination unacceptable. The *Brown* decision in 1954 forced Collins to deal with the issue.

Collins responded to the crisis on the basis of his heritage. Initially, the legacy of paternalistic racial traditions prevailed. Although defending the Supreme Court's authority, he instituted a program to meet the *Brown* decision's minimum demands. Such "moderate" leadership led Florida through a difficult period and resulted in fewer disruptions than in other southern states. Yet, by 1960 Collins recognized tokenism's inadequacy. His perception of practical and moral necessities led him to call for fundamental change in the state's racial customs.

As Collins's outspoken advocacy of revised racial codes moved him beyond traditional boundaries, he forfeited his political career. During the 1960s Florida politics demanded racial conservatism and sapped the strength of the New South movement. In a race-oriented campaign, Collins lost a 1968 bid for the U.S. Senate. When integration waned as a political issue during the 1970s, New South advocates once more concentrated the state's attention on governmental action to foster economic change. Many of the ideals and goals associated with LeRoy Collins's administration again became a part of Florida politics.

1

The Early Years of
a Hominy Husker:
1909–1932

Thomas LeRoy Collins, who would serve as Florida's governor from 1955 to 1961, was born at Tallahassee in 1909. The South's environment and heritage profoundly influenced southerners born in that era. A unique history, economy, and society convinced them of their distinctiveness. The tumultuous era of reform that had been initiated by New South advocates in the 1880s and intensified by the agrarian rebels of the 1890s had quieted. Southerners looked back. Many could remember an antebellum society based on slavery and the bittersweet years of Civil War and Reconstruction. In memory's silent shadows, myths and legends assumed the validity of history. W. J. Cash wrote that, at the dawn of the century, the South had reached "a sort of temporary equilibrium upon its ancient foundation."[1]

In 1900 Florida was the least populous (528,542) southern state. Most of its residents lived in the northern tier of counties, near the Georgia and Alabama borders. Except for a few isolated settlements, peninsular Florida was a frontierlike wilderness. A majority of the state's citizens worked in agriculture, earning an estimated annual per capita income little more than half the national average. Whites were then enacting measures to insure their political, social, and economic superiority over blacks. During the late 1800s, a poll tax and a multiple-ballot law removed most black people from the voting rolls; during the first decade of the 1900s, Jim Crow laws imposed a segregated society on Florida.[2]

As in other southern states, the Democratic party controlled the political system. After the Republicans' demise in the 1870s, Democrats divided into liberal and conservative factions on the issue of railroad legislation. Although conservatives dominated, liberal leaders, such as U.S. Senator Wilkinson Call, who served from 1879 to 1897, influenced state government. The Populist movement exerted less strength in Florida than in neighboring southern states, though the Farmers' Alliance Convention of 1890, in Ocala, formulated the national program for populism. The prestige of Henry M. Flagler and other wealthy northerners who came to the state in the nineties undermined the agrarian movement. The era of relative prosperity that followed the depression of 1894, as well as the absorption of many Populist demands by the liberal wing of the Democratic party, also diminished the reformers' strength.[3]

The Populist threat, though, forced the state's Democrats to recognize the need for reform. The election of the moderate William S. Jennings, in the gubernatorial contest of 1900, indicated the increasing liberal power. The trend culminated in 1904, when Napoleon Bonaparte Broward, a longtime supporter of reform demands, won the governorship. He began the "Broward Era" of liberal, or "progressive," government, which continued under his successors Albert W. Gilchrist and Park Trammell.[4]

Florida politics focused on Tallahassee, the capital city. Its history was rooted in the "Old South" tradition. Pioneers had established the town in 1824, three years after the United States gained title to the territory. During the four decades prior to the Civil War, planters from Virginia, the Carolinas, and Georgia settled large tracts of land in the area. They brought with them a plantation system of agriculture that was founded on slavery and cotton cultivation—as well as an aristocratic way of life that gave them political, economic, and social preeminence. Tallahassee and Leon County became Florida's center for cotton production. By 1860 the county's population of 12,343 included nearly three times as many blacks as whites, reflecting the area's dependence on slave-based agriculture.[5]

The Civil War caused fundamental change. Human costs were high because many local men answered the Confederacy's call for military service, but the area escaped the physical devastation common in the Upper South. Following the conflict, planters no longer could command black workers and lacked cash to hire laborers. Yet, by 1880 immigration from war-ravaged regions had increased the county's population to 16,840 blacks and 2,822 whites. A tenant farming system evolved to unite land and labor. Although white elites retained much of the property, black and white tenants farmed forty-acre tracts, sharing crops with the owner. Some marginal landholders retained their small farms by scratching out an existence growing cotton. Leon County's worn soil continued to produce this commodity as a cash crop until the arrival of the Mexican boll weevil in 1916.[6]

At the turn of the twentieth century, life in Tallahassee moved at a leisurely pace. Its five thousand citizens enjoyed the quiet, secure existence assured a generation that had accepted the ordered universe of the nineteenth century.[7] Social life consisted of visits with relatives and neighbors; church functions; and, for the affluent, parties at mansions such as the Columns, on West Park Avenue. Many people enjoyed theatrical productions at Munro's Opera House, on the corner of Jefferson and Adams streets. A Seaboard Airline passenger train's arrival always attracted a crowd. Drivers of "hacks," two-seated buggies owned by local livery stables, met each train in hopes of obtaining a fare for the unhurried ride across town beneath the overhanging live oaks, draped in Spanish moss. The condition of the unpaved streets, which were often rutted despite continual leveling by mule-drawn graders, determined the hacks' pace.[8]

On Saturdays, the streets were filled early with wagons carrying families from throughout Leon County. Often the farmers' countenances and physiques showed the effects of malnutrition, malaria, hookworm, and pellagra. Despite economic and health problems, hundreds of rural folks managed to make the Saturday-morning journey to town. While the women shopped at Byrd's, Mickler's, and Randolph's grocery stores or J. W. Collins and Company general store, the men gathered in Rascal Yard, near the state capitol, to discuss crops and politics.[9] The Saturday influx of farmers, the traditional importance of the church, the languid life-style, and the class-conscious society made Tallahassee a typical southern community.

But there were stirrings. The ossific society was being subtly transformed. The technological revolution, for example, led to pervasive changes. In the 1880s a railroad linked the city to Jacksonville and Pensacola. In 1903 it also obtained a northern rail connection when the Seaboard Airline company opened a Tallahassee–Bainbridge, Georgia, route. Two years later, an independent telephone company joined the capital to Southern Bell in Monticello. The noise of automobiles began to disrupt the tranquillity of quiet evenings sitting on the front porch. The *Weekly True Democrat,* the local newspaper, recorded the invention of a torch fueled by acetylene that could produce "the most terrific heat known to science." The newspaper also reported that a train going sixty miles per hour had received a "wirelessgram" for the conductor. "And thus," the journal proclaimed, "another wonder of the century is recorded."[10]

On March 10, 1909, two months after the conclusion of Broward's gubernatorial term and two days before the *Weekly True Democrat* trumpeted the wonders of the age, Thomas LeRoy Collins was born in Tallahassee. His paternal, immigrant ancestor was Shadrick Collins, an Irishman who had settled in North Carolina about 1800. Shadrick's son, William Blunt Collins, a physician, moved his family to Texas. In 1837 William Blunt's son, William Carey, was born in Orange, Texas. By the age of twelve, William Carey had committed himself to the Methodist church, and eight years later the East Texas Conference accepted him into the ministry. For nearly two decades—less the time he spent as a chaplain in the Confederate Army—he preached the gospel to the hardy pioneers of frontier Texas. In 1863 he married a North Carolina woman, Smithie Anna Herring. Her Scotch-Irish ancestors had come to the colonies prior to the American Revolution.[11]

The Reverend William Carey Collins transferred his ministry to the Florida Conference in 1875. Beginning with a circuit of churches in Leon County, he served fifteen pastorates over the next quarter of a century. His youngest child, Marvin Herring Collins, was born in 1877 at Pisgah, a rustic Methodist parsonage located eight miles northeast of Tallahassee. Marvin described his father as an erudite scholar whom church officials sometimes called on to debate biblical issues. Moreover, when the Reverend Collins preached, one observer testified, "his face fairly shone with light from the upper world." On November 8, 1900, he died from heart failure while in the pulpit of the Salem Church, in Gadsden County. Family legend held that he had just called for the congregation to sing his favorite hymn, "Nearer, My God, to Thee," when he suffered the fatal attack.[12]

In 1902 Marvin Herring Collins married Mattie Albritton Brandon, a native of Brooks County, Georgia. She was related to the aristocratic Thomas Jones family, a pioneering clan that had settled in southwest Georgia in the 1820s. During the post-Civil War era, families that had formerly taken wealth for granted suffered from poverty. Yet, education remained important, and in 1896 Mattie Brandon attended Georgia Normal and Industrial College, at Milledgeville. After two years of study, she moved to Tallahassee and passed the state teachers' certification examination. Prior to her marriage, she taught for a year in south Florida's wilderness region.[13]

Marvin and Mattie Collins began their married life in Tampa, where he worked as a grocery clerk. Their eldest sons, Brandon and Marvin, were born there. Later, the family moved to Tallahassee, where between 1907 and 1913 four more children—Alice, Thomas LeRoy, Arthur, and Mattie Sue—were born. They lived for several years on Duval Street, just south of the governor's mansion. In 1915 they built a five-bedroom home on East Park Avenue, near the edge of town.[14]

Mattie Brandon Collins's life centered on the home, the family, and the Trinity Methodist Church. She also belonged to the Garden Club and spent one day per week as a hospital volunteer. She tended the garden and kept the pantry filled with jellies and preserves. Her busy schedule left little time for frivolity or even casual conversation with her children. Her influence was by example. She dreamed of Roy (Thomas LeRoy's lifelong nickname) following in his grandfather Collins's footsteps by becoming a Methodist minister. She often half-teasingly referred to Roy as her "bald-headed bishop" (despite his healthy head of hair) after a church leader with a receding hairline visited the Collins home.[15]

Marvin Collins and his brother operated J. W. Collins and Company, a general store located on Monroe Street. Although eminently respectable and reasonably successful, Marvin struggled to support his large family. His dedication to business left him little time to share activities with his children, but he did impress upon them the fundamentals of integrity and honesty. His favorite pastime was fishing. He used a cane pole to land the lunker bass from Lake Jackson, just north of Tallahassee. Occasionally, he allowed Roy to go along on fishing trips. For the youth, paddling his father's homemade wooden boat was not only exhilarating but also a great privilege.[16]

The Marvin Herring-Mattie Brandon Collins family (*left to right*): Mattie Sue, Marvin, Mattie Brandon, Alice, Marvin Herring, Brandon, Arthur, and LeRoy. (*Courtesy, Alice Collins Wadsworth*)

The Trinity Methodist Church was a prominent part of Marvin's life. A quiet, reserved man, he served for years on the Board of Stewards, though he always worked as a committee member rather than as a leader. Once a new minister, unaware of his reticence, asked him to lead the congregation in prayer at a Wednesday evening church service. After an awkward pause, Collins began a faltering attempt at the Lord's Prayer, but he could not complete the familiar recitation. Although the minister rescued him by continuing it, he never again attended Wednesday services.[17]

Marvin always felt his children should work. As a boy, Roy started his days with the sun. He milked the family's cows and herded them to the pasture that his father rented. He walked to the elementary school, located on the southwest corner of Duval and Tennessee streets. After school, he rushed home to retrieve the cattle and deliver milk to customers in the neighborhood. He earned "spending money" by selling boiled peanuts and newspapers on the steps of the state capitol.[18]

Collins also worked on a farm owned by his maternal grandfather, Thomas Jones Brandon, who lived near Miccosukee, Florida, twenty miles north of Tallahassee. The land provided a subsistence livelihood and a small cotton crop for cash. Brandon came from a family of professional men (his father was a physician), but he rejected business and educational opportunities to pursue the agricultural vocation he loved. Although he lacked fingers on one hand, he managed the physically demanding tasks of premechanized farming.

Roy spent many summers on the farm running barefoot along country roads, fishing with bent pins in the slow-moving streams, and wandering through the woods and fields with his grandfather. By example and by design, Brandon communicated to his grandson a love and respect for nature. Roy also helped with the farm labor. The exhaustion and pain of gathering corn in the searing August heat left a lifelong impression on him.[19]

Every Sunday, the youth attended church with his family. At five years of age, he suffered the greatest public humiliation of his life in a children's day speech. His presentation required that he say the lines:

Two little eyes to look to God,
Two little ears to hear His words,
Two little feet to walk in His way,
Two little lips to sing His praise.

As he spoke the words, he was to point at the various parts of his body. He delivered the speech correctly, but unfortunately the synchronization with his hands broke down. As he referred to seeing, he pointed to his ears; as he mentioned hearing, he pointed to his eyes; his lips walked. When he concluded by proclaiming his ability to sing with his feet, the congregation dissolved in laughter, and he exited in tears.[20]

Although painful, the experience did not affect Collins's loyalty to the church, and, on April 30, 1916, he joined the Trinity Methodist congregation.[21] Throughout his youth, he and his sister Alice attended Epworth League meetings on Sunday afternoons. He often served as president and as discussion leader. Roy and Alice were always close. Two years older, she assumed responsibility for watching over him. The pair decided they would be foreign missionaries. "He was going to preach and I was going to play the piano," Alice recalled.[22]

Family life emphasized church activities. Neither Marvin nor Mattie Collins danced, played cards, or drank alcoholic beverages. They required their children to respect the Sabbath. "We were allowed to play quiet games," Alice remembered, "but not to go swimming or fishing." Church socials and worship services filled many evenings. Each year, Roy sold tickets to the church picnic, a major community event. The Collinses joined other families on a chartered train to Lanark, a Gulf Coast resort near Carrabelle. They spent the day picnicking, swimming, playing games, and visiting.[23]

Roy took part in the active, outdoor life afforded by a small southern town. He hunted rabbits in the fields near his home and explored the woods and countryside. A good athlete, he was reputed to have the best curveball on the local baseball team. He also played halfback on the neighborhood football team, the Magnolia All Stars, but work and other activities precluded his participation in athletics at Leon High School.[24]

Collins assumed a leadership role during his high school years. He helped to conduct morning chapel services, where the entire student body sang hymns and student leaders discussed scripture lessons. He recalled that the devotions and the football team were the major forces in bringing the faculty, administrators, and students together. In the school's production of *Mail Order Brides*, he took the leading role. He served as the senior class president and played the cornet in the high school as well as the city band.[25]

During the land-boom years of the twenties, a local auctioneer often hired the Tallahassee band to attract a crowd for his sales of town lots. "I became just absolutely fascinated by this auctioneer," Collins recollected. "He talked about the glory of this state's future and how people could invest in real estate and make big profits." At one auction, repeated appeals for bids on a lot elicited only silence. Finally, to aid the auctioneer in stimulating bidding, Collins called out an offer of twenty dollars. Before anyone else could bid, the auctioneer turned to the band, pointed to him, and shouted, "Sold!" He then told of his pride in a young man who had faith in Florida's future.

Collins was astounded. He had not thought of becoming a property owner. The down payment wiped out his bank account, and for many weeks the receipts from his newspaper route became real estate payments. Each weekend, he rode his bicycle to the lot and strode around the property, hoping someone would order him off so he could reveal the identity of the owner. At last, he made the final payment and received the deed. He went to the lot, walked out to the middle, knelt down, dug deeply in the soil, held up two fistfuls of dirt, and proclaimed, "It's mine! It's mine!"[26]

In addition to his other activities, Collins worked Friday afternoons and Saturdays at Byrd's grocery store. His association during his teenage years with Mr. and Mrs. Thomas B. Byrd exerted a strong influence on his life. Thomas Byrd, less dedicated to long hours of work than Marvin Collins, took time to talk to Roy of books and public affairs. The Byrd family recognized his talents and encouraged him to read and to think of furthering his education. Waiting on customers fostered his ability to meet people. At that time, boys greeted each customer, wrote out his or her order, obtained the goods from the shelves, and calculated the bill. The service included polite conversation about friends and family. Moreover, the traveling salesmen who routinely came to the store impressed the provincial Collins with stories of the world beyond Leon County.[27]

The work at the grocery also brought the youth into closer

contact with Tallahassee's black citizens. His parents insisted on kindness toward them, but did not question segregation. His experiences at the grocery created in him an uneasiness with racial customs. He did not immediately discard the prevailing view—and reality—that blacks were a separate class of citizens. Instead, his racial perceptions slowly evolved. He would live with a nagging conscience for many years.[28]

In a poem published in 1971, Collins described the social stratification of his boyhood community. He pictured a town divided into four distinct classes. The "golddusters," who were descendants of distinguished families and "rich as Croesus," dominated economically, socially, and politically. The "hominy huskers," middle-class businessmen, professionals, and artisans, founded their faith on evangelical religion, free enterprise, and public education. The "depot greasers" were the "unwashed, unshaved and unschooled" whites. Blacks held the lowest status. They did the heavy and the dirty work for low pay, while "hominy huskers" (such as Collins) joked about their "funny ways of shanty living." From the perspective of half a century's growth and experience, however, Collins had come to recognize the "cruel yoke of deprivation and humiliation" that had separated blacks from white society.[29]

Tallahassee's stratified society, which assigned a "place" and duties to each of its citizens, provided a secure setting for the growth of a talented, attractive, white boy. When Collins graduated from high school in January 1927, the senior yearbook noted, "everything about him [is] handsome."[30] He was more than six feet tall, with a slender, athletic build and dark hair and eyes. His most distinctive feature was a ready smile, which displayed a slight gap between his front teeth. Furthermore, a friend pointed out, "Roy was always hip-deep in personality."[31] Both teachers and students considered him to be the smartest boy in the school, and many persons in the community encouraged him to set high goals for his life. Yet, he was uncertain of his future when he completed high school. His sister Alice, who was attending the University of Michigan, wrote him often and imbued him with her excitement for college. He decided that, to achieve his vaguely defined ambitions, he would need to further his education.[32]

Although Marvin Collins never finished high school, he believed in the value of advanced education. He could not afford to send all his children to college. He also thought they would appreciate their education more if they worked for it. He proposed a plan: he would match each dollar they earned for a college education. By the summer of 1928, Roy had saved five hundred dollars and decided that, aided by his father's matching funds, he could finance one year of college.[33]

Roy, his brother Marvin, and a close friend, John Y. Humphress, enrolled at Eastman's Business School, in Poughkeepsie, New York. During the twenties, this institution enjoyed a good reputation throughout the South, and many Tallahasseans studied there. The young men took a Seaboard Airline train to Jacksonville in September 1928, and from there made the three-day journey to New York on a Clyde Line ship. In Poughkeepsie they shared accommodations at Mrs. Johnson's rooming house, two blocks from the campus. Their courses included accounting, salesmanship, advertising, and penmanship. They studied, dated often, and played on the school's winless football team. Collins also performed in a theater production at Vassar College, the famed women's school located nearby. He and his brother spent two weekends in New York City. They went to shows at the Roxy and Paramount theaters, where they especially enjoyed the vaudeville acts that entertained between the movies. In the late autumn, the three youths experienced their first cold weather and snow.[34]

By December the boys were homesick and determined to be in Tallahassee for Christmas. They concentrated on their studies, and five days before the holiday completed the equivalent of six months of academic work. Marvin returned to Florida by train, but the two younger men drove home in "The Spirit of the South," a Model T Ford they had bought for fifteen dollars.[35]

Roy moved back to his parents' home and worked as a teller at the Exchange Bank. He continued his interest in the theater, playing lead roles in several local productions. Often, though, he conflicted with the directors because of his insistence on ad-libbing when he felt he could contribute new insights or humor to the script. He hunted and fished with his friends and, on Saturday nights, borrowed his father's Buick for dates with students at the

Florida State College for Women (FSCW).[36] He appeared to have found his niche in Tallahassee society.

Yet, Collins was still restless. Neither his job nor his prospects for the future satisfied him. Still uncertain of his ultimate goals, he knew his objectives would never be reached by remaining a bank teller. He applied to the United States Naval Academy in hopes of receiving a free education, but he was not accepted. Justice William Glenn Terrell, of the Florida Supreme Court, who had written one of his letters of recommendation for the academy, suggested he try law school. He could not afford three more years of college, Collins protested, and, besides, he was not very interested in the law. The degree would be of value in any profession he chose, Terrell pointed out, and recommended attendance at Cumberland University, in Lebanon, Tennessee, which offered a one-year law curriculum. The judge convinced the ambitious young man to give up the security of his position at the bank to continue his education.[37]

By the autumn of 1930, Collins had saved five hundred dollars and, aided by his father's matching funds, entered Cumberland University. It lacked the prestige of the University of Florida's law school, let alone the glamour and reputation of an Ivy League institution. Yet, its faculty was sound, and it offered the crucial advantage of saving time and money for a young man who lacked much of either. Collins took part in many campus activities, but also committed himself to his studies. He acquired an interest in the law and looked forward to establishing his own practice. In the spring of 1931, he received an LL.B. degree, and his classmates voted him the outstanding member of the student body. After graduation, he returned to Tallahassee and passed the state bar exam. He recalled, "I came home, boldly hung out my shingle— and proceeded to starve."[38]

During those early years of the Great Depression, Floridians viewed lawyers as a luxury rather than a necessity. Even established, reputable lawyers searched for clients. The hard times left little work for a young man starting in the profession. One job stood out in Collins's memory of his first years of practice. As a favor, a local car dealer offered him some work. The businessman maintained a file of records on blacks who had purchased cars on credit by accepting liens on their possessions. Because most of them did not own homes, their goods consisted primarily of plows, mules, and household articles. Some had defaulted on their payments, and the car dealer arranged with Collins to foreclose on their property. The first home he approached was little more than a shack. The junky car, which had been purchased two months before, sat in the front yard, all four tires flat. Children, unwashed and nearly naked, played in the dirt around the dilapidated house. Collins looked at the "thoroughly miserable situation" and reassessed his decision to take the job. He needed the money. If he did not complete the task, he knew the businessman would simply hire another lawyer. Yet, he could not deprive the family of the few necessities it needed to scratch out a living. He turned back, returned the records to the car dealer, and explained he could not carry out the assignment.[30]

Another early case provided the basis—with some exaggeration—for a story Collins used as a staple in speeches years later. A Seaboard Airline train ran over and killed a farmer's valuable cow. (The way to breed a thoroughbred cow, Floridians then maintained, was to cross a broken-down range animal with a Seaboard Airline train.) The farmer hired Collins to sue for damages. The company, tired of exorbitant settlements, decided to make a test of the farmer's claim and sent to Tallahassee a battery of experienced Richmond lawyers to plead its case.

On the day of the trial, several railroad lawyers huddled around one table, while Collins and the farmer sat alone. Collins was quite pleased with his opening statement to the jury. A company lawyer then delivered an eloquent presentation that left both Collins and his client agape. The farmer quietly asked Collins if he would have another opportunity to speak to the jury. The latter assured his client that he would make a closing statement. "Good," the farmer said, "you tell them that the railroad company is a great big rich corporation and can get plenty of good lawyers, and I am just a poor old farmer and can't afford much." Collins always concluded the story by claiming that he won a five-hundred-dollar settlement and shortly thereafter started representing the Seaboard Airline company.[40]

After practicing on his own for two years, Collins formed a

partnership with Guyte P. McCord, an older, well-established lawyer. They formed a competent, cordial team, but made little money. When the Florida Supreme Court appointed McCord to be clerk in 1935, he and Collins ended their association. The latter then formed a partnership with Charles Ausley, a friend and political associate. Later, Ausley's brother John joined them. Until Collins became governor, the partnership prospered as one of Tallahassee's most influential law firms.[41]

While Collins struggled to establish his law practice, he began dating Mary Call Darby, a local girl he had known most of his life. She had been born on September 11, 1911, in New York City, where her father, Thomas Arthur Darby, held a seat on the New York Stock Exchange. He had investments in gold and coal mining in Alaska and in citrus groves in Putnam County, Florida. During the years 1895–97 he represented that county in the Florida senate. While in Tallahassee, he courted Jane Kirkman Brevard, the granddaughter of Richard Keith Call, an early territorial governor of Florida and a cousin of Wilkinson Call, the nineteenth-century U.S. senator. In 1909 Thomas Darby and Jane Brevard married and went to New York, where they lived two years prior to the birth of their only child. Mrs. Darby moved back to Tallahassee in 1913 and never returned to New York on a permanent basis. In 1918 her husband died during a downturn in his business affairs and left no substantial inheritance.

Mary Call Darby grew up in her grandmother's home, on the southwest corner of Brevard and Monroe streets. She often walked through the stand of oak trees that separated her residence from The Grove, a mansion that had been built by Richard Keith Call in the 1820s. During Mary Call's youth it belonged to Mrs. Reinette Long Hunt, a granddaughter of the former governor. Financial difficulties forced her to remodel The Grove into a boardinghouse. The cheapening renovations saddened Mary Call and she dreamed of some day restoring the Call family home to its antebellum beauty.

Mary Call's youth was spent in the same sort of relaxed existence enjoyed by most Tallahasseans. On warm summer days, she swam and picnicked. She and her mother often walked downtown, the excursions sometimes taking several hours, when her mother stopped at virtually every house to visit. Each weekend, Mary Call went with her uncle to the family's plantation, located on Lake Jackson. She played with black children during her visits there, but, for the most part, she seldom thought of race. Like other white southerners, she just accepted the view that blacks were different.

Mary Call attended kindergarten through the eighth grade at "The Model School," on the FSCW campus. Sue Collins, Roy's younger sister, was a classmate and friend. Mary Call often visited the Collins home, but she paid little attention to Sue's brother. The three-year difference in age was unbreachable at that time. Mary Call attended Leon High School, and, in the autumn of 1929, entered FSCW.

In September 1931, during her junior year, Roy Collins surprised her with a telephone call asking for a date. She declined because of prior plans, but he nevertheless brought to her home a box of candy he had asked his sister to make. Mary Call accepted his next invitation. They dated often in the following months and by the spring of 1932 wanted to marry. Collins, though, considered the income from his law practice insufficient to support a family. He decided to run for Leon County prosecutor. If he won the office, he concluded that his financial resources would be adequate for marriage.[42] The decision gave added importance to the success or failure of his first political venture.

2

The Legislative Forum:
1932–1953

LeRoy Collins established a career in public service during the period 1932–53, when Florida experienced fundamental economic and demographic changes. Yet, traditional social and governmental institutions held firm. Conflicts had to be resolved within the state's distinctive political environment. As a result of structural factors, such as the one-party system, each politician depended on his own skills to build a personal constituency. Collins's forum for leadership was the Florida legislature, where he served three terms in the house of representatives and six terms in the senate. Because citizens elected legislators by county districts, he relied on support from Tallahassee and Leon County.

By 1932, when Collins announced his candidacy for county prosecutor, Tallahassee had changed considerably since his boyhood. During the 1920s its population had nearly doubled.[1] More cars moved on more paved streets. Radio altered the leisure habits of the residents as they now spent many hours listening to entertainment, news, and sports. In 1928, for the first time, they followed a presidential campaign on radio. Motion pictures at the Daffin (later the State) and Ritz theaters brought Hollywood's depiction of the American ethos to the city.[2] The "wonders of the century" continued their transformation of southern life.

While changing, Tallahassee retained a small-town atmosphere. As always, life centered on the family and the church. On Saturdays, the streets were filled with wagons, despite the continual economic decline of small farmers. Health care had improved little: pellagra, typhoid, malaria, and ringworm continued to plague Floridians. Monroe Street still ended at the intersection with Gaines Street. Beyond that point was a sheer drop to a swamp covered with wild orchids.[3]

Although Tallahassee and much of the rural South clung to social institutions that had been forged in an earlier era, national influences altered the political environment. "Boosterism" dominated the country in the twenties. Because of the emphasis on business and industry, many southerners joined in the worship of money and economic growth. Babbitts could easily be found in Dixie.[4] The term "Atlanta Spirit" applied to a southern middle class that sought industrialization, urbanization, and northern capital to build a "New South." In 1924 one observer noted, "from the Potomac to Mobile Bay, from Hatteras to the Rio Grande there is no God but Advertising, and Atlanta is his prophet."[5]

The Atlanta Spirit appalled a minority of southerners, who condemned the evils of industrialism and urban society. The twelve southerners who wrote the book *I'll Take My Stand* in 1930 expressed this viewpoint. They romanticized the South's agrarian heritage and defended traditional values. This idealized vision of the region's economic, political, and social past had limited historical validity. Nevertheless, it attracted those who feared shifts in the South's foundations.[6]

Racial antagonism complicated the political environment. As rapid technological·and sociological alterations threatened traditional customs, many southerners opposed advances by blacks and resorted to violent repression to maintain their "precarious mastery." The schizophrenic struggle to be both progressive Americans and white supremacists muddled southern political ideology during the twenties and thirties.[7]

Florida reflected the conflicting trends in southern politics. In his distinguished history of the era, George Brown Tindall termed the prevailing southern ideology of the 1920s "business progressivism." The "neo-whiggish" leaders wanted good schools, road building, and governmental reform, he wrote, but "they stormed no citadels of entrenched 'privilege.' "[8] After Governor Broward's administration, the ideology of business progressivism characterized the leadership of Florida's Democratic party. Most of them professed reform goals while cooperating with corporations to stimulate the state's economy.

U.S. Senator Duncan U. Fletcher, who served from 1909 until his death in 1936, exemplified the business progressives. He advocated anticorporation reforms in the 1890s, in part to undermine the appeal of the more radical Populist platform. He later became a railroad lawyer and an investor in corporate enterprises. Yet, he still sought reform to insure "economic opportunity and social mobility."[9] After his death, a contemporary described him as "a man whose feet were on the ground, and yet whose mind penetrated into the ethereal realms of idealism."[10] The theme of "practical idealism" predominated for the next half-century in Florida politics. Men who contended that reform in government, education, and public services facilitated the growth of business and prosperity became the statewide leaders in the Democratic party.

Between 1916 and 1928 opponents mounted an assault on the dominion of the business progressives. Sidney J. Catts, a native of Dallas County, Alabama, led the challenge. In 1911 he had moved to Walton County, Florida, where he served as a Baptist minister. He soon became an itinerant insurance salesman. During his travels throughout the Panhandle, he gained an appreciation for the indignation of the "crackers" over business control of the government. He became the spokesman for their cause. Closed off from the normal avenues to party leadership, he used the emotional issue of anti-Catholicism to win the governorship in 1916. Once in office, the religious question became secondary. Instead, Catts emphasized antibusiness measures, such as tax reform and labor laws. His program reflected the anticorporate, traditionalist principles of agrarian north Florida. "In a sense, Catts became a surrogate for populism come to Florida two decades late," his biographer contended. The business progressives blocked Catts's reforms by accentuating his buffoonery, bigotry, and radicalism to deflect attention from the merits of his platform.[11]

During the early 1920s, booming prosperity came to the state as tourism and manufacturing joined agriculture as major components of the economy. Although the good times aided his opponents, Catts carried on his challenge to the business progressives. He ran in vain for the U.S. Senate in 1920 against Fletcher and for the governorship in 1924 against John W. Martin. The state's farmers did not share in the affluence of the decade. The real estate collapse and great hurricane of 1926 brought economic distress to other Floridians. Aided by the state's financial plight, Catts led one final crusade against business dominance. In 1928 Doyle E. Carlton, of Hardee County, narrowly defeated him for the governorship.[12]

Even though the business progressives suppressed the agrarians' political challenge, the traditionalists maintained their determination to blunt the effects of modernization. In 1920 a University of Florida professor who was deemed to be too "radical" was fired. Eight years later, FSCW came under attack for circulating "obscene books" and teaching immorality. The Ku Klux Klan flourished in Florida as a refuge for people who found their fundamental social and religious customs menaced. Herbert Hoover's 1928 victory in the Florida presidential balloting—the first time a Republican had won the state since 1876—reflected the fears as much as the faith of the citizens. Many of them voted not for Hoover as an agent of business progressivism, but against Alfred E. Smith, who, as a Roman Catholic and a "wet" on the prohibition issue, threatened their traditional values.[13] Nor did the state escape the tide of racial violence that swept the South during the twenties and thirties. The 1934 lynching of Claude Neal in Marianna, a Panhandle community seventy miles west of Tallahassee, was so grotesque that George Brown Tindall described the man's death as a "carnival of sadism."[14]

Manifestations of rural disaffection with rapid urbanization, economic change, and transformation of social mores remained a part of the environment. The traditionalists held racial segregation, their most treasured social heritage, sacrosanct. Control of the malapportioned legislature gave the agrarians an influential position in state government. During the next four decades, they would use this status to impede reform.

After the defeat of the Catts movement and the emergence of a consensus on the values of business progressivism, ideology exercised little force in statewide politics. Instead, the Democratic party became what V. O. Key, Jr. termed as "an incredibly complex mélange of amorphous factions." Transitory coalitions based on personalities, single issues, and financial self-interest characterized the system. Geographical dispersion, a diversified economy, and a heterogenous population contributed to weak statewide leadership. "Political atomization" led to a party code of "every man for himself." The open primary allowed anyone who could pay the filing fee to become a gubernatorial candidate. Temporary organizations based on expediency resulted in "political pulverization," as in 1936, when fourteen candidates competed in the gubernatorial primary. Writing in the 1940s, Key concluded, "Florida is not only unbossed, it is also unled. Anything can happen in elections, and does."[15]

Once elected, the governor possessed little power to manage the government. The cabinet, in which he was one of seven members, functioned as a collective executive branch. The governor chaired meetings, but he held no special status. The cabinet performed vital executive duties, such as administering state institutions and determining the budget. Other cabinet officers, unlike the governor, could be elected to consecutive terms. Because they often held their posts for extended periods, they sometimes considered the governor to be a "junior partner" in the executive branch. Commissioner of Agriculture Nathan Mayo, for example, served from 1923 to 1960 in nine different administrations. Such leaders built their own constituency in the bureaucracy, the legislature, and the electorate. As a result, the public often held the governor responsible for executive actions that were, in fact, beyond his control.[16]

The governor, furthermore, could not impose his program on the legislature. He depended on urban voters for election because he had to canvass statewide. On the other hand, malapportionment gave rural Floridians overrepresentation in legislative districts. The governor could use only patronage, persuasion, and the veto to influence the lawmakers. At any rate, the legislature met for just sixty days every two years, and the cabinet carried out much of the daily administrative detail.[17] Thus, the government functioned without strong gubernatorial control over the cabinet, the bureaucracy, or the legislature.

When LeRoy Collins decided to enter Florida's turbulent political scene in 1932, he faced formidable opposition. The "courthouse crowd" treated his challenge of powerful county prosecutor Clyde W. Atkinson as a joke. Collins, though, campaigned extensively throughout Leon County. Mary Call worked nearly as hard, but she refused to deliver speeches. Although she was good at campaigning on a personal level, she was too reserved to speak before a crowd. Collins painted a sign on his car proclaiming the merits of his candidacy. When he and Mary Call went on a date, he insisted on parking the car in a prominent place so that the sign would be read.[18]

Democrats voted on June 7, 1932. That evening, city officials blocked off Adams Street and set up bleachers in front of the *Daily Democrat* building. A large crowd gathered to hear Claude Pepper, later U.S. senator and congressman, report the election returns over a loudspeaker mounted in a window of the building. Collins and Mary Call joined the throng and listened dejectedly as the final tally showed Atkinson to be the victor by 268 votes. Despite the defeat, Collins realized his strong showing had made him well known in the county. The increased recognition would aid his law practice and any future venture into politics.[19]

Mary Call had never concurred with Collins's practical, but unromantic, assertion that their marriage depended on an electoral victory. After the election, he, too, entertained second thoughts. They married three weeks later, on June 29, 1932. Collins's law practice remained small, which limited his new bride to a five-dollar-per-week household budget. He supplemented his income with a Works Progress Administration job indexing compilations of laws. For entertainment, the Collinses exchanged visits with other couples and often picnicked at Saint Teresa Beach. An occasional night out for a movie or a play highlighted their social life. Collins continued to take part in campus productions at FSCW. Mary Call had enjoyed seeing her handsome boyfriend on stage, but, after their marriage, she became increasingly less thrilled by the long hours her husband spent rehearsing plays on the all-girl campus.

Nevertheless, he retained his love for the glamour and excitement associated with the theater.[20]

During the early years of their marriage, the Collinses rented the upstairs of their home to a young married couple. The woman claimed mystical powers through numerology. Once she tearfully confronted Collins with a dire prediction. She said her calculations proved that the name Thomas LeRoy Collins augured certain disaster. She pleaded with him to change it. "I didn't believe what she said was true, but I saw no need to take chances," he recalled. "Nobody ever calls me Thomas," he told her. "Would you check with your sources and see what will happen if I just use LeRoy Collins?" If he did not employ the name Thomas, she subsequently informed him, then he was destined for success. Thereafter, he signed all personal and legal documents "LeRoy Collins."[21]

Collins continued to be active in civic affairs. He helped to found the Junior Chamber of Commerce and the Leon County Young Democrats to stimulate new local leadership. He and some friends also formed the Catfish Club, a group of eleven young Tallahasseans who wanted to prod their city into moving in a progressive direction. The club met every week or so in a member's home to discuss problems confronting the city, state, and nation. President Franklin D. Roosevelt was the idol of the members and they enthusiastically spoke up for New Deal reforms. Their pressure for improved community health and welfare services, however, did not impress the city's conservative leaders.[22]

Collins had enjoyed the 1932 campaign and remained an ambitious young man. He looked to a seat in the state legislature as an opportunity for service and as a boon for his law career. Because he had not attended the University of Florida Law School, he had made few friends in the state's legal profession. He believed a term in the legislature would allow him to expand his contacts. Besides, he did not want to quit politics a loser. In 1934 he announced his candidacy for state representative from Leon County.[23]

Financial necessity forced Collins to run a "homemade type" campaign. He and his wife traveled to meetings across the county, and friends helped paint signs for cars and billboards. George I. Martin, the incumbent representative, was confident of victory. He anticipated that, because four candidates were in the race,

Roy and Mary Call Collins on their wedding day, June 29, 1932. (*Courtesy, Roy and Mary Call Collins*)

none would receive a majority in the first primary. A runoff election between the two garnering the highest number of votes seemed certain. Pursuing such logic, Martin held back much of his campaign money for the second election. In the June 5 primary, Collins displayed remarkable voter support. The *Daily Democrat* declared, "The primary election was signalized by the sensational race of LeRoy Collins, young Tallahassee attorney, who swept into office with almost three times the votes of his opponents to lead the entire county ticket." When he took the oath of office on April 2, 1935, he was twenty-six years old, the second youngest legislator in the state.[24]

During his first legislative session, Collins demonstrated no clear philosophical stance. Resisting measures that he considered morally wrong, he voted against "quickie" divorces and the sale of liquor by the drink. He opposed in vain a bill to legalize slot machines, which Governor David Sholtz had proposed to pay for educational reform. On the other hand, Collins indicated his progressive inclinations by sponsoring a bill that gave equal property rights to women.[25]

In 1936 Collins again won the Democratic nomination in the first primary. He ran under the slogan "One Good Term Deserves Another," and, for the first time, used the radio for an election-eve speech.[26] The 1937 legislature vindicated his position by repealing the slot machine bill. Men, desperate for a stake to escape from depression poverty, had gambled their meager resources in the ubiquitous machines, which appeared in restaurants, pool halls, bars, and special parlors. A mania for gambling gripped many Floridians, and large numbers of families sank further into destitution. After two years, an overwhelming majority of voters demanded repeal of the law.[27]

Although Collins opposed Sholtz's innovative financing plan, he provided leadership in educational reform throughout his career. He cosponsored a 1937 bill for a statewide teacher retirement system. After his unopposed reelection in 1938, he served as chairman of the House Education Committee in the next legislative session. He supported measures to modernize the school system and to protect teachers from political interference.[28] After three terms in the house of representatives, he was a respected, effective legislator whose record of voter support in his home district was outstanding.

During legislative sessions, the Collinses led busy lives. In addition to his official duties, he maintained an expanding law practice. His wife attended the normal round of teas and receptions. She also put on her white gloves, took her calling cards, and visited each of the legislators' wives. In addition, she entertained each member of the legislature at either a breakfast meeting or a dinner party. The pace of the Collinses' lives slowed when the biennial sessions ended. They visited friends, attended football games, and spent some time each summer at their Saint Teresa beach house. They had three children during the first decade of their marriage: Thomas LeRoy Collins, Jr., in 1934, Jane Brevard Collins in 1936, and Mary Call Collins in 1940.[29]

A lifelong dream of Mrs. Collins came true when she and her husband purchased The Grove in 1941. During Reinette Long Hunt's lengthy struggle to keep it in the Call family, it had fallen into disrepair and the grounds had become a virtual jungle. The new owners first painted over the sign on the front gate advertising "Hotel Accommodations." They removed the partitions Mrs. Hunt had added and began clearing the dense foliage that surrounded the home. For several Saturdays, the entire family went to the municipal junkyard, where they reclaimed the bricks that had once paved Monroe Street. They used them to build a large patio on the east side of The Grove.[30] During the same year the family changed residences, Collins moved from the house to the senate chamber at the state capitol.

In January 1940 Senator William C. ("Homestead Bill") Hodges, of Leon County, died after an eighteen-year political career. His sponsorship of the Homestead Exemption Bill, which reduced taxes for the state's home owners, and his aid to many Tallahasseans during the depression had made him virtually invincible in local politics. He had also entertained often at Goodwood, his plantation home outside the city. These factors made the Hodges name a formidable political asset in the county.[31]

When Hodges died, Collins was forced to make an important decision. He had narrowly lost a bid to become Speaker of the house of representatives in the 1940 session. If he remained in that body, he seemed assured of being elected to the speakership in the next session. However, lured by the greater status and influence of the senate, he chose to run for the vacated senate seat and supported the successful candidacy of his close friend, Daniel T. McCarty of Fort Pierce, for Speaker of the house. Collins appeared certain of victory until Margaret W. Hodges, the senator's widow, decided to contest the election. Combining genuine grief with political savvy, she appealed to the voters' sympathies by appearing at rallies in a mourning veil and using a handkerchief to dab tears from her eyes. She also began calling in the political debts owed her husband and ran under the slogan "Homesteads Are Safer With Hodges."[32]

Had the election been held early in the year, Mrs. Hodges probably would have won. But, as the campaign progressed, voter sympathy for her decreased, and her lack of qualifications became more evident. One anecdote, in particular, helped the Collins campaign. When confronted by a Hodges supporter, a local auto mechanic asked what the man would do if his surgeon died halfway through an operation. Would he request the surgeon's wife to complete the operation? The mechanic asserted that the Hodges adherents should apply the same criteria to choosing their state senator. The story spread quickly and made sense to many voters. Collins refused to attack Mrs. Hodges, and suggestions that he was being unchivalrous by continuing the campaign angered him. His tactics paid off in a victory of nearly two thousand votes.[33]

The senate leadership appointed Collins as chairman of the Education Committee, where he continued his support for bills he had first introduced in the house. The measures included a teacher retirement fund, a state system of public instruction, and education for the physically handicapped. Also urging a ban on secret societies in high schools, he asserted that such social organizations "foster a clannish, undemocratic spirit in the public schools." Further, he proposed laws to improve medical care for expectant mothers, for newborn babies, and for blind people. He sponsored bills imposing a levy on intangible personal property and a state corporation tax. He also continued his work to gain equal property rights for women.[34]

During the 1943 session, Collins was chairman of the Finance and Taxation Committee. Welfare and reform retained their importance to him. He fought in vain to make the state's adoption system more professional by placing adoptive children under the guardianship of the State Welfare Board; advocated increased aid to the indigent; and condemned an appropriation for elderly Floridians as "an idle gesture to fool the old people." He also supported a bill extending unemployment compensation benefits to women who needed to leave their jobs because of pregnancy and favored measures allowing women to serve on juries and giving them equal property and legal rights.[35]

Although an influential senator, Collins did not belong to the formal leadership group. His colleagues respected his character and ability, but north Florida agrarian interests controlled the legislative process. Because of malapportionment, the small counties were heavily overrepresented in the senate and their representatives could frustrate efforts to revise the state's antiquated governmental system. Collins's progressive record on education, taxation, welfare, and constitutional reform was anathema to these conservatives.[36]

In Florida politics, no marked distinction existed between liberals and conservatives. The term "conservative" was used to describe those who were concerned with maintaining rural control of the legislature and traditional social values. Conservatives also opposed state interference in county affairs, where local political and economic elites exercised power. Normally, local issues concerned liberals less. They emphasized the principles of business progressivism: governmental reform and economic development. Most gubernatorial candidates assumed a moderate-to-liberal stance because they were forced to appeal to major business interests and to urban voters in statewide campaigns.[37]

Commentators consistently linked Collins with the liberal faction, yet he retained solid support in his north Florida district. The presence of two state colleges and the governmental bureaucracy contributed to a more progressive constituency than in other Panhandle counties. More importantly, though, personality, ability, and hard work explained Collins's electoral success. Regardless of his achievements, by the autumn of 1943 he had lost his enthusiasm for politics. Perhaps the frustrations inherent in the state's legislative system contributed to his ennui. He wrote to a friend:

> I have definitely agreed that I will not run for anything, and in fact I have lost what little ambition I used to have to some day run for a state-wide office. I am thoroughly convinced that the happiness, peace and security of my family will be much better advanced if I will follow a business career rather than a political one.[38]

The Second World War interrupted Collins's speculations on his future. He volunteered for naval service in 1943, but was rejected because of his age. The following year, however, the navy accepted his application when it formed a special team of government experts to prepare for the occupation of Japanese-held territory. After attending Officer Indoctrination School at Hollywood, Florida, the men moved to Princeton University, where they studied the history, economy, and society of Taiwan. They were then transferred to Monterey, California, for language study. Mrs. Collins and the family drove to California to be with Collins before he went overseas. The government decided, though, to use the Philippines, rather than Taiwan, as its base for operations against Japan and disbanded the group. The navy stationed Collins in Seattle, Washington, where he spent the remainder of the war prosecuting courts-martial. He completed his naval service in 1946, without ever having been on board a ship.[39]

After two years of disruption, the Collinses were anxious to renew the slower-paced routine of life in Tallahassee. On their return, they found The Grove in serious disrepair, and they devoted much time and money during the next few years to refurbishing it. Their amusements remained simple. They and several friends formed a play-reading group called the Possum Club. The members took turns hosting the club in their homes and choosing the plays to read. Collins taught Sunday school class at the Trinity Methodist Church and sometimes led a nondenominational service held in a local theater. In 1946 he and his son joined St. John's Episcopal Church, his wife's congregation. On Sunday afternoons all of Marvin and Mattie Collins's children and their families usually gathered at the family home on Park Avenue. In 1950 Sarah Darby, the Roy Collinses' fourth child, was born.[40]

The wartime service away from the daily frustrations of Florida politics apparently restored Collins's interest in public life. While in Seattle, he had qualified to run for the senate seat he had given up and which Charles Ausley, his law partner, had held during his absence. Although the voters had viewed him as a stand-in for Collins, he seemed reluctant to relinquish the post. Collins forced him to withdraw by declaring his own candidacy. Ausley recognized the futility of challenging in the primary, and Collins was elected without opposition. Despite this disagreement, the two men continued to be business partners and friends.[41]

When he returned to legislative duties in 1947, Collins again served as chairman of the Education Committee. He figured prominently in the establishment of the "minimum foundation" program. This idea resulted from a reform study that had been initiated during the final months of Governor Spessard Holland's term and continued during the Millard Caldwell administration. The panel designed a plan that required the state to insure a minimum level of financial aid for each student. Reformers wanted to equalize educational support between the wealthy and poor counties and among schools within each county.[42]

The Minimum Foundation Bill was a remarkable effort to modernize Florida's educational system. For the first time, the state would contribute to funding school construction and to paying operating expenses. Further, the bill mandated nine-month terms, called for consolidation of school systems within each county, required each superintendent to possess a college degree, and geared teachers' salaries to their educational attainments.[43]

The minimum foundation proposal elicited strong opposition. Antagonists disliked the measure because it necessitated increased taxes. They also believed that the formula to measure the relative worth of the counties was too complex. Moreover, they resisted state control over appropriations for the counties. Some teachers and school superintendents disliked the bill because of the more demanding educational requirements. During the debate on the issue, thirty of the thirty-eight senators signed a telegram to the Florida Education Association convention, in Tampa, that called for an alliance in opposition to the minimum foundation plan. In return, the senators promised the teachers a pay raise regardless of educational status. Some of the educators agreed to oppose the bill.[44]

Collins led the battle in the senate for the Minimum Foundation Bill. He provided crucial support for Governor Caldwell, who pressed strongly for the measure. During the next decade, personal, political, and philosophical differences would create a broad schism between the two men. In 1947, though, the fate of the Minimum Foundation Bill depended on their cooperation. Collins steered the bill through the parliamentary maze and defended it in often-bitter debate. Meanwhile, Caldwell threatened to veto any education bill that did not include the entire minimum foundation plan. The dissenting teachers realized they needed to accept the educational requirements or they would receive no pay raise. When these teachers withdrew their opposition, the coalition against the bill crumbled. The minimum foundation program ultimately passed the senate with only one dissenting vote. However, the conflict further alienated Collins from the conservative leadership in the senate.[45]

Collins added to his progressive credentials during later senate terms. As chairman of the Appropriations Committee in 1949, he advocated to no avail the imposition of personal and corporate income taxes to lessen the sales-tax burden. Two years later, he urged the state to accept responsibility for automobile safety. "We must do something to stop the slaughter on the highways," he argued. In 1953 he sponsored a plan for free county libraries. That same year, he also proposed the establishment of a committee to study governmental reorganization. He supported Governor Fuller Warren's 1951 bill aimed at the Ku Klux Klan, which forbade the wearing of masks in public demonstrations. During those years, though, race seldom emerged as a legislative issue. No debate ever forced Collins to adopt a position that might have demonstrated an ideological gulf between himself and his constituents on the race question.[46]

Throughout these years, Collins worked closely with Speaker McCarty to foster progressive legislation. The press dubbed the two men the "White Knights" and recognized them as leaders in the Democratic party. In 1947 the capital press correspondents selected Collins as the "most valuable senator." Six years later, his colleagues voted him the "most valuable member" and chose him as the "most effective in debate."[47]

In 1952 McCarty was elected as governor. He pledged to end patronage abuses and to fill government offices on a merit basis. The day after his inauguration, he fired four hundred Road Department employees and halted six million dollars' worth of highway projects. Extensive reorganization of governmental departments followed.[48] Moreover, a journalist noted, "McCarty offered the most comprehensive program for governmental reform that any chief executive has proposed in Florida history."[49] The cutbacks, merit appointments, and reform plans angered many legislators. McCarty's adherents, though, looked forward to an era of progressive government.[50]

Unfortunately, the governor suffered a heart attack on February 25, 1953, just a month after his inauguration, and could not provide effective leadership during the legislative session. On September 28 he died at the age of forty-one, his weakened body unable to withstand a slight case of pneumonia. In accordance with the Florida constitution, the president of the senate, Charley Eugene Johns, became the acting governor.[51]

Johns was a conservative Democrat from the northeast Florida community of Starke. He had supported McCarty in 1952, but coolness had arisen between him and the administration over senatorial prerogatives in dispensing patronage. When Johns became acting governor, he asked for the resignation of the Road Board, the Turnpike Commission, and the Racing Commission. These positions had, in the past, gone to political associates. Johns wanted to use the patronage to build a political organization for the special election that was to be held in 1954. When the McCarty appointees refused to resign, Johns suspended them, which created a furor throughout the state.[52]

Johns's action shocked the McCarty faction. "It is heart-breaking to see dissipated before your eyes gains a friend gave his life to achieve," Collins said. "We must not fool ourselves. The cause of good government has suffered a setback." The McCarty group began planning for the 1954 campaign. The former governor's younger brother, John McCarty, claimed that he deserved the support of the progressive forces. Collins disagreed. He argued that his legislative record and his close association with Governor McCarty made him the logical choice for the liberals. As in the senatorial campaign of 1946, Collins forced his potential adversary to withdraw or challenge him in the primary. McCarty decided to withdraw. On December 13, 1953, Collins announced his candidacy for the governorship.[53]

3

Qualities of the Spirit:

The Election of 1954 and
a Philosophy of Government

Florida Democrats chose their candidate for governor on May 25, 1954. During the evening of that hot and humid election day, Tallahasseans began to gather at the Collins headquarters, located in the first block of East Park Avenue. The campaign workers arrived earliest, climbing the dark staircase to the large, barnlike room. They had spent hundreds of hours that spring passing out campaign buttons, blowing up balloons, and organizing fish fries. On election day, they had gotten out early to drive people to the polls and to make last-minute phone calls to assure themselves that every Collins adherent voted. The campaign workers greeted one another with quiet handshakes and optimistic forecasts about the election results, but their words belied the underlying tenseness: the fear that, for all their work, their candidate would lose.

The committed were soon joined by the curious. A long line—including Collins's old friends, community leaders, and casual strangers attracted by the excitement—began to form as Tallahasseans queued up on Park Avenue to enter the headquarters. Ten minutes after the polls closed at seven o'clock, the candidate and his family arrived to await the decision with their supporters. During the evening, more and more people came, jamming the room and the staircase. They milled about talking excitedly and struggling to catch a breath of fresh air. Finally, officials posted guards at the door to tell the disappointed mass spilling over into

Park Avenue that no more room was available. Those left outside complained and cajoled to no avail and then gathered into groups while waiting to have the results relayed to them.[1]

The first returns would come from the southern counties that used voting machines. The Collins advocates realized these initial tallies would determine the outcome of the election. Their candidate needed large pluralities in the south to offset Johns's northern strength.[2] The candidate, the workers, and the crowd awaited the totals that they hoped would reward six months of campaigning.

The candidacy of Brailey Odham, a former state senator from Sanford, had thwarted Collins's goal of uniting the progressive wing of the Democratic party behind his campaign. Odham had run a strong race against Dan McCarty in the 1952 election, and he enjoyed well-organized support throughout the state. The division of the liberal faction and the acting governor's control of the various state agencies led some observers to suggest that Johns might poll a majority of the votes in the first primary, which would make a runoff election unnecessary. But on May 4 Florida Democrats gave the former railroad conductor from Starke only a 33,000-vote lead over Collins, the runner-up. Odham received 187,000 votes. Both Collins and Johns recognized that the candidate who attracted Odham's supporters would prevail in the runoff election. Johns claimed he would win 75 percent of these votes, even though Odham offered his support to Collins.[3]

In the 1954 gubernatorial primary, Floridians faced a distinct choice of candidates and philosophies. McCarty's death had placed a representative of the Democratic party's conservative wing in the governorship. Johns's personal philosophy paralleled that of the agrarians, who for three decades had called on southerners to maintain their traditions against the encroachment of northern, industrial influences. Collins led the business progressive faction in the Democratic party, which urged Floridians to build a new state based firmly on an urban, industrial economy. Because the election centered on candidates whose philosophies and constituencies were clearly defined, it engendered both personal and political hostility between the candidates and their backers.[4]

Johns styled himself the "poor man's candidate" and described Collins as a "big utility lawyer who lives in a $200,000 colonial mansion." The latter, whose firm represented such clients as Southern Bell Telephone Company and Hialeah Race Track, had anticipated criticism as the corporations' candidate. He contended, "My firm has represented 'big business' because it is logical for these concerns to want top grade attorneys. We also represent the Boy Scouts, widows and many small business firms. Had I been crooked in any way, my people would not have kept reelecting me"[5] The issue illustrated the conflicting viewpoints of the agrarians and the business progressives. To Johns's constituents, the title "corporation lawyer" identified a lackey of the enemy. To Collins's proponents, corporations deserved respect and support as the fundamental building blocks for a prosperous state.

Collins countered by charging Johns with running a "government by crony" and using the state payroll to build a political machine. Alluding to Johns's offers of patronage in return for political support, Collins later asserted that he ran against "the muster of the vultures."[6] Again, the factions used different vocabularies. "Cronyism" to the business progressives was politics to the agrarians. At the courthouse or at the statehouse, the successful rural politician rewarded his friends and punished his enemies. That was the tradition. From the agrarians' viewpoint, Johns had a right and, in fact, a duty, to replace McCarty's appointees with his loyal followers.

Collins combined conventional and innovative canvassing tactics. He made traditional "stump tours," traveling by auto accompanied by a sound truck, stopping in nearly every community, and delivering as many as a dozen speeches per day. Yet, he—and, to a lesser extent, the other candidates—injected new ideas into state politics. "Collins, more than anyone else, sensed that the smart candidate did most of his campaigning where the voters were," a reporter pointed out. Collins chartered an airplane to speed his travel between the state's three population centers: the Gold Coast, in southeastern Florida; the Tampa Bay region; and Jacksonville. He also became the first state politician to master television, a medium he would use both as a campaign tool and as an instrument of popular leadership.[7]

When Collins announced his candidacy, he assumed most Floridians knew of his background and record. Like other legislators, he later observed, he had read his own press clippings and presumed the voters had too. He soon realized his mistake. Because most Floridians had never heard of him, he needed to publicize his name and record. He emphasized his support for education and profited from his image as the "Father of the Minimum Foundation Program." He also often pointed out that Senator Johns had cast the only dissenting vote to the Minimum Foundation Bill.[8]

Rather than his record, though, a singular event gave Collins the voter recognition he sought: his opponent agreed to a televised debate, which exerted a decisive impact on the 1954 election. Early in the year, Collins suggested a series of meetings throughout the state. Johns's advisers warned him to avoid a face-to-face confrontation. They pointed out that Collins appeared polished and urbane and feared their candidate would not make a comparable impression. Johns heeded their advice prior to the first primary, but, after this narrow victory, he insisted on accepting the challenge. "I now have overruled my friends," the acting governor boasted, "and don't you worry about Charley Johns taking care of himself." The contestants arranged the debate for May 13, in the studio of Miami television station WTVJ. Fifteen radio stations carried the audio portion of the program statewide.[9]

The Miami debate was catastrophic for Johns's campaign. Performing well on television, Collins projected a cool, yet personable, image. Before the debate began, Johns appeared to be confident. But a mistake made by his campaign staff soon turned the event into a debacle. The Dade County Johns Committee had inserted an advertisement in the Friday, May 14, Miami *Herald* that gloated over their candidate's victory in the debate. The advertisement charged, "Well Senator Collins (wherever you are) we told you what would happen. You asked for it on television last night—AND YOU GOT IT. . . . We hope you're satisfied now, Senator. But if you want some more—maybe we can arrange it." Unfortunately for Johns, the Miami *Herald*, a morning newspaper, printed early editions the evening before. As a result, the Friday newspaper was being sold prior to the Thursday night debate.[10]

Chosen to speak first, Collins immediately produced the newspaper, read the advertisement, and declared, "That's the sort of advertising that's been run two hours before the meeting and I've already been convicted." Johns could only weakly reply, "I do not have anything to do with advertising. I didn't know about it." Throughout the debate, Collins never lost the momentum his initial thrust had provided. As a senator, Johns had refused to support the measure to unmask the Ku Klux Klan. When Collins attacked him for his stance, Johns explained, "I made a mistake. Of course, you never made a mistake." Collins scored a major victory. Although stoutly pro-Collins and thus hardly unbiased, the Miami *Herald* spoke for many people when it editorialized, "Although some TV viewers may have been confused by the welter of charges and counter-charges, they could not fail to note the contrast between Johns' shiftiness and the forthrightness of Collins."[11]

Eleven days later, the two candidates received the verdict of the voters. In the jam-packed Collins headquarters, the crowd nervously anticipated the all-important returns from south Florida. Finally, the vote count began to come in. The totals from Hillsborough County, which included Tampa, gave Collins a twelve-thousand-vote lead. Broward County, where Fort Lauderdale was the major city, extended Collins's advantage by five thousand votes. The crowd hushed as an official posted the returns for Dade County, which included Miami. The totals were Collins 101,709 and Johns 44,564. The incredible plurality of nearly sixty thousand votes gave Collins an insurmountable lead. The Tallahasseans exploded in celebration of their impending victory; each new total brought resounding cheers from the crowd. Johns finally spoke on radio and television, conceding, "God's will be done. God's will was that we lose."[12]

After Johns's concession, the excited throng in the Collins headquarters erupted in the most prolonged demonstration of the evening. The floor vibrated so violently that some feared it would collapse. When the uproar had settled, the partisans began to chant for a speech. Collins had shown his greatest strength in south Florida, yet he had carried Leon County by two thousand votes and believed he could always depend upon his community's support. "I am so proud of the final vote and of course am extremely happy," he told his followers. "But the wonderful expression of confidence makes me humble and determined to make Florida the

Collins, as candidate for governor, voting on May 4, 1954. (*Courtesy, Florida State Archives*)

kind of governor and do the kind of job for our state that our citizens want and deserve."[13]

Collins subsequently excused himself from the celebration and telephoned his son LeRoy, a midshipman at the United States Naval Academy, in Annapolis, Maryland. The Collinses then walked two blocks to the St. John's Episcopal Church, where the pastor held a special service.[14] Following these devotions, the Collinses returned to The Grove, which, after 125 years, would again house Florida's first family.

Collins had seven months to savor the primary victory before his inauguration. J. Tom Watson, of Tampa, the Republican gubernatorial nominee, died on October 24, which ended the party's token opposition to Collins. After the November balloting, the governor-elect and his wife toured Latin America. The trip was not only for rest and relaxation after a hectic election year but also to publicize the Inter-American Cultural and Trade Center then being constructed in Miami to provide a permanent showcase for the arts and products of North and South America. Florida hoped to take the lead in fostering closer social and economic relations between the hemispheric neighbors. Mixing politics with southern hospitality, Collins invited each of the dignitaries who entertained him and his spouse on the tour to attend his inaugural.[15]

Much to Collins's surprise, twenty-one Latin Americans, including the wife of the president of Panama, the vice-president of Panama, and numerous ambassadors from other countries, announced their intention to attend the inauguration. Tallahassee was not prepared to entertain such a large number of important guests. In addition to a lack of housing, the governor's mansion was run-down and inadequate for entertaining. Mary Call Collins called on her friends to help. They responded by contributing silver and china as well as helping to serve the eighty dignitaries who attended the inaugural dinner at The Grove.[16]

The dinner proved to be a memorable occasion. An Atlanta firm catered the affair, using local waiters. Because of insufficient kitchen facilities at the Collins home, a portion of the cooking had to be done at the executive mansion, located just across the street from The Grove. Waiters made dozens of trips carrying pots, pans, and platters from one house to the other. Despite the use of the

second kitchen, the burden overloaded the antiquated wiring at
The Grove, and the lights dimmed intermittently throughout the
evening. Inasmuch as Collins did not serve alcoholic beverages
while governor, various friends hosted predinner cocktail parties,
which created a difficult transportation problem. Moreover, because the preparation of the meal took extra time, the cocktail
parties ran well over schedule and several guests were too intoxi-
cated to appreciate the southern cooking. Despite the many problems, Tallahasseans managed to entertain the distinguished
inaugural guests graciously.[17]

On January 4, 1955, Collins was inaugurated as Florida's thirty-
third governor. Supreme Court Justice Glenn Terrell, who had
guided him toward the legal profession, administered the oath of
office. Collins then spoke to the crowd about his goals for the state.
He established the theme for his administration when he asserted,
"Florida stands on the threshold of greatness. Our future is limited
only by the range of our vision, the quality of our leadership, and
the desire of our people."[18]

Collins's philosophical roots were in the tradition of the New
South creed. Although he disliked being labeled as a "liberal" and
understood the value of "the balance wheel of conservatism," he
recognized the need for basic change in southern institutions.[19] He
believed that adjustments in political and economic structures
were essential if Florida was to join the modern industrial society
of the mid-twentieth century.

Collins considered change in political institutions the fundamental prerequisite for modernizing the state. In his inaugural address,
he pointed out, "progress in business, industry, and human welfare can only go so far with a ward-healing, back-scratching,
self-promoting political system." During the campaign, he had
urged Florida to replace its 1885 constitution with a new one and to
adopt a more equitable system of legislative apportionment. Furthermore, he had suggested the increased use of the merit system
to end the flagrant abuse of patronage. Yet, the new governor
believed that change in the political system went beyond written
revision. "Government cannot live by taxes alone, or by jobs alone,
or even by roads alone," he argued. "Government, too, must have
qualities of the spirit." He asked his fellow citizens to offer truth,

justice, fairness, and unselfish service to their state. "Without these qualities," he said, "there is no worthwhile leadership, and we grapple and grope in a moral wilderness."[20]

Collins also insisted that Floridians, as well as other southerners, needed to revise their views of states' rights and responsibilities. Like most of his constituents, he preferred local and state governmental action to federal intervention. "But," he warned, "the important thing to remember is that the services must be performed." If the local and state governments failed to serve their constituents, then the people would turn to Washington. The states must adjust to meet problems, or forfeit their right to action. "If more people would be concerned with states' responsibilities instead of states' rights," he concluded, "there would be little loss of those rights."[21]

Collins recognized the difficulties awaiting a leader who sought to change long-established traditions. Echoing a sentiment once used to describe Duncan U. Fletcher, a close Collins friend noted that the governor "always had his head in a cloud, although he was normally pretty practical."[22] Collins's philosophy reflected the "practical idealism" that characterized Florida's business progressives. His awareness of people's reluctance to accept rapid change tempered his ideals. In a speech to a group of southern governors, he observed:

> Effective public leadership requires more than the vision to see and the courage to act, although both these qualities are essential. A leader must also have the discretion and judgment required to raise a standard out front, but not so far that it is beyond the horizon of the people, and, therefore, cannot be seen and understood and followed by them.[23]

Collins was determined to retain contact with his constituents. He encouraged their influence in policy formulation by creating citizens' committees on virtually every issue. He further urged the state to adopt a "sunshine law," which would open all governmental meetings to the public. Shortly after the inaugural, he began monthly radio reports to the people. By 1956 eighteen stations carried his taped report. During his second administration, he added a monthly television program. While on the air, he answered a portion of the letters written to him and chatted about issues of concern to the state.[24]

Collins also established a good rapport with the large, and sometimes abrasive, capital press corps. He eventually held weekly, transcribed news conferences. His office distributed the transcripts to each editor, columnist, radio station, and television news desk in Florida. The written record, which identified the questioners, added to the statewide stature of the newspersons who covered his administration. This procedure also prompted them to ask precise, penetrating questions because their employers and peers would later read the transcripts. A sprightly interchange of insight and humor resulted. After the "hard news" session ended, Collins often sat with the reporters around a conference table for an hour or more talking of events in an informal manner. During these discussions, he sometimes subtly inserted "trial balloons," ideas the reporters might pick up and include in columns or editorials. If the public received the proposal well, then he adopted it as his own. He recognized the value of the press as a tool for communication with his constituents and handled it fairly and skillfully. In return, he received virtually universal respect from the capital correspondents.[25]

When Collins became governor, Florida was again experiencing an economic boom. After the Second World War, southern "boosters" regained the momentum they had lost during the depression. The "Sunshine State" led the region in economic growth.[26] Collins identified with the booster tradition and considered stimulation of the economy to be an important function of the governor.

Although Collins advocated economic development, he recognized the perils of uncontrolled growth. He insisted that "we [must] keep the rest of our house in order." First, he sought to avoid the ruinous cycle of a boom-and-bust economy that was overly dependent on the vagaries of tourism and real estate activity. He contended, "Florida stands on three sturdy legs. Tourism. Industry. Agriculture. The ultimate potential of all three has hardly been sighted, but all three must grow and strive together, or none can survive." Collins also rejected the image of the state as a playground for the rich. He opposed "quickie" divorces and legalized gambling. Tourism was important, but a moral atmosphere conducive to family life was even more valuable. He believed, moreover, that "natural advantages" should not be sacrificed to economic advancement.[27] As a person who had always lived close to nature, he loved the pine forests and the gulf beaches, where he had spent many hours as a child and as an adult. He considered a broadened industrial base to be essential for a new Florida, but not at the cost of the old Florida's natural beauty.

As Collins assumed the duties of governor, his philosophical precepts stressed the need for well-ordered change in governmental and economic structures. Modernized, efficient governing institutions could work with the business establishment to the benefit of all the citizens. Utilizing the business progressives' practical idealism and the hominy huskers' faith in free enterprise, Collins planned to carry out a reform program that would insure the state's prosperous future.

4

Lambchoppers, Porkchoppers, and Steakhouse Society:
Reapportionment and Reform, 1955

Governor LeRoy Collins began his administration with a sense of urgency. Because he assumed the constitutional prohibition against consecutive terms would apply to his partial-term governorship, he believed the 1955 legislative session would afford him his single opportunity to enact a reform agenda.[1] Yet, he expected to encounter formidable resistance. The agrarians and the business progressives held different visions of the state's future. In 1955 Collins's call for reform would confront the conservatives' determined defense of traditional standards. The conflict would spawn one of Florida's harshest seasons of political strife.

Following the inauguration, the Collinses moved across the street to the governor's mansion. Their new home was located between First Avenue and Brevard Street, on property formerly owned by the Call family. Shortly after the new residents settled in, state engineers advised them that deterioration had made the old mansion dangerous for occupancy. They moved back to The Grove, which served as the executive residence for the next two years.[2]

The youthful, active Collins family attracted extensive media attention. The governor appointed his wife to serve on the Mansion Committee, which supervised the construction of a new home for the chief executive. She was the most important influence on the choice of furnishings for the mansion. LeRoy Collins, Jr., was in his second year at the United States Naval Academy, fulfilling one of his father's youthful dreams. Tallahasseans still referred to the midshipman as "little Roy," though he was taller than his father. Jane was in her junior year at Leon High School, and Mary Call attended Elizabeth Cobb Junior High School. Darby, then four years old, most often "stole the show" from the other family members, including the governor. A newspaper described her as "something of a firecracker," and she was always the center of attention for the photographers. Because the Collinses lived in their own home, their life-style changed little, though the executive's heavy work load left him less time for family activities.[3]

Collins's initial task was to appoint his administrative officials and personal staff. He first reinstated the seventeen McCarty administrators that Johns had suspended. He also appointed the first woman in the state's history to serve in the "Little Cabinet," which consisted of those agency supervisors and board members who were directly responsible to the governor. Ina Thompson, of Defuniak Springs, formerly Walton County school supervisor, became motor vehicle commissioner. Joe Grotegut, a Daytona Beach reporter, headed the governor's staff and provided a buffer between him and the public and special interests. Constituents who had problems spoke first to Grotegut, who then researched the matter and presented it to Collins at a convenient time. As a newspaperman, he had a knack for sifting out the facts and presenting them clearly and concisely.[4]

Collins's staff included other influential advisers. Robert Fokes, a close friend who had managed the campaign, accepted an administrative position. The Lake City native previously had served as an executive assistant to U.S. Senator Claude Pepper. In the Collins administration, Fokes acted as liaison to the cities and counties and handled patronage. Two of the staff held strongly liberal credentials. James W. Prothro, a political science professor at Florida State University, served as an informal adviser. John Perry, a reporter for the St. Petersburg *Times*, handled press relations. More importantly, he contributed ideas and language to Collins's speeches. The governor liked "the stretch of his ideas and his visions of things to come." Increasingly, Perry and Prothro exerted a vigorous progressive influence on him.[5]

Collins used his staff well. He liked to talk issues out, pacing about the office and eliciting ideas. The atmosphere was normally relaxed and informal. The governor, his receptionist noted, was "never very far from frivolity." He loved to lean back in his chair, put his feet on the desk, and laugh uproariously at tales told by his staff or friends. He often contributed stories, normally told at his own expense, concerning family or political experiences.[6]

Collins followed a busy schedule. He installed offices in the basement of The Grove, where he and his staff started their day with an hour's work. During legislative sessions, he would work late into the night at The Grove and then arise at dawn to continue his efforts. He also traveled across Florida and the United States. But, if no issues pressed for decision, he would take a respite from his normally frenetic pace to enjoy his family and friends. He sometimes arrived at the capitol late and left early. Admitting that "I am constitutionally incapable of working by the clock," he required pressure to perform at the highest level.[7]

Many of the trappings and resultant restrictions that would later characterize the office of governor were not present during Collins's administration. Visitors to his home passed through no checkpoints because no security guards were posted. Anyone could drive up to the house, knock on the door, and be greeted by the governor or a member of his family. The same situation existed with phone calls. On most mornings, Collins walked the nine blocks to the capitol. Friends, wanting to discuss fishing or football, often joined him on the stroll. He normally stopped at Fain's Drug Store for coffee and a visit with the "regulars" who gathered there.[8]

By the 1950s Tallahassee had lost its rural atmosphere. During the preceding decades, the establishment of quail plantations had dealt "a deadly blow" to agriculture in Leon County. Wealthy northerners bought the land, restricted cultivation, and built private hunting preserves. The urban population continued to increase dramatically.[9] Most of Tallahassee's stores and offices remained downtown, but during the decade, a forward-looking corporation built on Apalachee Parkway the city's first shopping center. Although the city had been transformed, the people retained certain customs. The bicameral legislative sessions were still major events. Recurrent rumors that the capital would be moved to Orlando spurred the city's social leaders to extravagant lengths in entertaining the visiting legislators. Racial traditions also had not changed. Schools, churches, theaters, buses, and restaurants remained segregated. As one resident remembered, "There were two communities."[10]

A common lobbying custom, termed "Steakhouse Society," characterized the social setting during legislative sessions. Representatives of special interests entertained lawmakers at local restaurants, normally the Silver Slipper, on South Monroe Street, or Joe's Steakhouse, on East Tennessee Street. Both had private dining rooms with their own outside doors so that customers could enter and leave unnoticed. Political alliances could be forged or undermined in secret. Because Leon County was "dry," the private rooms also permitted the diners to bring their own liquor and imbibe unobserved.[11] Men furtively entering the restaurants with their bottles concealed in brown paper bags would remain an awkward memory for many Florida politicians.

The effectiveness of such lobbying practices in influencing legislation could never be verified. Yet, in their study of Florida politics during this period, William C. Havard and Loren P. Beth judged the "social lobby" to be a significant factor. "The very volume and intensity of social activity in Tallahassee during legislative sessions would lead one to conclude it has some importance," they pointed out. Such "activities are expensive and would hardly be undertaken without some hope of gain thereby." Collins later noted that the lobbyists often served a positive role by providing information to the legislators. He maintained, "Not all lobbyists were evil, nor did they all have evil schemes. But some did; some did."[12] Whatever their effect, the "Steakhouse Society" set the tone for the transaction of legislative business during his governorship.

In the 1955 legislative session, Collins fulfilled one campaign pledge by persuading the lawmakers to establish the Florida Constitution Advisory Committee, whose mission was to present proposals for a new state charter to the 1957 legislature. Collins wanted the new constitution to include a revised plan for gubernatorial succession, executive reorganization, and new guidelines for apportionment of the legislature.[13] The apportionment problem, though, could not be delayed. The existing charter required that the legislature be reapportioned each decade. The last apportionment plan having been designed in 1945, the constitutional prescription necessitated an immediate redistribution of districts.

Because Collins had been serving in the U.S. Navy in 1945, he had taken no part in the bitter legislative battle on reapportionment. Nevertheless, he had expressed his opinion on redistricting in a letter to the editor of the Fort Myers *News-Press*. Collins noted that the constitution required districts to "be as nearly equal in population as practicable." He believed the provision should be enforced because the law required it, basic fairness dictated it, and the maintenance of mutual respect between north and south Florida demanded it. The senate's frustration of efforts at fair apportionment, he charged, represented "an unconscionable effort on the part of 23 men to oppress nearly 2,000,000 citizens."[14] A decade later, his position remained unchanged.

When Collins became governor, Florida possessed one of the nation's most malapportioned legislatures. In the house, one representative served 2,199 constituents, but another served 165,028. The population of the smallest senatorial district was 10,413 people; the largest, 495,084. The malapportionment was actually worse than two decades before. In 1937 some 26.1 percent of the voters elected a majority in the senate; in 1955, 17.7 percent. The house of representatives had experienced a similar decline in the number of voters necessary to elect a majority.[15]

Despite the statistical proof of malapportionment, Collins confronted enormous difficulties in his demand for reform. Johns, Collins's "mortal political foe," had returned to the senate after his brief stay in the executive mansion. Most of the senators had supported him in the 1954 primary. He belonged to an "Old Guard" of senior senators who controlled the legislative process in the upper house. The group also included S. D. Clark, of Monticello, Wilson Carraway, of Tallahassee, and Merrill P. Barber, of Vero Beach, all of whom represented banking interests. William A. Shands, of Gainesville, was, perhaps, the senate's most influential member. Among his many business interests, he owned one of the state's largest billboard companies and used his influence to insure that no antibillboard legislation passed. On the the issue of reapportionment, the Old Guard combined with approximately fifteen other "small county" senators to form a majority in the thirty-eight-member upper house. They vowed to oppose all reapportionment plans that would increase the size of any of their districts.[16]

In a July 13, 1955, Tampa *Tribune* editorial, James A. Clendinen termed the antireapportionment faction the "Pork Chop Gang." Floridians later called those who favored redistricting the "Lambchoppers." Although initially applied only to the factions in the reapportionment dispute, the terms "Porkchoppers" and "Lambchoppers" soon became popular designations for the agrarian and the business progressive wings of the Democratic party. State Senator Verle A. Pope, of St. Augustine, who served from 1948 to 1972, was considered to be a leader of the Lambchoppers. He later distinguished between the groups by contending that statewide issues interested the Lambchoppers and that the Porkchoppers, because of the economic needs of their communities, were mostly concerned with finding jobs for their constituents.[17]

The Porkchoppers, moreover, realized the state's population boom threatened their position as arbiters of its government. Since 1920 the population had changed from two-thirds rural to two-thirds urban. The Porkchoppers wanted to retain the agrarian traditions of southern politics. But more than keeping a nostalgic grip on an older era prompted their opposition to reapportionment. Redistribution of senate seats threatened their power over state revenues and patronage, the weapons they used to build and maintain their political strength. Even if a small-county senator sympathized with the need for reapportionment, he could not support revision and hope to be reelected. The folks back home would charge him with "selling out" to the big cities.[18] Reapportionment's foes often summoned Populist themes as the rural elements struggled to preserve their world.

Collins recognized the political problems that reapportionment presented to the small-county senators, but he pleaded with them to "be big" in the interest of improving the government. He also warned the Porkchoppers that, if they continued, in effect, to disenfranchise a large portion of the population, the federal government would be forced to act. Refusing to use his patronage power or his influence on the building of roads to pressure the obstructionist senators, he argued, "It takes a gradual shaping of public opinion to win the really big fights."[19] Instead of coercing the recalcitrant senators, he chose to trust the democratic process to force the necessary change.

During the regular session of the 1955 legislature, the senate blocked all proposals for reapportionment. Collins, citing the constitutional requirement for redistricting, called for an extraordinary legislative session. Throughout the long, excruciating Tallahassee summer, the deadlocked legislature grappled with its seemingly insoluble problem. Tempers rose with the temperature. Havard and Beth wrote, "It is difficult to think of a move known to the history of the reapportionment struggle in the state that was not employed, and several additional ones were especially invented for the occasion." Two reapportionment bills finally passed, but Collins vetoed both. In a statewide broadcast, he declared that the bills did not meet the constitutional requirement that the districts "be as nearly equal in population as practicable." Thereafter, the struggle "settled into a sort of trench warfare."[20]

Finally, in September, the governor broke the deadlock by suggesting that the legislature propose a constitutional amendment on reapportionment and present it to the voters in the 1956 general election. At any rate, because the legislators refused to provide an equitable apportionment plan, he could not accept the useless expense of continuing the session. "If you are to violate the Constitution, it is far better that you do it on your own time," he charged. "There can be only one recourse then for me, and those who fight with us in every corner of Florida, and that is to take the issue to the people in the elections next spring." He promised the legislators that "the full weight and force and influence I possess and can honorably use will be thrown into this fight for fair play for all of the people of Florida." That same month, speaking in Dunnellon, home of Senator L. K. Edwards, Jr., a Porkchopper, Collins termed his opponents "greedy and selfish" and condemned their defiance of the constitution. His words added to the bitterness engendered by the reapportionment battle.[21]

The lawmakers passed an amendment calling for one senator from each of the sixty-seven counties and increasing the number of representatives to 135. The new house seats were to be given to the larger counties. Collins opposed the amendment because it would allow the small counties to retain their death-grip on the senate. "It constitutes a compounding of the inequity and inequality of the present apportionment of representation," he contended. Floridians rejected the amendment.[22] The governor, legislature, and citizenry had no choice but to await the Constitution Advisory Commission's recommendations to the 1957 legislature.

Some Lambchoppers blamed Collins for not pressing reapportionment more forcefully. Representative C. Farris Bryant, of Ocala, a presumed gubernatorial candidate in 1956, claimed that "the battle for reapportionment was lost, in the last analysis, by the deliberate and calculated refusal of the Governor to use that influence and prestige entrusted to him by the sovereign people of this state to assist him in upholding the Constitution of the State of Florida." Collins expressed amazement at the charge. Was he expected to bargain on the appointment of judges or to penalize universities in Porkchop areas? "Is [Bryant] suggesting that I should stop the State's road construction program in his own county of Marion because its own Senator will not vote for fair reapportionment?" Collins asked. Refusing to take such actions, he vowed instead to use "every honorable means at my command to win this fight."[23]

Collins tried to keep the constitutional reform controversy from affecting his other proposals. Although at odds with the Porkchoppers on the reapportionment problem, he recognized the need for cooperation on other issues. This contributed to his reluctance to use his executive powers to force compliance from the small-county senators. He also possessed sufficient political acumen to use the Old Guard senators as sponsors for bills in areas of agreement. Shands, for example, whose district included the University of Florida, was a respected proponent of higher education. Collins enlisted his support for reform of the state's university system, and, together, they accomplished a great deal.[24] By using such political strategies, the governor prevented the complete alienation of Porkchoppers from his administration.

Collins succeeded in pushing some important measures through the stubborn 1955 legislature. South Floridians thought that the state-long turnpike bill was a significant victory. Many of them considered the turnpike, which made all the state more accessible to auto travel, to be a vital spur to tourism in their region. The legislature also responded to Collins's call for an extended merit system by allowing him and cabinet officers to institute such programs in their areas of authority. He immediately placed the Hotel and Restaurant Commission, the Motor Vehicle Commission, the State Board of Conservation, the State Racing Commission, and the State Road Department under the merit system.[25]

Collins also convinced the legislature to establish an agency to spur the state's economic growth. The lawmakers created the Florida Development Commission to "stimulate and promote the coordinated, efficient, and beneficial development of the state." It was responsible for tourist services, nationwide advertising, attraction of new industry, coordination of urban planning, enhancement of international trade, and a number of other tasks formerly left undone or inefficiently divided among state agencies. In addition, Collins sponsored the Florida Development Credit Corporation, which encouraged the state's 234 banks to pool credit for the purpose of luring new industry. His effort to centralize responsibility in state agencies paid dividends as early as 1956, when, compared to the previous year, nearly twice as many industries initiated steps to establish themselves in the state. He pushed for industrial expansion, but warned citizens of the vitally important goal of protecting their environment. He attempted to attract low-waste, high-employment industries such as electronics, aircraft, and research and development.[26]

On northern goodwill tours, Collins actively sought new industry. Other governors had made similar tours, though he added an emphasis on industry to the two earlier primary concerns of tourism and agriculture. In July 1955 he and a delegation of about thirty businessmen traveled to New York, Boston, and Philadelphia. The next February, a similar contingent visited Cleveland, Detroit, and Chicago. Members of the governor's staff, representatives from the State Development Commission, and newspersons from the capital press corps accompanied the tours. In each city, Collins met privately with local politicians and business leaders, spoke at luncheons and dinners, held press conferences, and made radio and television appearances. In part, he tried to convince bankers and financiers of Florida's economic soundness. He wanted to attract them to county and municipal bond issues, which would result in lower interest rates. Emphasizing his belief in the state's prosperous future, he claimed it was "alive with opportunity" and represented "the best investment on earth."[27]

Collins enjoyed a good relationship with businessmen. Florida's leading capitalists and its leading business progressive shared a goal. They wanted to modernize the government so that it could be an active force in stimulating prosperity. To the business community's delight, Collins welcomed the salesman's role and excelled at the task. He insisted, "In our efforts to encourage Florida's sound industrial development, we must not overlook the importance of salesmanship. These tours . . . afford a wonderful opportunity for selling Florida." The trips also strengthened his close affinity with the state's financial leaders. They traveled by train, sharing accommodations in a string of private cars. The leisurely pace provided the businessmen time to become personally acquainted with Collins. A newsman who went on the tours recalled that the opportunity "to rub elbows" with the governor appealed to the "tycoons."[28]

One of Collins's major efforts to attract a new industry in the end proved to be unsuccessful. On January 9, 1956, he flew to California on a secret mission. After he had left, John Perry informed the press of his departure and explained only that the trip was "of vital importance in connection with Florida's industrial expansion."[29] In fact, Collins had gone to California to confer with reclusive and eccentric billionaire Howard Hughes, who had insisted on secrecy. During a series of meetings, the governor learned of one of the most exciting development proposals in Florida's history.

For nearly a year, south Floridians had conjectured on the activities at a Hughes office in Miami Beach. Reports that he had leased a waterfront estate further stimulated rumors. The press knew that, for some time, representatives of Hughes, Dade County, and the University of Miami had talked confidentially of a medical research project. The county had set aside sixty acres for this project. A final clue had come at a January 3 cabinet meeting, when Collins requested the officials to make available for development an industrial site at Clewiston, in south Florida. Although these actions fueled speculation, the public learned nothing of negotiations that had been taking place for several months.[30]

Del Webb, a wealthy Phoenix, Arizona, contractor who supervised construction for Hughes, had initiated the talks with Collins. In a series of phone calls, Webb informed the governor that his client was contemplating large investments in Florida and wanted a guarantee of cooperation from the state government. Collins's enthusiastic response led to several telephone conversations with Hughes. The industrialist outlined plans for a south Florida factory to manufacture aircraft engines. Finally, he promised to detail his proposals if Collins would meet with him in California.[31]

In response to this invitation, Collins and a small group of Floridians flew to Los Angeles on January 9. Webb met the party at the airport and escorted it to the Beverly Hilton Hotel, where Hughes maintained his West Coast residence. Discussions were held with Hughes that evening and throughout the next day. Collins and Hughes also met privately. Hughes pledged all the participants to secrecy. Intermittently during the discussions he would put a finger to his lips, ask for silence, stealthily cross the room, and fling open the door, looking for eavesdroppers. During these meetings, he expanded on his plans to build a factory in Florida.[32]

Hughes also mentioned for the first time a more dramatic proposal. He planned to finance the world's largest medical research center as his gift to the nation. The complex would be constructed on islands off the coast of southeast Florida that would be created by dredging the ocean floor and building up shallow areas. A research center would then be erected on the islands and provided with the finest equipment and staff from around the world. The project would also include housing and recreational facilities for the employees. Hughes intended to pay for the construction, but wanted assurances from the state and local governments that he would be accorded virtually absolute control over the area.[33]

Hughes had obviously studied the project carefully. Collins believed he was sincere. Webb, who would be responsible for constructing the center, also felt the same way. Collins told

Hughes that Florida would be delighted to obtain such a facility. Collins was allowed to issue a press release announcing that Hughes planned "new ventures, including a new industrial plant, and research development in other important and challenging fields as well." Hughes's statement praised Collins's "alert and aggressive manner."[34] Beyond these declarations, they maintained secrecy.

Hughes asked Collins to stay over an extra day so that they could talk more about the project. The next morning, the industrialist took the Floridians on a tour of his aircraft plant and showed them the "Spruce Goose," his huge wooden transport plane that had left its hangar only once. For lunch, they flew to Palm Springs. Hughes insisted that the flight crew move back to the cabin while he piloted the airplane and Collins sat in the copilot's seat. Collins, who knew nothing of flying, remembered, "It scared me to death, I'll tell you that. I didn't want to do the wrong thing because I felt like we had something tremendous in our grasp. . . . But I still didn't like the prospect of doing that." Hughes decided to give Collins a scenic tour, once virtually turning the plane on its side to provide him with a clear view. "I would have taken his word happily on anything that was out there," Collins recalled, "but I didn't have any choice since he was being such a fine host." On the return flight, Hughes flew far out over the Pacific Ocean and circled until dusk so that the governor could see the beauty of Los Angeles's lights when approached from the west. Throughout the day, Collins tried to make appropriate responses to Hughes's constant conversation while clutching tightly to the arms of the copilot's seat. When he returned home, he believed he had played a part in an economic and promotional coup for his state.[35]

Hughes never completed his grand design. According to Collins, Hughes Tool Company submitted the low bid to the federal government for producing the aircraft engines, but was denied the contract on what Hughes considered to be a technicality. In a telephone conversation with Collins, he was furious about the decision. Although he restated his determination to build the medical research center, he never carried through. He did give several million dollars to a medical research project that was established in Miami Beach, but his contributions never approached the scale he had described. Collins and Webb concluded that the conflict over the federal contract undercut his interest in the research center. They decided he wanted to avoid any projects which might require the federal government's cooperation. After the grandiose projections of the potential value of the schemes for Florida, Hughes's failure to fulfill them created some embarrassment for Collins. Critics claimed they were a hoax for political gain, and for several years he was forced to answer hostile questions and jibes concerning them.[36]

Collins's achievements in attracting new industry lessened his disappointment with the failure of the Hughes projects. Similarly, reform accomplishments mitigated the frustrations of the reapportionment battle. In normal times, the first two years of Collins's governorship would have been judged a successful extension of the business progressive tradition. But he did not serve during normal times. In 1954 a decision of the U.S. Supreme Court initiated a social revolution in America. Blacks began to demand a change in their second-class status. The conscience of the nation challenged the South's inviolate racial customs. Ultimately, neither Collins's successes nor his failures in reform and economic promotions would provide the basis for evaluating his governorship. Instead, his leadership in the racial crisis would furnish the criterion for measuring the worth of his political career.

5

The Authority of Law:
The Racial Crisis, 1955–1956

The unexpected emergence of a social reform issue hindered Collins's attempt to concentrate the state's energies on governmental and economic changes. On May 17, 1954, one week prior to the Democratic primary election between him and Johns, the U.S. Supreme Court had ruled that segregated school systems were unconstitutional. The decision, in *Brown* v. *Board of Education of Topeka, Kansas*, asserted that the "separate but equal" concept, which had been expressed by the Court in the 1896 *Plessy* v. *Ferguson* ruling, did not conform to the demands of the Fourteenth Amendment. Chief Justice Earl Warren, in writing the unanimous verdict, cited psychological and sociological studies to support the Court's contention that segregated schools detrimentally affected black children. "Separate educational facilities are inherently unequal," he concluded.[1]

In the aftermath of the ruling, Governor Collins would become a spokesman for the "southern moderates," an epithet used to describe those who defended segregation but condemned defiance of the Supreme Court.[2] Initially, most white Floridians appeared to share his commitment to moderation. The interjection of militant segregationism into the 1956 gubernatorial primary changed the political climate. Although Collins won reelection, the militants' strength posed a challenge to his moderate leadership.

Reactions to the *Brown* decision in the spring of 1954 did not indicate the intensity of the opposition that would later emerge. President Dwight D. Eisenhower called for the desegregation of the schools in Washington, District of Columbia, and ordered the integration of schools on military bases. Some border and non-southern states that maintained dual school systems formulated desegregation plans immediately after the Court's ruling. In the Deep South, however, the *Brown* decision elicited unrestrained rhetorical abuse. Governor Herman Talmadge, of Georgia, declared that the Supreme Court had "blatantly ignored all law and precedent and usurped from the Congress and the people the power to amend the Constitution and from Congress the authority to make the laws of the land." Although such bombastic flurries were common in the Congress, the newspapers, and the pulpits, few people talked of open defiance. The South seemed resigned.[3]

Florida responded more dispassionately to the *Brown* decision than did the other Deep South states. The most influential newspapers called for "a period of thoughtful calm," and U.S. Senators Spessard Holland and George Smathers concurred.[4] The state's comparatively small black population, the large immigrant population, extensive urbanization, and economic dependence on tourism contributed to the moderate response. Furthermore, the Supreme Court's deferral of arguments on carrying out desegregation lessened the immediate impact of the decision.[5]

During the gubernatorial campaign, Collins reacted to the *Brown* decision by affirming segregation as a part of the state's custom and law and by pledging to use all the legal powers of the governor's office to preserve the dual school system.[6] Following his election, he supported Attorney General Richard W. Ervin, who filed a brief with the Supreme Court urging a policy of "gradualism." The May 31, 1955, ruling that allowed compliance "with all deliberate speed" appeared to reflect the Ervin position. Collins promised that Florida would "continue to deal with this matter soundly and sensibly and without furor or hysteria."[7]

Despite this assurance, some observers anticipated a battle in the 1955 legislative session between those who accepted "gradualism" and those who desired more dramatic action. In his address to the legislature, Collins restated his determination to use all of the governor's legal powers to preserve segregation. Representative

Prentice P. Pruitt, of Jefferson County, and Senator Johns led proponents of the activist position. They were unable to pass a measure calling for a constitutional amendment to reverse the Supreme Court's decision. Johns, though, authored and gained passage of a Pupil Assignment Law, which gave local school boards final responsibility for the placement of students. Collins signed the bill.[8]

The signing of this bill underscored Collins's determination to retain segregation by legal means. The "legal opposition" view constituted the initial basis for his actions on integration. He opposed integration because he believed "the end of segregation, if and when it comes, will be a result of a basic change in attitudes and thinking. . . . It can only come when acceptance of non-segregation is developed in the hearts and minds of people."[9] At the same time, his refusal to countenance defiance of the Supreme Court made him a leader among the "moderate segregationists."

Although the *Brown* decision had not been clarified and the potential for reversal remained, Collins recognized the probability that segregation would need to end. Political factors, though, convinced him not to state his evaluation publicly. To provide moderate leadership, he maintained that he could not adopt a pose "beyond the horizon" of his constituents. Furthermore, he hesitated to sacrifice support for his governmental reform program by advancing too far on the question of desegregation. Moreover, he had assumed he would not be allowed to seek a second term. However, the Florida Supreme Court ruled that he would be eligible to run for office in 1956 because he was completing the McCarty administration.[10] Collins desired reelection and presumably recognized that an unpopular position on the race issue could cost him the nomination. Political realities led him to support the use of legal methods to preserve the state's dual school system.

In 1956 all of the public schools and universities were segregated. A Gallup poll indicated that four out of five white Floridians opposed the *Brown* decision.[11] Yet, they appeared willing to accept the concept of gradualism. They had displayed no defiance of the initial *Brown* ruling nor of the implementation guidelines. One observer called Florida a "wait-and-see" state that was controlled by moderates.[12] The injection of the racial question into the 1956 election, however, prodded it toward the ranks of the "resisting states."[13] Helen L. Jacobstein, a historian who studied the campaign, concluded, "The Florida Democratic gubernatorial primary of 1956 represented a crucial decision in Florida's racial history."[14]

Six candidates contested for the 1956 Democratic gubernatorial nomination. In addition to Collins, three of the candidates enjoyed major stature. Fuller Warren, of Miami (though a native of Blountstown in the Panhandle), had served four turbulent years as governor from 1949 to 1953. He excelled at "stump speaking" and possessed much wit and charm. C. Farris Bryant, of Ocala, a graduate of the University of Florida who held a law degree from Harvard, was a widely respected legislator. He had served as Speaker of the house in 1953 and had supported much of Collins's program in the 1955 legislature. Sumter L. Lowry, the final major candidate, was a retired National Guard lieutenant general and prominent businessman from Tampa. He possessed neither an engaging personality nor political experience, but he brought a record of business success and military service to the campaign.[15]

Lowry, an avowed white-supremacy candidate, based his campaign solely on the issue of race. Stating that integration "was thought up and organized years ago by the international Communist conspiracy," he feared a three-pronged Communist attack on the United States through integration, world government, and infiltration of the Christian church. He argued that no Democratic officeholder should be allowed "to hedge and pussyfoot" on the issue of segregation.[16]

Lowry characterized Collins as a part of the conspiracy threatening the nation's institutions. In a particular flight of fantasy, he charged, "Collins was a leader of the World Federalist Movement and during the 1951 legislature he led a last ditch fight for World Federalism." When Collins suggested that racial extremism would undermine Florida's economic growth, Lowry responded, "He would sell out the children of the state for the dollar bill," and added, "the people are tired of governors who pussyfoot and evade this issue while the NAACP program of integration marches on." Collins was deemed to be "caught in his own web of gradualism" and accused of being "a professional hypocrite." Lowry proposed to save Florida from the evils of integration by the passage of an interposition resolution.[17]

The concept of interposition was not new to American politics. Its advocates sought to interpose state authority between the federal government and the citizens if national officers adopted a position the state considered to be unconstitutional. In the Kentucky and Virginia Resolutions of 1798–99, Thomas Jefferson and James Madison contended that the states possessed such power. Those in New England took a similar stance in their protest against the War of 1812. Two decades later, John C. Calhoun argued, "It is this negative power—the power of preventing or arresting the action of Government—be it called by what term it may—veto, interposition, nullification, check or balance of power—which in fact forms the constitution." The Civil War resolved the dispute over the predominance of federal law, but, for many southerners, the myth of state supremacy remained a cornerstone of their political philosophy. During the 1950s, they again seized upon the concept of interposition as a means to avoid carrying out the Supreme Court's desegregation order.[18]

Lowry's polemics on interposition and segregation made race a volatile issue in the state and even injected the potential for physical disruption into the debate. Although recommending the peaceful maintenance of segregation, Lowry warned, "You'll have violence . . . if integration is attempted." He also suggested that those who agreed with him might "march on Washington and overthrow the Supreme Court, if necessary, to prevent integration."[19] As the campaign progressed, increasing numbers of Floridians rallied to his vigorous defense of the South's racial traditions, and he became the primary threat to Collins's hopes for a second term as governor.

Collins followed a simple campaign formula. He later admitted, "My strategy was to work hard all through the campaign at being governor and to stay away from Sumter Lowry." The governor refused to debate, maintaining that such meetings simply attracted large audiences for his opponents that they could not draw on their own. Although he had successfully used the "stump tour" technique two years before, he placed more emphasis on a media-oriented campaign in 1956. The impact of his radio and television appearances compelled the other candidates to depend more on the electronic media than ever before in Florida politics. Such campaigning was expensive. Collins, as the front-runner and incumbent, could raise money more easily than his less well-known opponents. He spent $291,183 on the campaign, compared to Warren's $194,682, Lowry's $115,216, and Bryant's $63,048.[20] His financial resources, successes as governor, experienced campaign organization, and name recognition throughout the state gave him considerable advantages in the campaign.

The integration question, however, could not be avoided. The pressure created by Lowry's campaign forced Collins to take a stronger stand on the race issue. He noted that Floridians overwhelmingly supported segregation and reassured the voters that he stood "firmly and squarely" with them on the issue. But, he said he represented "orderly and effective assertion of our rights under the authority of law." He added, "We will have segregation in this state by lawful and peaceful means, and we will not have our state—our Florida which has such a bright future—torn asunder by rioting and disorder and violence and the sort of thing this man is seeking to incite."[21]

Collins, moreover, rejected the blatant racism of the Lowry campaign. In a statement prepared for the press but not released, he intimated his moral concern. "I do not pretend that segregation in public schools, or at public meetings, or on public conveyances is consistent as a matter of principle with Christianity or the basic American ideal of equality before the law," he said. "And to both of these faiths I am dedicated." Publicly, he claimed that race hatred could only serve as a destructive force in the creation of a modern Florida. "If you want a governor who is determined to have the white people of this state hating the colored people and the colored people hating the white people, you don't want LeRoy Collins," he insisted.[22]

Three racially related events combined with Lowry's rhetoric to make integration a key issue in the primary. The first concerned a commuted sentence for a black man convicted of raping a white woman. Collins opposed capital punishment; during his second administration, he would seek legislation to abolish the death sentence. The punishment might have legal justification, he argued, if it deterred others. Yet, he claimed, scientific studies proved "capital punishment does not deter." He, moreover, considered the action morally wrong, recommending, "We should take Florida out of this barbaric business of State killing. Only God can give human life. Man should not take it away." Despite moral reservations, however, Collins felt legally bound to carry out executive duties, including the signing of death warrants. In each case, though, the trial and appeal records were studied thoroughly. If any legal justification could be found, he commuted the sentence.[23]

One such commutation, in the Groveland rape case, created a highly charged campaign issue. On July 16, 1949, near Groveland, Florida, four black men allegedly kidnapped and raped a white, seventeen-year-old housewife. In retaliation, white mobs attacked local blacks and burned several homes. Only the National Guard's intervention restored order in Lake County. A posse killed one of the accused before an arrest could be made. A sixteen-year-old defendant received a life sentence. Two others charged with the crime, Samuel Sheppard and Walter Lee Irvin, were convicted and condemned to death. The Florida Supreme Court upheld the verdict. In April 1951 the United States Supreme Court, though, ordered a new trial on the basis that the all-white jury and emotional atmosphere had not been fair to the black men.[24]

On the night of November 6, 1951, as Sheriff Willis McCall escorted the defendants from the state prison back to Lake County for retrial, he shot and killed Sheppard and seriously wounded Irvin. McCall claimed the prisoners tried to escape, but Irvin testified that he fired without provocation. The U.S. Department of Justice and Governor Fuller Warren investigated the incident, but uncovered no evidence to support Irvin's charge. A Lake County coroner's jury ruled that the shooting was "justifiable" because McCall had acted "in the line of duty and in defense of his own life." At his second trial, Irvin was again found guilty and sentenced to death. This time, both the Florida and United States supreme courts upheld the conviction.[25]

Shortly after Collins became governor, Irvin's supporters began to exert pressure for commutation. The St. Petersburg *Times* stated that its investigators had followed the case closely and asserted, "On the basis of their findings, there is great doubt that Irvin is guilty." The report concluded, "Florida cannot afford to ignore the principles of justice in favor of mob rule and bigotry, both of which Lake County has had more than its share." The newspaper's stance provoked a deluge of letters to Collins on Irvin's behalf. For example, Mary McLeod Bethune, black educational leader and founder of Bethune-Cookman College, at Daytona Beach, called on the governor to take personal responsibility for preventing Irvin's execution and for further investigation of the crime. "We, the citizens of Florida, are depending upon God and you," she pleaded.[26]

Collins did not like the way Lake County authorities had carried out the arrests or the trial. The violence, emotionalism, and McCall's actions appalled him. He asked two lawyers to assist him in extensively researching the case. According to Collins, they discovered that the prosecution's only physical evidence consisted of tire tracks at the scene of the crime that matched the imprints from Irvin's car. The lack of physical evidence suggested a legal justification for overturning the death sentence. When McCall had made the arrest, a deputy drove Irvin's car to the sheriff's office. Conceivably the deputy could have gone to the crime scene, made the tire tracks, and then returned to the office. Collins grasped upon the idea to justify commutation. He told the State Pardon Board that Irvin's guilt had not been established "in an absolute and conclusive manner." On December 15, 1955, Collins and the board unanimously commuted the death sentence to life imprisonment.[27]

The board's decision elicited some negative reaction. One criminal court judge detailed his legal opposition to the commutation and then charged, "this action is a surrender to the left-wing press." A constituent warned Collins, "I am afraid I can't support you any longer, unless you and the board rescind your action and admit a mistake." Yet, for the most part, Floridians expressed little anger at the commutation.[28]

As the political climate heated up, though, two of Collins's foes used the commutation to create problems for him. The first was Circuit Judge Truman G. Futch, whose district included Lake

County. He enjoyed some renown as the "stick-whittling judge" because he littered the floor with cedar shavings while presiding.[29] On February 16 he ordered a grand jury investigation of the commutation proceedings and explained that this unprecedented action was a response to petitions requesting an inquiry signed by 121 citizens of his district. In his charge to the grand jury, he clarified his political interest, saying, "You have the right to inquire and determine if you can the authority, reasons and motives, political or otherwise, which impelled the governor to commute the sentence."[30]

Collins, accepting full responsibility for the commutation, pointed out that he had recommended the action and the board had simply agreed. At the same time, he refused to testify before the grand jury. "There is nothing to investigate except LeRoy Collins' judgment and conscience," he said. "Both are beyond the control or coercion of a grand jury. They are subject to review by God and the people of Florida."[31]

Futch's challenge and Collins's response brought an emotional reaction from people on both sides of the issue. Describing the National Association for the Advancement of Colored People (NAACP) as a "Communistically sponsored organization, headed by a Chicago Jew," a Virginian wrote Collins, "The NAACP is very gleeful over your COMMUTATION of the death sentence of the RAPIST."[32] One constituent declared: "You don't have to take ordur [sic] from the negroes and Jews who are causing all this trouble over segregation."[33] Collins received more messages of support than condemnation, though. One citizen wrote, "God bless men who have the strength to back their convictions," and another expressed "gratitude for your gallant stand in the defense of justice."[34] A West Palm Beach resident added: "I find your stand a convincing demonstration that all honor and decency have not disappeared from American public life."[35]

After several weeks of investigation, the grand jury announced that Collins had acted within his legal rights in commuting Irvin's sentence. The report noted: "This Grand Jury feels that both the prosecution and defense were negligent in failing to use all available scientific, clinical, and medical means of investigation." Even Judge Futch now excused Collins as "an innocent victim of the

Communists by helping to save a Negro in the Groveland rape case from the electric chair."[36]

The pardon in the *Groveland* case added to the bitterness between Collins and Sheriff McCall. Collins opposed his political and racial views and also suspected him of corruption. The governor always regretted his inability to gather sufficient evidence of wrongdoing to suspend him. The headlines given Futch's grand-jury investigation provided the sheriff with an opportunity to embarrass Collins. On February 22, 1956, McCall arranged an incident at Eustis, where Collins was to ride in a parade. As the governor and his wife sat in a car awaiting the start of the festivities, the alleged Groveland rape victim approached them, escorted by McCall's deputies. The press, which had been alerted to expect the confrontation, crowded around to record the event. When the woman reached the car, she yelled something to the following effect: "You're the one who let off the nigger that raped me. Would you have done that if it had been your wife?" The incident disgusted and angered Collins.[37]

Some contemporary observers believed the furor over Irvin's commutation stemmed from political motives. Bob Delaney, a newspaper columnist, pointed out that Collins could hardly have hoped to win votes by commuting the sentence of a black rapist. "Simple mathematics shows that the politically expedient thing would have been to let the death sentence stand," he wrote, "but a man of courage and integrity could not do it, no matter how advantageous, [when] he had honest doubts." Yet, Delaney described "the current ruckus in Lake County" as "quite obviously designed to discredit Gov. LeRoy Collins."[38]

The governor's adversaries in the Democratic primary tried to capitalize on the issue. Condemnation of the commutation became a staple in Lowry's speeches and advertising. Warren asked, "Will LeRoy Collins ever explain to the citizens of Florida his shame and why he excused this Negro to the shame of every decent white woman of our state?"[39] Although infuriating for Collins, the commutation issue probably had little impact on the electoral results. The strong segregationist candidates more than likely already enjoyed the support of those voters who were influenced by such political machinations.

A U.S. Supreme Court decision handed down in the midst of the gubernatorial primary presented a more serious danger to Collins because it threatened the foundation of his moderate segregationist platform. In April 1949 Virgil D. Hawkins, a black Floridian, applied for admission to the University of Florida Law School. When university officials denied his application, he sought a legal remedy. In 1950 the Florida Supreme Court ruled that a proposed law school at Florida Agricultural and Mechanical University (FAMU), the state-supported black college, would satisfy Hawkins's rights under the Fourteenth Amendment. He disagreed and appealed to the U.S. Supreme Court which, on May 24, 1954, directed the state court to reconsider the case in light of the *Brown* decision. On October 19, 1955, Florida's highest tribunal decreed a postponement of Hawkins's admission pending a study to determine potential problems. Hawkins, by then a forty-eight-year-old public relations director at Bethune-Cookman College, in Daytona Beach, asked the U.S. Supreme Court to overturn the delaying action. On March 12, 1956, the Court ordered Hawkins's immediate admission to the law school.[40]

The decision posed a problem for Collins, for it appeared to undermine the concept of gradualism that had formed the basis of the state's response to the *Brown* decision. Collins vowed, "We will not surrender in our battle to protect our state's customs and traditions." He promised to present Florida's case personally if the Supreme Court granted a review. He also called a conference of the state's educational leaders in Tallahassee to devise a coordinated response. In his opening address, he warned the conferees to reject radical actions. Listing several "danger signs" of extremism growing out of the gubernatorial campaign, he admitted, "I am gravely concerned about what is happening to the minds of the people."[41]

The Tallahassee conference concurred with Collins's suggestion that the southern governors meet with President Eisenhower to explain the extent of segregationist sentiment. Such an assembly, the governor asserted, would let the president know "of the great concern we in the South have about any efforts to coerce integration." Collins later telegraphed a request to President Eisenhower for a meeting to discuss the integration issue. The president agreed

to consider this action if Congress did not accept his plan for a
bipartisan commission to study the problem.[42]

The meeting of educators in Tallahassee also asked for the
appointment of a committee to recommend legally sound segregationist measures. The governor pledged to summon a special
legislative session if the committee's proposals were legal and
effective. His careful wording portended his opposition to a special
session at which an interposition resolution would be a primary
order of business. He appointed L. L. Fabisinski, of Pensacola, a
retired circuit judge, to chair the committee.[43]

The adoption of the committee plan was a wise political move. It
delayed specific proposals to counteract the *Hawkins* decision until
after the primary voting. In conjunction with his pledge to retain
segregation, Collins's actions effectively limited the ruling's impact
on the election. Nevertheless, the other candidates attempted to
use the issue. Lowry blasted the Tallahassee conference as a
"whitewash," and Bryant advocated an interposition resolution as a
useful "protest." Warren added sensationalism to the debate by
charging that Hawkins had brutally beaten two students while
teaching in Lake County years earlier. Warren considered the
incident sufficient cause to deny him admission to law school.
Hawkins denied the charge, and Lake County officials did not
substantiate the accusation. Yet, in the emotional campaign atmosphere, Warren's statement publicized his forceful segregationist
stance.[44]

The third campaign incident calling attention to the segregation
issue concerned Henry H. Arrington, a black assistant state attorney in Miami. Collins's appointment of Arrington—who was to
participate in the prosecution of black defendants—partially fulfilled a 1954 campaign pledge to Dade County's black leaders.
Before the gubernatorial primary, the appointment drew little
notice. On February 25, 1956, Arrington served on a radio panel,
answering questions called in by listeners. In his responses, he
supposedly implied that not all his cases involved blacks and that
he worked with an integrated office staff. Warren and Lowry seized
on Arrington's purported statements to demonstrate Collins's soft-
ness on integration. Lowry charged, "Arrington chortles to the
Communist-inspired NAACP that 'I have a white secretary and the

office is fully integrated' despite the fact Collins claims there is no integration in Florida." Arrington's superior, State Attorney George Brautigan, of Miami, accused him of making "false and misleading" statements and pressured Collins to act on the controversy. The latter fired Arrington, which eliminated the incident from constant news coverage and lessened its impact on the election.[45]

The black community's subsequent electoral support for Collins indicated that it apparently held no grudge over the action. Indeed, Arrington later acknowledged that "it was a wise move for him to make at the time."[46] Yet, black people had little choice. Perhaps, despite the action, they simply found Collins to be the least offensive of the major candidates. The firing certainly tarnished his image of moral courage in the racial crisis. It underscored the fact that, in both his elections to statewide office, he vocally supported segregation. Philosophical distinctions between him and his constituents on the racial issue appeared only after his second election, as he became more liberal and a majority of Floridians became more conservative. The Arrington incident also illustrated that a racist campaign, such as Lowry's, exerted strong pressure on moderate candidates to adopt a more militant posture.

Collins tried to defuse the racial issue by emphasizing his business progressive credentials and by claiming that racial strife would sap Florida's economic strength. "Nothing will turn . . . investors away quicker than the prospect of finding here communities hopped up by demagoguery and seething under the tension and turmoil of race hatred," he said. His campaign material portrayed him as the state's "super salesman." In April, Del Webb announced Howard Hughes's plans for investment in Florida and read Hughes's statement describing Collins as "just about the best salesman any state ever had." The governor's "victory tune" quickly incorporated the good news:

He made the legislature legislate
He put roads in places that help the state
  He went travlin' North, met the V.I.P.s
  And he brought back millions in new industries
Invested 16 bucks where we never got one
He made folks like Florida's favorite son

Floridians, here's a governor we must choose
Or we'll lose that project with Howard Hughes.[47]

Collins's economic successes and moderate racial stance brought
him recognition and support from the state and national press. All
but one of Florida's daily newspapers that endorsed a candidate
chose him. Beginning in 1955 and continuing throughout the
campaign, articles on the state appeared in national periodicals.
The magazines praised Collins's economic salesmanship and racial
views. In light of the widespread media support, he recalled, "It
was like the old line. I had to pinch myself to make sure I wasn't
dreaming."[48]

The other candidates suspected intrigue. Bryant called the flood
of national interest "peculiar," and Warren credited a "big time
New York advertising agency" with publicizing the governor. In
fact, the state of Florida did have a New York "press representative," Hal Leyshon and Associates. This agency helped to organize
the northern promotional tours and to gain attention for Florida—
and thus for Collins.[49] Self-promotion, though, did not explain
completely the media fascination. It also resulted from curiosity
about the state's remarkable economic growth. The national press
may have wished, moreover, to aid the campaign of a southerner
who disavowed violent resistance to integration.

Collins won the election with an unprecedented victory margin.
He received 434,274 votes, compared to 179,019 votes for Lowry,
who finished second. The other candidates garnered a total of
226,787 votes. Collins amassed 14,000 votes more than the combined total of his five opponents, which gave him a first-ballot
sweep unprecedented in the history of Florida's Democratic party.
He gained 61.94 percent of the vote in thirty-one southern counties, though he carried only Leon County in the north. Thirty-two
percent of eligible blacks registered in 1956, and they overwhelmingly supported him at the ballot box. In Jacksonville, for example,
thirteen black precincts reported 9,920 votes for him and a total of
803 for his opponents. Citing the magnitude of the victory, commentators lauded his success as a triumph for racial moderation.[50]
The gubernatorial primary demonstrated that in 1956 a majority of
the voters opposed extremism in defense of segregation.

The Roy-Mary Call Collins family on inauguration day, January 8, 1957 (*left to right*): Thomas LeRoy, Jr., Jane, Governor Collins, Mary Call, Sarah Darby (in front of her mother), and young Mary Call. (*Courtesy, Florida State Archives*)

The returns, though, held other portents for the future. First, considering Bryant's lack of financing and prior organization, his 110,469 votes testified to the soundness of his candidacy, and in effect made him the front-runner for the 1960 nomination. A rational, competent conservative, he had established an anti-Collins base during the campaign. Second, the returns illustrated the viability of a strategy centered on emotional racism. Lowry scored a remarkable total for a political novice, signifying the strong undercurrent of extremism in the state.[51] No doubt, southern politicians, such as Orval E. Faubus, in Arkansas, Ross Barnett, in Mississippi, and George C. Wallace, in Alabama, recognized the significance of Lowry's electoral strength. For Collins and the South, Florida's 1956 gubernatorial primary marked the emergence of a new, more perilous period in the racial crisis.

6

The Call of History:
The Racial Crisis, 1956–1957

During 1956 white southerners would intensify their opposition to integration, while Collins would move toward compromise. Events influenced his perception of the realities confronting the South and convinced him of the need for change. The introduction of an interposition resolution in the legislature, which reflected the extremist attitude first evidenced in the gubernatorial primary, and the initiation of a bus boycott in Tallahassee, which attested to the potential of racial violence, caused him to reevaluate the issue. He used his second inaugural address, in January 1957, to express his belief in the inevitability of revised racial codes.

On July 20, 1956, Collins called an extraordinary legislative session to act on the Fabisinski Committee's report. In his opening address, he urged the lawmakers not to exceed its suggestions. The legislature furthered the recommendations by enacting a more effective Pupil Placement Law to supplant the 1955 measure and a teacher assignment edict to prevent the integration of faculties. Another statute empowered the governor to enforce "rules," meaning segregation regulations, on public lands or in public facilities, if law and order were threatened. Finally, the lawmakers entrusted the governor with the authority to proclaim a state of emergency and to use law officers or the militia to suppress disorder.[1]

For many conservatives, the Fabisinski Committee's proposals appeared to be too mild. Led by Representatives Prentice Pruitt, of Monticello, and J. Kenneth Ballinger, of Tallahassee, they demanded stronger action. Pruitt introduced an interposition resolution. The maneuver posed problems for some house members. Many recognized the unconstitutionality of the resolution, yet realized that opposing it might trigger an emotional reaction from their constituents. The senate completed its work on the Fabisinski proposals, but was forced to wait while the house debated the interposition issue. The resolution seemed certain to pass despite Collins's opposition. Seeking to prevent a vote, he grasped upon the constitutional provision authorizing the governor to dismiss the legislature if the two houses could not agree on a time for adjournment. On August 1, while the house was in the midst of its debate, he sent a note to the Speaker stating that, under his constitutional authority, he declared the legislature adjourned.[2]

This unprecedented action caught interposition's proponents completely unprepared. They felt betrayed. "I think it was a low blow when this house was deliberating in good faith," charged Pruitt. Representative Bryant, another interposition advocate, observed simply, "We've had it." During the moments of shock following the dissolution order, Senator William Neblett, of Key West, told Bryant, "Well, I guess that's interposition. The governor interposed."[3] Although Collins's timely intervention forestalled interposition in 1956, the legislators' anger insured that the issue would surface again in the next year's regular legislative session.

A crisis in Tallahassee further added to Collins's concerns on the race question. In May 1956 two black women students from FAMU boarded a bus and sat in the only empty seats, which happened to be in front of some white patrons. When the driver ordered the students to stand in the back of the bus, they refused. Police arrested them on the grounds that they had placed themselves in a position to cause a riot. Officials dropped the charges, but two days later angry whites burned a cross on the front lawn of the house in which the students lived. Tallahassee's black leaders used the incident to press for an end to segregated buses.[4]

Six months earlier, a similar incident had resulted in a boycott of the bus services in Montgomery, Alabama. On December 1, 1955, Rosa Parks, a black seamstress, declined when a driver demanded that she give her seat to a white man. She insisted that, after a long day's work, her feet hurt too much to stand on the ride home. She was arrested and fined fourteen dollars. Montgomery's black citizens began a bus boycott under the leadership of Dr. Martin Luther King, Jr., minister of the Dexter Avenue Baptist Church. In January 1956 his home was bombed. Montgomery officials later arrested and fined him for violating an obscure state law that prohibited boycotts. Filing suit in federal court, the blacks asked for an end to segregated buses. Throughout 1956 the litigation and the boycott continued. The Montgomery protest inaugurated a period of resistance and rebellion in America. King's nonviolent strategy provided a model for those seeking institutional change.[5] The vehemence of the white reaction served as a warning of the storm that was to follow.

Even though black leaders in Tallahassee realized action aimed at ending segregation would be difficult and dangerous, they instituted a bus boycott on May 28, 1956. Led by the Reverend C. K. Steele, minister of the Bethel Baptist Church, they organized the Negro Inter Civic Council (ICC) to coordinate their effort. It established a car pool that operated from a grocery store owned by Dan Speed. The economic squeeze forced the bus company to discontinue service on July 1. The day after the buses stopped running, Collins attacked the NAACP for "a miscarriage of ambition" and urged blacks to reach a compromise on their grievances. The ICC voted to continue the boycott. During the next month, bus service began again, but the company required financial assistance from the city.[6]

In August city officials arrested the leaders of the car pool and charged them with violating an ordinance requiring vehicles for hire to have special licenses. Two months later, Judge John Rudd convicted all the blacks for failure to possess them and imposed on all the individuals involved five-hundred-dollar fines, sixty-day suspended sentences, and one-year probations. Rudd also forced the ICC to withdraw its support from the car pool.[7] Despite the legal setbacks, the boycott continued.

On November 13, 1956, the U.S. Supreme Court ruled that the Montgomery bus segregation law was unconstitutional. Shortly after this decision, leaders of Tallahassee's boycott decided to return to the buses and sit in the front seats. Fearing violent confrontation, they postponed action until the students at Florida State University (FSU) and FAMU left the city for Christmas vacation. On Christmas Eve, Steele and seven other ICC members boarded buses and took seats in the front. The city council, under the leadership of Mayor John Y. Humphress, Collins's boyhood friend, ordered the drivers to enforce segregation. The company refused to comply, and on December 27 police arrested nine drivers for failure to enforce the city ordinance.[8]

On that same afternoon, the ICC resolved to test the city law with a mass demonstration. Speed, chairman of the organization's transportation section, announced that at 3:30 fifty blacks would board buses at the downtown bus stop. A crowd of two hundred whites gathered at the site and waited for the blacks to appear. When Steele arrived, he recognized the tense atmosphere and called off the demonstration. He vowed to continue his policy of avoiding violent confrontation.[9]

Other incidents added to the strain on the capital city. On December 28 the Reverend J. Metz Rollins, an ICC leader, received a telephone threat on his life. The Leon County White Citizens Council held a meeting on New Year's Eve and passed a resolution asking Collins to use his emergency powers under the Fabisinski laws to take control of the municipal buses. One speaker at the meeting asked, "Since when has it become a sin to be primarily a white American?" He implored whites "to lend your support to the cause as best you can."[10] Such calls to action from whites heightened tensions in the city.

During the early morning hours of New Year's Day, the volatile situation exploded. Rocks broke four windows in the Steele home. At about the same time, shotgun blasts were fired into Speed Brothers' Grocery, in a case of mistaken identity; Cornelius and Daniel Speed, cousins of the ICC leader, owned the store. Neither of them had participated in the boycott. The vandals had obviously meant their message for Dan Speed, whose store was located in another section of town.[11] After months of steadily growing pressure, the unexpected violence shocked the capital city.

Collins issued a proclamation blaming "irresponsible Negro leadership" and "extreme, rabid pro-segregationists" for creating the disorder. Using the emergency powers granted him by the 1956 legislature, he ordered the buses to cease operation. Protesting the action, Steele charged that Collins had fallen into a trap set by the White Citizens Council. Collins denied being influenced by the racist organization and maintained he wanted only to prevent further violence. He received editorial support for his action from newspapers statewide.[12]

Collins's action did not end the crisis. A few days later, a cross was burned in front of Steele's home. Although most Tallahasseans decried the incident, the cross-burning suggested that the potential for violence remained. During the same week, a federal judge ruled that Miami's segregated buses were unconstitutional. Reacting to the decision, the Tallahassee city council rescinded its order on segregated busing and adopted a new ordinance that required drivers to assign seats on the basis of passengers' "health, safety, and welfare."[13] This action indicated that white leaders were not prepared to concede defeat.

On January 11, 1957, Collins lifted his ban on bus service, but emphasized that his action did not mean he approved the city ordinance giving the drivers authority to assign seats. The next day, buses began to operate once again, yet the tension remained. On January 17 shotgun blasts fired through the windows of Steele's home shattered the relative calm. Police Chief Frank Stoutamire vowed to end the violence. Collins, too, had had enough. "This kind of lawlessness is inexcusable and must be stopped," he exclaimed. If local officials did not take prompt and effective action, he promised to take personal responsibility for enforcing the law in the city.[14] The violence and the unequivocal responses of Stoutamire and Collins stunned the residents. Eventually, they agreed to a compromise that desegregated buses on predominantly black routes.[15]

The violent confrontations in Collins's hometown created special problems for him. His longtime friends and associates were the city's bankers, businessmen, and politicians. Although he and the members of his family had less time to spend with old acquaintances, they continued many of their local activities. The Possum Club remained an outlet for Collins's theatrical proclivities. He also hunted and fished with friends when time permitted. He reserved Sunday mornings for church, though a lack of preparation time forced him to give up teaching a Sunday school class.[16]

This intimate involvement with Tallahassee society made it difficult for the governor to assume a dispassionate attitude on the bus boycott. He understood the difficulty white residents experienced in accepting changes in their racial traditions. Yet, he also recognized that blacks had legitimate grievances and would continue their demands. He sought compromise, a moderate solution that rejected "radical leadership" on either side. His second inaugural gave him an opportunity to tell all Floridians his feelings on the segregation issue.[17]

Early in the morning of January 8, 1957, a crowd of several thousand began arriving at the capitol for the inaugural festivities. Most of them were in shirt-sleeves and some wore shorts because of the bright winter sun. The warmth of the day and the festive spirit of the crowd belied the tense atmosphere the bus boycott had created. The forty-seven-year-old governor seemed in high spirits as he joked with reporters about his embarrassment at needing to wear a top hat, but his jovial attitude did not reflect the emotional strain he faced. He knew his words would shock some Floridians, but he felt compelled to state his views on the racial crisis.[18]

The governor was sworn in for a second term at 10:30 on inaugural morning, a break with the traditional noon ceremony. In his address, he first discussed the accomplishments and goals of his administration. He turned next to the issue of segregation. He pointed out that southerners were not lawbreakers. The South had followed a policy of legal segregation supported by Supreme Court decisions. Southerners were not prepared for such inexact fields as psychology and sociology suddenly to be placed on the scales of justice and overturn three generations of attitudes and traditions. To that point, Collins had simply rehashed the traditional apologies for the South's refusal to accept change in its customs.

The governor, however, then turned from his understanding assessment of whites' attitudes to a demand that they recognize the realities of their position. Ultimately, he insisted, the South would be forced to alter its traditions. In answer to those who preached defiance, he said:

In the first place, it will do us no good whatever to defy the United States Supreme Court. Actually, this Court is an essential institution for the preservation of our form of government. It is little short of rebellion and anarchy to suggest that any state can isolate and quarantine itself against the effect of a decision of the United States Supreme Court.

If such a proposal could possibly have any legal efficacy, we would have no Union and the power of the Court to protect the people in the enjoyment of their freedoms would be severely impugned and imperiled. We should frankly admit this and put the true label of demagoguery on any doctrine of nullification.

Collins then stated his support for legal opposition to school integration:

It is my judgment that [the Fabisinski] laws—in line with the court's recognition that local conditions must be taken into full account— give us assurance that there will be no integration in our public schools so long as it is not wise in the light of the social, economic and health facts of life as they exist in various localities of our State.

His program, the governor reasoned, would prevent school integration "in the foreseeable future." He again pledged to use all the powers of his office to preserve school segregation.

In other areas, however, Collins made a dramatic plea for white people to understand the legitimacy of black demands. He charged, "We should admit that our attitude generally in the past has been obstructive all along the line." Although urging blacks to abstain from militancy in protesting their status, he insisted that whites admit their errors. "I am convinced, for example," he said, "that the average white citizen does not object to nonsegregated seating in buses." He urged white Floridians to recognize the realities of their society: "We can find wise solutions if the white citizens will face up to the fact that the Negro does not now have equal opportunities, that he is morally and legally entitled to progress more rapidly, and that a full good-faith effort should be made forthwith to help him move forward in the improvement of all his standards."

Collins then issued an inspirational call for citizens to display courage in the crisis confronting their state. He declared, "There must be change, and change usually comes hard." He quoted from a hymn by James Russell Lowell, a nineteenth-century abolitionist, that began:

> Once to every man and nation
> Comes the moment to decide,
> In the strife of truth with falsehood,
> For the Good or Evil side.

Collins charged, "The cause is with us now." Not all that he and his adherents sought could be achieved, but their efforts would make change easier for those who followed. They must begin. He pleaded, "God forbid that it shall ever be said of our administration, 'They did not have the vision to see,' or seeing, 'They did not have the will to try.'"

The governor renewed his demand for change by again quoting from the Lowell hymn:

> New occasions teach new duties,
> Time makes ancient good uncouth;
> They must upward still and onward
> Who would keep abreast of truth.

Collins concluded, "This is the call of history—a history which grows impatient. Ours is the generation in which great decisions can no longer be passed to the next. We have a State to build—a South to save—a nation to convince—and a God to serve."[19]

As one Florida newspaper pointed out, the speech had "required political courage and personal soul-searching." Others also complimented the governor's courage in forthrightly stating what many southerners believed but feared to say. *Newsweek* observed, "a calm and remarkably candid voice came out of Florida's hill capital of Tallahassee." Many commentators emphasized the stirring quality of the speech, which they called "splendid" and "magnificent." The Pensacola *Journal* stressed Collins's "masterly eloquence," and the Ocala *Star Banner* praised the "statesman like inaugural address." The state's newspapers expressed overwhelming support for the governor's stand.[20]

The Miami *Herald* cautioned that no matter how commendable Collins's principles, their application would depend upon his relationship with the legislature. For the most part, the reaction of lawmakers who attended the inaugural seemed positive. Representative John Shipp, of Jackson County, considered it "a wonderful speech"; and Representative S. D. Saunders, of Clay County, called it "one of the most constructive speeches I have ever heard." Representative John Orr of Dade County believed Collins's "greatest virtue is his capacity for moral leadership." Not all agreed. Senator James E. Conner, of Inverness, disputed with the governor on the legitimacy of Supreme Court decisions. "They are not based on federal law, but on politics. I follow the Florida Constitution on segregation," he said. "Now that [Collins] has yielded to the philosophy of the U.S. Supreme Court," Senator Harry Stratton, of Callahan, added, "I guess we are officially integrated."[21]

The address brought a mixed reaction from the state's black leaders. The Reverend Joseph A. Reddick, of Miami, state president of the NAACP, thought Collins had set a good example for other public officials. "My faith in him is very definitely justified," Reddick said. A black leader from Jacksonville believed the governor had taken "a realistic approach to the great problem of trying to get the public to accept the fact segregation has in fact been outlawed by the Supreme Court." Black Tallahasseans, on the other hand, expressed little enthusiasm for the speech. The Reverend Steele evinced "no particular reaction that would be quotable."[22] For many blacks, Collins's support for segregated schools and his plea for an end to militance may have appeared more significant than his call for change in other customs.

Indeed, Collins had drawn an exceedingly fine line. He insisted on respect for decisions of the U.S. Supreme Court, yet promised to maintain segregated schools. He sympathized with the whites' opposition to school integration, yet urged change in other segregated customs. He implored blacks to reject "radical" leadership, yet offered no cooperation in carrying out the *Brown* decision. The paradoxical principles muddled the generally favorable reaction.[23] Senator Shands, for example, said, "I am in general agreement with his segregation ideas." Senator Newman Bracken, of Crestview, thought, "The governor gave a splendid appraisal of the segregation issue"; and Senator Dewey M. Johnson, of Quincy, concluded, "There was good sense in his segregation statements."

Similarly, several editorials included praise for Collins's defense of school segregation.[24] Was the positive response of Floridians then determined primarily by his segregationist stance, or by his call for change?

In retrospect, the speech seemed to express a curious innocence. Did Collins expect white extremists to forbear violence; blacks to wait for evolutionary change; and moderate whites to accept integrated buses, beaches, neighborhoods, and lunch counters? Perhaps he did. It was the age of innocence in the American civil rights movement. People and ideas were being tested. Collins sought solutions based on the practical idealism that was characteristic of a business progressive. An "agrarian" governor might have offered an emotional defense of cherished, if doomed, traditions. Collins recognized realities. He felt obligated, as one newspaper pointed out, to lay "the facts of life in this 1957 democracy before the people of Florida." He "put the plain unvarnished, if unwelcome, truth before the people."[25]

According to Collins, white southerners had to accept certain verities. The Supreme Court had allowed "all deliberate speed" on school desegregation, which could delay implementation in the "foreseeable future." Acceptance of school integration was certainly "beyond the horizon" of Collins's constituents. Yet, change was coming. Blacks would no longer accept second-class citizenship. Violence would not keep them "in their place." Defiance would not impede the Supreme Court. The 1956 gubernatorial primary had illustrated the danger; a large minority of Floridians had expressed their acceptance of extremist rhetoric. The Tallahassee bus boycott had shown that events could translate such words into actions. A dramatic confrontation on school integration could loosen the moderates' tenuous hold on the majority. The South faced a crisis; choices had to be made; that was the "call of history." Collins was in the process of defining a moderate course for southerners to follow. After his inaugural address, one Florida newspaper rejoiced, "Thank God that after these two and a half years of a South crying its distress in the wilderness, we have leadership."[26]

7

Little Rock:

The Racial Crisis, 1957

By 1957 southerners recognized the finality of the Supreme Court's desegregation decision, which had been handed down three years before. No judicial appeals remained; the Court would not reverse its opinion. This awareness brought diverse reactions in Dixie. Blacks became more adamant in their demand for integration. Many whites wished to resist implementation, but others pointed out the futility of defiance and urged acceptance of new racial customs. Most white southerners, though, remained uncommitted to either view. Opposing violent resistance but fearing change, they sought guidance from their political leaders. Collins and other moderates would recommend new racial codes to create a stable, prosperous South. A majority of whites, however, would follow leaders who were determined to defend ancient customs. Choices made during those crucial months would condemn the region to a fruitless decade of defiance.

Southerners seeking alternatives to political extremism received no positive guidance at the national level. President Dwight D. Eisenhower's unenthusiastic response to the Supreme Court's decision convinced many people that resistance had silent support in the White House. Instead of endorsing the Court's position, he offered bland statements on the inability of laws to change people's beliefs. The vacuum of presidential leadership encouraged those who were demanding defiance of the federal courts.[1]

Extremists also received reassurance from southern representatives in Congress. In 1956 the legislators issued a "Declaration of Constitutional Principles," which came to be called "The Southern Manifesto." It pledged "to use all lawful means to bring about a reversal of this decision which is contrary to the Constitution, and to prevent the use of force in its implementation." Although the solons urged southerners "to scrupulously refrain from disorders and lawless acts," the tone of the document was more bellicose. Anthony Lewis, a nationally syndicated columnist, noted, "The true meaning of their Manifesto was to make defiance of the Supreme Court and the Constitution socially acceptable in the South—to give resistance to the law the approval of the Southern Establishment."[2]

The Southern Manifesto constituted one portion of a broader program of opposition to the *Brown* decision. Commentators applied the term "massive resistance" to the efforts of southern conservatives who advocated extreme measures to stop integration. The movement's "saints" included Thomas Jefferson, James Madison, John C. Calhoun, and Jefferson Davis. The concepts of white supremacy and states' rights formed the basis of its ideology. Senators Harry F. Byrd, of Virginia, Richard Russell, of Georgia, Strom Thurmond, of South Carolina, and James Eastland, of Mississippi, provided national leadership. Many social scientists and journalists gave the movement intellectual support. Dr. Lindley Stiles, dean of education at the University of Virginia, and Professor Henry E. Garret, of the Columbia University psychology department, asserted the superiority of segregated education. James J. Kilpatrick, Jr., editor of the Richmond *News Leader*, furnished the most important journalistic influence on the massive resistance movement.[3]

The Citizens' Councils of America supplied the grass roots political organization for the movement. In July 1954 segregationists formed the first council at Indianola, Mississippi. Within three years, the membership of the organization was estimated at 250,000. Its leaders wanted to unite white southerners in opposition to integration. Roy V. Harris, of Augusta, Georgia, the president, argued, "We are engaged in the greatest crusade in the history of mankind. If you're a white man, then it's time to stand up with us, or black your face and get on the other side." Social, economic, and political pressures exerted by the councils prodded many southerners into more intransigent positions. Ralph McGill, publisher of the Atlanta *Constitution*, observed, "public opinion itself became a sort of mob which terrorized or silenced any who might dare oppose it."[4]

The massive resistance advocates initially fought for the passage of interposition resolutions in southern legislatures. Virginia acted first, followed by Alabama, Mississippi, Georgia, South Carolina, and Louisiana. The resisters applied pressure on other southern legislatures to join their sister states in opposing the federal government. Although filled with ambiguities and fantasies, the concept of interposition implied one basic fact: many southerners were ready to use state power to oppose changes in their racial traditions.[5]

Although Collins appeared willing to take a stand against the massive resistance movement, he faced problems inherent in his state's political structure. First, the factionalized Democratic party provided him with no local political base upon which to build support for his views. Furthermore, the malapportioned legislature gave disproportionate power to the smaller counties, where segregationist thought was strongest and his influence was weakest. He also conflicted with the Florida Supreme Court, which had declared a " 'states rights' doctrine reported to be the strongest of any state court."[6]

Agencies in the state bureaucracy that exercised power beyond gubernatorial control compounded Collins's difficulties. During his second administration, for example, he urged the Board of Control, which governed higher education, to follow the lead of other southern states and allow blacks to enter graduate programs. The board rejected the proposal and vowed to continue its opposition to integration.[7] The cabinet system, which traditionally exercised power beyond the governor's influence, also created difficulties for Collins. He could not force the members to abide by his policy of moderation on the racial issue.

The contrasting goals of Attorney General Ervin and Collins in the 1957 legislature demonstrated the problem of gubernatorial control. In 1954 the former had advocated "gradualism." Two years later, however, an electoral challenge from segregationist Representative Prentice Pruitt influenced him to adopt a more adamant stance. Before the opening of the legislature, Ervin submitted recommendations for laws to prevent integration. He proposed establishing a new commission on race relations to continue the work begun by the Fabisinski Committee in 1956. He also suggested that the legislature set up procedures for counties, municipalities, and school districts to vote on desegregation issues. The law's purpose was to allow a vote to close schools if violence seemed imminent. Finally, the attorney general asked the legislature to propose an amendment to the U.S. Constitution "specially setting out certain of the powers reserved to the states under the tenth amendment of the United States Constitution."[8]

In his speech opening the 1957 legislative session, Collins accepted Ervin's suggestion for an advisory commission on race relations. He ignored the other proposals. The legislature quickly empowered the governor to appoint a commission and then passed "the last resort bill," a measure for closing the public schools. Collins vetoed it. "I will never approve any plan to abolish any public school, anywhere," he asserted. The Fabisinski laws of 1956 had given him the power to close the schools if necessary to prevent violence. He feared that allowing a vote on the issue would lead to the closing of public schools just to maintain segregation. He considered the house vote sustaining his veto "a very significant victory for reason." It meant Floridians were "determined that the agitator and the extremist shall not take over."[9]

Segregationist lawmakers—many of whom felt the governor had used trickery in adjourning the legislature to avoid passage of the interposition measure in the previous session—were determined to pass the resolution in 1957. On April 5 the house agreed to interposition by a voice vote. The resolution accused the U.S. Supreme Court of usurping state prerogatives in several areas, including education, and declared decisions weakening state powers in those fields to be "null, void and of no effect."[10]

The battle then shifted to the senate. Verle Pope, of St. Augustine, and Doyle Carlton, Jr., of Wauchula, led the fight against the resolution. A statement issued by Ervin hampered the efforts of those opposing interposition. When an undecided senator requested his opinion on the value of interposition, he admitted the concept lacked any real legal significance. But, he continued, the state's school system stood on "the brink of disaster," and forced integration could topple it over. Interposition, he conjectured, might cause the federal courts to pause for further study before implementing the *Brown* decision. On April 18 the opposition failed by one vote in an effort to have the resolution returned to committee. This defeat ended resistance to the measure, and the resolution passed.[11]

Comments in the days following the interposition vote further illustrated the division between Collins and Ervin. The governor asserted, "It can do no good whatever, and those who say it can perpetrate a cruel hoax on the people." In a television interview, Ervin again spoke of the measure's moral value. Collins, responding to a question at his weekly news conference, charged, "The resolution is on its face a lie. I cannot attribute any moral value to a lie. Nor can I attribute any moral value to defiance of this nature."[12]

Because interposition passed the legislature as a resolution, rather than as a law, the governor did not possess the power to veto it. He forwarded the resolution to President Eisenhower as the legislature had instructed, but attached a note declaring his personal opposition. On the original resolution, filed in the office of the secretary of state, Collins wrote:

> This concurrent resolution of "Interposition" crosses the Governor's desk as a matter of routine. I have no authority to veto it. I take this means however to advise the student of government, who may examine this document in the archives of the state in the years to come that the Governor of Florida expressed open and vigorous opposition thereto. I feel that the U.S. Supreme Court has improperly usurped powers reserved to the states under the constitution. I have joined in protesting such and in seeking legal means of avoidance. But if this resolution declaring decisions of the court to be "null and void" is to be taken seriously, it is anarchy and rebellion against the nation which must remain "indivisible under God" if it is to survive. Not only will I not condone "Interposition" as so many have sought me to do, I decry it as an evil thing, whipped up by the demagogues and carried on the hot and erratic winds of passion, prejudice, and hysteria. If history judges me right

this day, I want it known that I did my best to avert this blot. If I am judged wrong, then here in my own handwriting and over my signature is the proof of guilt to support my conviction.[13]

The interposition conflict demonstrated the widening gap between Collins and those southerners who were urging massive resistance to the *Brown* decision. He had never supported defiance of the Supreme Court. He had urged legal opposition to integration, but several factors were causing an evolution in his position. First, he realized the finality of the Court's decision. Moreover, his reelection removed some political pressure and, assured of four full years, he could "call himself to a sense of duty." He increasingly recognized a sense of responsibility for all of the state's citizens, black as well as white.[14]

As Collins moved toward acceptance, many people veered toward resistance. At certain junctures during his governorship, he and a majority of white Floridians would follow separate paths on the desegregation issue. Ultimately, they would arrive at widely disparate views. The second inaugural address was one turning point; the interposition resolution was another. The integration conflict in Little Rock, Arkansas, also signaled the increasing division between Collins and his constituents.[15]

The "massive resisters," though a minority, were prepared to rally southerners if an incident gave them an opportunity. Governor Orval E. Faubus, of Arkansas, provided it in the autumn of 1957. He "set the south on fire" by his use of armed state troops in an attempt to nullify the *Brown* decision. Prior to his defiant stand on school integration, he had been considered a moderate on the race issue. Following his 1954 election to the governorship, he encouraged the integration of the state Democratic party and removed racial barriers on the undergraduate level at state universities. Although a Citizens' Councils organizer and three other candidates opposed him in the 1956 Democratic primary, he won a first-ballot victory.[16] He appeared to have established a moderate position on the integration issue.

Little Rock, moreover, seemed an unlikely site for a momentous confrontation between state and federal power. The Arkansas capital was noted for its tradition of racial harmony. In 1955 the city began planning for gradual desegregation; previously all-white Central High School was designated to initiate the process. During the two years of preparation for integration, the massive resistance movement weakened the position of the city's moderate leaders.[17]

Faubus had previously avoided the issue by insisting on local control of integration decisions. In the Little Rock situation, however, an absence of leadership in the city government forced him to assume responsibility. When opposition to integration intensified in the summer of 1957, he requested federal assistance in maintaining order. The Eisenhower administration refused to become involved in a local school dispute. The president offered no support for the moderates and at one point remarked about southern concern for "mongrelization of the race." The irresolute moderate leadership and the persistent clamor of the resisters led Faubus to intervene on September 2, 1957. In defiance of a federal court order, he dispatched 270 Arkansas National Guardsmen to Central High School to block the entrance of nine black students.[18]

Faubus later claimed his actions during the crisis were not motivated by racial prejudice but by his belief in states' rights. "For too long the national government had been usurping the peoples' rights, and cramming unpopular policies down their throats without any consideration for their feelings," he charged.[19] Critics, though, believed the growing strength of those championing defiance influenced his actions because he was worried about his reelection campaign in 1958. He feared alienating support, they argued, and evinced a willingness to adopt the position most advantageous for his political future.[20]

Faubus kept the guardsmen on duty at Central High School while federal judge Ronald N. Davies considered the issue. The governor maintained that he had acted only to prevent violence.[21] Professing fear of arrest, he dramatically surrounded the executive mansion with guardsmen. "The blood that may be shed," he said in a telegram to Eisenhower, "will be on the hands of the federal government and its agents."[22] This audacity thrilled southerners who were angered by what they viewed as unwarranted attacks on their traditions.

On September 20 Davies enjoined Faubus from blocking the

integration of Central High School. The governor withdrew the National Guard, warned of violence if the court forced integration, and left for the Southern Governors' Conference at Sea Island, Georgia.[23]

Collins was scheduled to deliver the opening address there. The speech, in the midst of the Little Rock crisis, provided him with a forum to challenge the "massive resisters." He had entitled his address "Can a Southerner Be Elected President?" North Carolina Governor Luther H. Hodges, chairman of the conference, had originally assigned the topic, "Why Can't a Southerner Be Elected President of the United States of America?" He wrote Governor James P. Coleman, of Mississippi, "I thought that would get more attention, but, of course, the subject means the same thing."[24]

Collins, though, did not consider the two topics identical. Although he avoided preconference comments on his conclusions, the press conjectured he might answer in the affirmative. The subject was accorded special significance because he was being considered as a potential vice-presidential candidate in 1960. Also, reports that the speech had been revised several times during the Little Rock confrontation led to suggestions it would be a response to Faubus's action. These speculations resulted in an unprecedented buildup by the national press.[25]

Collins received warnings of the political dangers in advancing too far on the racial issue. Faubus spoke for many southerners when he later characterized his section of the country as "an unwanted stepchild in the family of states." He continued, "Naturally, if any Southerner were to be considered for a national role, he must openly conform to the political views prevalent in other sections even if it meant the denial of his own region." Reflecting this view, Governor Marvin S. Griffin, of Georgia, charged prior to Collins's speech that a southerner could not be elected as president "without knifing his own people."[26]

In order to obtain a Floridian's reaction, Collins gave Malcolm B. Johnson, editor of the Tallahassee *Democrat* and an old friend, an advance copy of the speech. Johnson advised him that it was too liberal and would cost him political support.[27] Collins, though, appeared determined that his message reach his constituents.

During the week prior to the meeting, he recorded a thirty-minute excerpt of the speech for radio and filmed passages for television that he offered to the state's media for presentation after the live address.[28]

The weekend before the conference, an incident occurred that further impressed on Collins the potential hazards in challenging the resisters. Several of the governors gathered in Atlanta for a meeting of the Southern Regional Education Board. On Saturday night, they attended a Georgia-Texas football game. Shortly after the second-half kickoff, they were introduced. Some were amiably booed, though Collins received polite applause. In contrast to the disinterest shown in the other governors, the announcement of Faubus's name evoked an unrestrained emotional outburst from the 33,000 southerners. Officials delayed the game several minutes as wave after wave of applause poured down upon the Arkansas governor. People jammed the aisles and leaped over seats to get nearer. The press swarmed over Faubus. Order was finally restored, but, following the game, crowds thronged through the streets shouting, "Faubus! Faubus!"[29] Dixie had a new folk hero.

The demonstration reinforced for Collins the earlier warnings on the price of moderation. He had not planned, in fact, to attack Faubus and considered his address a statesmanlike position. Besides, the governors had reached tacit agreement that segregation would not be discussed in the formal gatherings. Prior to the conference, Governor Hodges reminded Collins: "We don't want to make any scare headlines out of this meeting." Yet, the racial crisis could not be ignored. Collins knew that any stance opposing defiance of the federal government would be interpreted as a denunciation of Faubus.[30]

On Monday, September 23, the day of Collins's speech, the governors received ominous reports from Little Rock. Over the weekend, Mayor Woodrow W. Mann had belatedly sought assistance. The police department offered only halfhearted assurances of maintaining order and refused to guarantee the black children's safety. The national government rejected requests for marshals to help avoid conflict, even though the mayor was under federal court order to carry through on integration. Mann had no other choice than to use the reluctant police force to prevent violence. On Monday morning, the black students entered Central High School, but by noon a belligerent mob outside the building had forced their removal.[31]

The mounting crisis in Arkansas added drama to Collins's luncheon address. He began by stating that a southerner could indeed be elected as president. The candidate would need outstanding competence, allegiance to the national interest, and an ability to sell himself. Equally important, he advised, a southern candidacy would require well-defined goals.

Collins suggested that one goal should be the realignment of federal-state relations. He did not consider the demand for greater state responsibility necessarily a conservative view. The states could lead in progressivism. But states' rights adherents had to understand, the governor stressed, "many of the responsibilities which should have been assumed by the states have gone to the federal government largely by default because state and local governments have often failed to serve or to protect their people." States' rights proponents needed to accept the complementary goal of states' responsibilities.

Collins also recommended that a southern candidate advocate new foreign policy standards. The presidential aspirant should pledge to reduce the defense budget and dissolve the cold war by accepting Wendell Willkie's concept of "One World." Foreign policy must consist of more than condemnation of communism. Ultimately, the United States had to offer the "uncommitted" areas of the world something better than the repression of national aspirations in return for military bases. Collins, in effect, demanded that morality be a component of American foreign policy.

Having answered the "states' righters" and "Communist crusaders," the governor turned to the racial issue. "An essential goal which any serious presidential candidate must seek," he contended, "is that of racial harmony and progress." He appreciated the difficulties confronting southerners who worked for "the brotherhood of mankind, and the dignity of the law, in areas alive with emotions deeply rooted in the past." The leader must not advance too far in front of his followers. Yet, he must advance.

Collins believed Americans realized the problems and would respect a southerner who dealt with the race issue in a calm, lawful, courageous manner:

> I am convinced that the prevailing sentiment in this nation is not radical. It is realistic and understanding. It does not condone arrogance and the irresponsible forcing of issues. It believes that the decisions of the United States Supreme Court are the law of the land and insists that ours be a land of the law. It does not sanction violence, defiance and disorder. Above all, it abhors hate.

Collins charged that southern leaders must understand and accept these sentiments to be in harmony with the rest of the nation.

Southerners were also urged to tolerate change in their customs. "They must not forget that the first law of nature is change," Collins entreated, "and that the second is the survival of those who put themselves in accord with this change." The South should resist wrapping itself in a "confederate blanket" and consuming itself in racial furor. To repudiate change, the governor concluded, would be to miss the region's best opportunity for progress and to bury itself politically for decades.[32]

The address defined a new course for personal leadership. Collins could not return to a position of legal opposition to the Supreme Court and remain consistent with the tone of the Sea Island speech. Instead, he moved to a policy of "legal implementation." His duty, and that of other southerners, was to carry out the law as defined by the Supreme Court.

Collins's fellow executives gave him a standing ovation at the end of the speech. Governors Frank G. Clement, of Tennessee, and Hodges agreed that the address was "magnificent." The Republican governor of West Virginia, Cecil H. Underwood, called it "a marvelous speech." Oklahoma Governor Raymond Gary considered it to be "a masterpiece."[33]

Not all the governors responded so enthusiastically. Alabama's picturesque governor, James E. Folsom, remained in the bar to avoid what he termed "Collins's filibuster." Governors Earl K. Long, of Louisiana, and Griffin, of Georgia, described the speech as good but unrealistic. Griffin later added that, of course, he did not agree with Collins's interpretation of the Constitution. Governor George B. Timmerman was more direct. "We in South Carolina will run our own affairs," he declared, "regardless of what other people want." Initially, Faubus evaluated the address as "a fine speech" and refused further comment. Privately, though, he believed, "Collins had prostituted himself to non-Southern interests in hopes of a vice-presidential spot on the Democratic ticket or favor with an anti-South administration."[34]

Collins received praise from across the nation. Eleanor Roosevelt congratulated him. Vice-President Richard M. Nixon contended, "I think that the true majority opinion in the South is represented by the statesmanlike position taken by Governor Collins in his speech." Some newspapers viewed the address as a response to the events in Little Rock. By direct implication, Collins had "spanked" Faubus, one wrote. Another asserted that the speech illustrated the contrast between the Old South, represented by Faubus, and the New South, represented by Collins. *Newsweek* asked, "wouldn't LeRoy Collins make a good [national] candidate?"[35]

Southern moderates also voiced support for Collins. The Atlanta *Constitution* judged the address to be an "eloquent testimony of faith." Another Georgia paper wrote, "Never has there been an appeal in modern times for great leadership so well, so eloquently, and so powerfully expressed."[36] A Louisiana college professor praised the governor for striking "the golden mean" between two groups of extremists. One South Carolina scholar understood the real significance of the speech. "It may be a paradox," he pointed out, "but in times like these it takes a bold man to be moderate."[37]

Many Floridians also complimented Collins. Several politicians, including Senator George Smathers, commended the speech.[38] A Miami newsman thought it established Collins as the leader of southern moderates. Another journalist submitted that Florida's chief executive had stolen the show from Arkansas's governor. Some Floridians wanted Collins to begin organizing his campaign for president. The directors of the Annual Destin Fishing Tournament urged him to establish his summer "White House" in their city.[39]

Other constituents were less supportive. The Martha Reid Chapter, United Daughters of the Confederacy, of Jacksonville, adopted a resolution stating, "[Collins] has preached the 'moderate approach' on the problems of integration which is the doctrine of meek submission to the NAACP." The women criticized him for "courting the Northern radical wing of the Democratic Party, the NAACP, and the negro vote in the large cities of the East and Middle West" in order to satisfy his ambition for national political office. They concluded by condemning "slurs on our Southern customs and traditions by Governor LeRoy Collins."[40] Despite the attitude of such resisters, the public response to the address was essentially positive.

Events in Little Rock soon transformed southern opinion. On the afternoon that Collins spoke to the governors' conference, Mayor Mann again requested federal assistance. Eisenhower issued a cease-and-desist order demanding noninterference with the Court-ordered integration, but he had withheld his influence too long. On Tuesday, the mob again formed at Central High School. That evening, the president federalized the Arkansas National Guard and dispatched a thousand soldiers from the 101st Airborne Division to the city. On Wednesday morning, federal troops escorted the black students into Central High School and dispersed the demonstrators.[41]

Eisenhower's action shocked the South. The governors at Sea Island expressed virtual unanimity in their opposition; only Maryland's Theodore R. McKeldin, a Republican, endorsed the deployment of troops. In a statement supported by Folsom and Long, Timmerman charged, "[Eisenhower] is attempting to set himself up as a dictator, and this may be taken as a further evidence of an effort to communize America." Collins had warned that the use of troops would be a "grievous error" and disapproved of the president's action. He did not restrict his scorn to Eisenhower, though. "The whole mess out there [in Little Rock] is sickening," he said.[42]

On the morning the troops escorted blacks into Central High School, the governors chose Collins as their new chairman. McKeldin had been the preconference favorite for the position, and the nominating committee had proposed Griffin. However, the enthusiastic response to his speech and the help of Hodges made Collins the surprise choice. Observers viewed his selection as a victory for southern liberals.[43]

On Clement's suggestion, the governors appointed a committee to negotiate with Eisenhower for the withdrawal of federal troops. They chose Hodges as chairman of the group, which also included Collins, Clement, McKeldin, and Griffin. Faubus, who had returned to Little Rock, agreed to support the action.[44] Eisenhower accepted the request for a meeting "to discuss the problems of school integration." Acknowledging the president's response, Collins emphasized that the committee had been instructed to consider only the Little Rock issue. He added, "As individual Governors, however, each of us will be free to discuss any phase of the integration problems."

Governor Griffin then backed out, charging that Collins had given in to the president's request for a more wide-ranging discussion. He wired Collins: "I cannot accept your suggestion that as Governor of Georgia I should undertake to discuss with the President at this meeting the operation of the public schools of Georgia." Collins responded that he had made "crystal clear" the limitations on the governors. "You place the other members of our committee in an awkward position," he added.[45] Without Griffin, the extreme segregationist viewpoint was not represented.

For four hours on the morning of October 1, 1957, the governors held a strategy meeting at the Mayflower Hotel, in Washington. After agreeing that the conference would need to be limited to the removal of federal troops, they composed an opening statement expressing their goal. If Faubus pledged to maintain law and order, then the president should withdraw the troops. The conferees contacted Faubus to outline their plan. Although requesting that he be informed of later developments, he said, "All right, that's all right."[46]

At 2:30 that afternoon, the committee met with Eisenhower. Before the formal conference began, he served coffee to the governors on the Rose Garden patio. Noticing that Collins was momentarily separated from the others, Eisenhower walked over to speak to him confidentially.[47] Perhaps Eisenhower recalled Collins's telegram in March 1956 conveying the Tallahassee conference's sentiments on integration. At that time, Collins had requested a meeting between the southern governors and the president to describe the intensity of segregationist opinion. Ei-

senhower must have recognized neither the political pressures on
Collins in 1956, nor his changing perspective during the succeeding eighteen months.

At any rate, the president chose this opportunity to explain his
views on the racial crisis. He expressed his hope that the people of
the South understood his position. He deemed the southern way of
life perfectly all right. Yet, the Supreme Court had ruled on the
law, and his duty was to enforce the decision. If the Court had
ruled the other way, he disclosed, he would be just as anxious to
support the verdict.[48]

Collins was astounded. The president had misjudged him. Collins later asserted that Eisenhower must have viewed him as a
typical southern governor and, believing the group to be homoge-
neous in its opinion, thought his disclaimer of responsibility would
be well received. He was wrong. Collins believed that the president owed the country more positive leadership. Although Collins
subsequently often "replayed" the conversation in his mind, in-
serting the comments he wished he had made at the time, he was
for the moment virtually speechless. He could only mumble,
"Thank you, Mr. President."[49]

After a ten-minute picture-taking session, the conferees moved
into Eisenhower's west-wing office. Frank Bane, the executive
secretary of the Council of State Governments, joined the negotiations. Presidential press secretary James Hagerty and presidential
aides Howard Pyle and Sherman Adams also participated. Attorney General Herbert Brownell, recognizing the South's anger at
his role in the Little Rock controversy, decided the talks would be
friendlier without his presence, but remained nearby for consulta-
tion with the president.[50]

The southerners began the negotiations by warning Eisenhower
that the removal of military forces from Little Rock was essential to
resolving the integration crisis. He could not withdraw the federal
troops, he responded, without assurance that state authorities
would protect the right of children to attend school. He recalled, "I
told them, I was ready to join in issuing a statement that Faubus
had promised to assume full responsibility for law and order in
Little Rock and promised to help carry out the order of the court,
and that therefore I would direct the withdrawal of troops and the

defederalization of the national guard." As Adams observed, "The problem boiled down to drafting a declaration of peaceful intentions for Faubus to send to the President so that the troops could be removed."[51]

After talking for more than an hour, the committee moved to another room and began drafting a message for Faubus to send the president. Meanwhile, Eisenhower discussed possible wordings of the statement with Brownell. When the governors drafted a document that the attorney general agreed would indicate Faubus's good intentions, Eisenhower approved it.[52]

The governors then sought Faubus's concurrence. A series of telephone calls, long waits, revisions, and frequent consultations with Hagerty, Pyle, and Adams ensued. When the committee formulated a statement acceptable to all sides, Hodges and Bane talked to Faubus personally to be certain he agreed with the wording.[53] Eisenhower was skeptical. "For the Lord's sake," he demanded, "get it sound and solid so it won't be necessary to go through this again." The governors sent a telegram to Faubus to make sure he understood the phraseology. Faubus was to say, in part, "I now declare, that upon the withdrawal of federal troops, I will again assume full responsibility, in cooperation with local authorities, for the maintenance of law and order, and that the orders of the Federal Courts will not be obstructed." When Faubus agreed to issue the statement, Eisenhower promised to withdraw the troops.[54]

The conferees were jubilant. One newspaper wrote that the pressure from the four governors had influenced Faubus's "head- long retreat."[55] The pact would be formalized when Faubus released the statement from Little Rock. Because of the demands of a special legislative session, Collins returned to Tallahassee immediately after the meeting, but the other governors remained in Washington. Two hours later, Faubus's message arrived. When the governors were informed of the wording, they were stunned. Collins did not learn until the next morning that Faubus had revised the accord.[56]

The Arkansas governor had inserted the words "by me" at the end. Eisenhower believed this changed the meaning of the document. He charged Faubus with repudiating his obligation to see that others followed the law. When questioned on the issue of protecting the black children, Faubus parried, "I don't have to do that. The federal government's in charge at the moment. I'll consider that possibility whenever it becomes my responsibility." He later denied any agreement to a specifically phrased statement and considered the original wording to be "a perfidious effort to entrap me into doing the dirty and unpleasant enforcement of the federal court orders." Eisenhower recalled, "I had no choice."[57] The troops remained in Little Rock.

Faubus's action disgusted Collins, who insisted, "We went over every word of every statement very carefully with Governor Faubus and it was my understanding that he specifically agreed to everything verbatim just as the President did." Collins telephoned Eisenhower to express his approval of the president's cooperation and his disappointment with Faubus. The Floridian thought that Eisenhower's position was reasonable. The president had been willing to accept Faubus's word, which Collins would not have done.[58]

On September 30 the Florida legislature had convened in special session to consider constitutional revision. Many legislators, however, considered the events in Little Rock more important than drafting a new constitution. They wanted to block any attempt by the federal government to force integration in Florida. Ervin's "last resort" school-closing bill appeared to be an attractive alternative to imposed desegregation.[59]

The proponents of the school-closing measure faced a difficult problem. Because Collins had called the special session only to consider constitutional revision, passage of bills on other subjects required a two-thirds vote. Staunch segregationist Senators W. Randolph Hodges, of Cedar Key, and H. H. Hair, Jr., of Live Oak, introduced the last-resort proposal. Hodges charged, "We are faced with the fact that we will have the Supreme Court order enforced with the cold steel of bayonets." The bill easily passed the senate by a vote of thirty-one to five.[60]

The house of representatives had upheld Collins's veto in the spring. The governor and State School Superintendent Thomas D. Bailey concentrated their efforts on stopping the measure in the house. On October 2 the bill fell five votes short of the required two-thirds majority for passage. That evening, the proposal's advocates applied pressure to house members in an attempt to force passage of the bill the next day. The second ballot on the measure failed to pass by three votes.

As a compromise, Collins signed a bill that allowed the closing of schools if the federal government used troops to force integration. He justified his action by saying, "it is almost ridiculous to assume that any sound education could be carried on under pressure of armed guards, and as a parent, I would rather have my children at home." He had been concerned that racist agitators would aggravate the situation to obtain a vote to close the schools.[61] The compromise bill prevented this possibility. Collins had succeeded, for the moment, in blocking the initiation of massive resistance in the state.

Collins remained determined to present a moderate alternative to an increasingly intractable South. On October 10, just nine days after the White House conference, he again enjoyed an opportunity to challenge the resisters. The sponsors of the Presbyterian Men's Convention, in Miami, invited him to deliver a welcoming address. According to a church journal, the delegates expected "the mild and somewhat meaningless words" that normally characterized such speeches. Instead, Collins used the occasion to issue a call for action to southern moderates. Although the churchmen were later addressed by such notables as Billy Graham, observers conceded that, after Collins's opening speech, the other orations were "largely anticlimatic."[62]

The governor based his comments on the theme of a Robert Sherwood play, *The Trial of Pontius Pilate*. In Collins's view, the drama illustrated that, in the biblical story, Pilate, not Christ, was on trial. When the mob threatened, Pilate washed his hands of the incident and said, "See to it yourself." Sherwood implied that Pilate's guilt resulted from his failure to act.

Collins told the churchmen, "You and I today are under the pressure of a mob." Challenging the Presbyterians on the theme of their convention, he asked, "when the mob is howling at your door and when the pressure comes, will you then be *All the Way for Christ?*" Collins believed the racial crisis had put southern moderates on trial. Their failure to act would be an admission of guilt.

The governor used two examples from his own state to illustrate his concern. During his battle with the legislature on the interposition resolution, he had hoped for support from lawyers "who knew better." "But the mob was howling," he asserted, "so they washed their hands of it and they said, 'See to it yourself.' " As a result, the legislature passed a resolution that was "anarchistic in its very nature."[63]

Collins also told the convention of an incident involving Dr. Deborah Coggins, a health officer for three north Florida counties. In August 1956 she had needed to confer with a black nurse who worked under her. Pressed for time, she met her colleague in the back room of a restaurant, where they talked while eating lunch. When local citizens learned of the "integrated" luncheon, a mob gathered at the county courthouse demanding that the doctor be discharged. The county commissioners subsequently fired her.

At the time of the incident, Collins said, "I am sick about it. The action cannot be squared with the right and justice and conscience, and, if I didn't speak up and say so, I feel that I would, by my silence, condone an evil act." In his speech to the Miami convention, he asked:

> Where in that situation were our Presbyterians? Where were our Methodists? Our Episcopalians? Where were all of our churchmen? Where were all of our people who are dedicated to this proposition of *All for Christ?* Did they go before these county commissioners and say, "Don't! This is wrong!"? No, they called for the bowl, and they washed their hands, and they said, just as Pontius Pilate said, "The blood of this innocent, righteous person won't be on my hands. See to it yourself." And she was fired, to the everlasting shame of our citizens.

The governor concluded his address with an appeal for "dedication to action" to provide a moderate alternative during the crisis facing the South.[64]

The Little Rock conflict marked a turning point for Collins, Faubus, and the South. The confrontation offered the region a choice. White southerners could choose the path of defiance, following leaders such as Faubus, or they could choose the path of moderation, led by men such as Collins. Faubus would serve six successive terms as governor of Arkansas, whereas Collins would never again hold elective office. By choosing the path of defiance, a majority of white southerners accepted a commitment to years of conflict on the issue of race.

8

The Campaign for
Half a Loaf:

Reapportionment and Reform,
1957–1959

While the racial crisis haunted the South, Collins would try to maintain interest and support for the modernization of his state's institutions. Although his crusade for constitutional revision ultimately foundered on the reapportionment issue, he achieved other reforms in the 1957 and 1959 legislatures. Meanwhile, he continued to gain national attention for his stance on the racial issue, for his role in the National Governors' Conference, and for his efforts to stimulate Florida's economy. By 1960 one reporter believed the governor had "achieved a stature outside the state no other Florida chief executive has enjoyed."[1]

Despite the racial furor in 1957, Collins claimed that governmental change was the state's most important problem. In his second inaugural address, he charged, "First and foremost among governmental reforms, we need a new constitution." The Constitution Advisory Commission, which had been established in 1955, presented its recommendations to the 1957 legislature: the new charter should include provisions for a lieutenant governor and limited home rule, two of Collins's long-standing demands; and the supreme court ought to possess the power to reapportion if the legislature could not reach an agreement. In his opening message, Collins commended the report and urged the lawmakers to place duty above partisan politics in designing a new constitution.[2]

The Porkchoppers, though, did not intend to forsake their cause.

They had won in 1955 and expected to repeat their success. The reapportionment battle had scarred executive-legislative relations. Collins's pledge to appeal "over the heads" of the legislators directly to the voters especially incensed his opponents. They considered the ploy outside the tradition of resolving governmental disputes by interpersonal give-and-take. The Porkchoppers also believed Collins had pressed a hopeless cause too far. They contended he should have accepted their legislative formulas as the best measures possible. His intransigence had caused the deadlock in 1955, the opposition claimed. Reapportionment warfare had intensified small-county unity and the Porkchoppers' intractable attitude.[3]

Some of Collins's urban allies also criticized his reapportionment strategy. A few believed a personal appeal to two or three marginal senators might have broken the 1955 deadlock. Collins's effort to prevent the estrangement of the Porkchoppers from his administration brought more criticism. Some Lambchoppers claimed that he could have forced concessions by using his power over road construction and patronage. They accused him of demonstrating more friendship with his opponents than with his allies. The Tampa *Morning Tribune* advised, "The only language which many legislators understand is the rough talk of support denied and patronage withheld." The Miami *Daily News* declared, "the real question is not whether the Florida Legislature is ready to deal with the problem but whether the Florida Governor is."[4] In the 1957 session, the Lambchoppers and Porkchoppers were bitterly hostile, and both groups held grievances against Collins.

William A. Shands, president of the senate, appointed a special committee to study the proposed charter; a Porkchopper, Dewey Johnson, of Quincy, was designated as chairman. For vice-chairman, Shands chose John Rawls, of Marianna, one of Collins's strongest critics in the 1955 reapportionment battle. Eleven of the thirteen-member committee opposed the governor's position on constitutional change. The small-county bloc also controlled the Constitutional Revision Committee, in the house of representatives. Such committee "stacking" was a time-honored ploy in state politics, yet the tactic evoked bitterness from those who considered it to be unfair.[5]

The legislature refused to call a constitutional convention, which would have been beyond its control. Instead, the lawmakers amended the state charter article by article. They linked the changes by a "daisy chain," requiring acceptance of all or none. The house committee wanted to retain the same number of legislative seats and take away the governor's veto power on reapportionment decisions. The senate concurred with the proposal to strip the governor of the veto and to keep the same number of house seats. In an attempt to placate the large counties, though, the Porkchoppers agreed to expand the senate from thirty-eight to forty-two members.[6] In effect, the legislative measures would have maintained the status quo, while removing executive influence on reapportionment.

Collins was not pleased. He termed the senate recommendation, "the most unsound, unacceptable, and abominable suggestion I have seen advanced in the field of constitutional revision." He countered by suggesting an increase of twenty representatives and five senators. When the house defeated the proposal by three votes, he and the legislature seemed destined for another deadlock.[7]

Rather than calling a special session with little hope of success, Collins agreed that a joint legislative committee could continue the work after adjournment. A breakthrough on reapportionment came late in the summer. On September 6, the Porkchop "gang" gathered at an Aucilla River fishing camp to consider redistricting proposals. The majority agreed to add seven senators, four of whom would be from south Florida. Although this proposal offered little to the underrepresented sections, Collins vowed his support if the proposal would include "a substantial increase in the house membership to offset the weakened position of the populous areas under the senate plan." On September 21 a house caucus voted to add nineteen seats to its ninety-five-member chamber. The governor and the joint legislative committee accepted the plan.[8]

Collins called a special session on constitutional revision for September 30, 1957. The legislators battled over the "last resort" school-closing bill before turning to consideration of constitutional reform. Because the provision on reapportionment had already been formulated, the solons quickly agreed on fourteen amendments to modernize the constitution. The proposals included a much weaker home-rule amendment than the governor desired. The legislators, though, acceded to his request for a lieutenant governor to prevent a succession crisis such as had occurred following McCarty's death.[9] The voters were to judge the amendments in November 1958.

Many Lambchoppers protested that the apportionment provision did not go far enough and condemned Collins's support for the plan. One urban newspaper described the plan as a continuation of "rural rule." For one of the few times in his political career, Collins's integrity was questioned. The Tampa *Daily Times* termed his compromise a "capitulation," and the Daytona Beach *Morning Journal* accused him of lying about the plan. The Orlando *Sentinel* concluded, "To say we are disappointed in our alert and ebullient

Governor Collins and his father admire catch from 1958 fishing trip. (*Courtesy, Florida State Archives*)

young governor is to put it mildly."[10] The larger counties appeared unwilling to accept a partial victory.

Collins led the campaign for ratification. "We can't get adequate reapportionment until we get better apportionment than we have now," he argued. "The new apportionment plan gives us vastly improved representation for our most underrepresented areas and new legislative strength and leadership for further improvement." The debate ended when the Florida Supreme Court forbade the referendum on the basis that the linkage of the amendments into a "daisy chain" contradicted the dictates of the state's constitution. Although Floridians enjoyed no opportunity to vote, opposition in the urban areas would have virtually assured defeat of the amendments.[11] Reapportionment had to be delayed until the next legislative session.

By 1959 Collins's influence had waned. The reapportionment battle had cost him support. Furthermore, one observer pointed out, some legislators entertained "a deep-seated hostility toward him for his stand on racial legislation." Dubbed the "Wrecking Crew," these legislators were determined to defeat any of his proposals "partly for spite and partly from pure cussedness."[12] He, himself, had pushed reforms that further weakened his office. The merit system removed much of his patronage power. He also insisted on appointing judges and county officers on merit, rather than making deals with local leaders. Moreover, he instituted a system of highway allocation based on a formula to determine need rather than trading road construction for votes. Finally, many Florida Democrats considered him to be a lame-duck governor and were thinking of the primary coming in the spring of 1960. Under the circumstances, a columnist wrote, some legislators believed "the governor's support for a measure might kiss it to death."[13]

Despite these problems, Collins did not concede defeat on reapportionment. Following the supreme court ruling, he appointed a new committee, which presented constitutionally valid changes to the 1959 legislature. In an address to the lawmakers, he predicted a devastating era of sectionalism if they denied equitable apportionment. "The people of south Florida—the people in our population center—feel that they are not being treated fairly, in the matter of legislative representation, and they are right," he asserted.[14] "Governor Collins might as well have been talking into a dead mike," a newsman noted.[15]

The legislators knew that, for their part, the reapportionment war was over. The Porkchoppers had vanquished all challenges to their hegemony. "The attacking forces seemed to have exhausted themselves in the long struggle, and the defensive alignment displayed the magnanimity expected of so powerful a foe," commentators suggested. Both sides searched for an "honorable truce." The Porkchoppers refused to consider constitutional revision and, instead, attempted to solve only the reapportionment problem. Ultimately, they agreed to an amendment adding six senators and eight representatives. In return, the small counties were assured an equal division of racetrack money regardless of size.[16]

Prior to the November 1959 vote on the amendment, Collins campaigned throughout the state. Applying the political axiom "half a loaf is better than none" to the reapportionment issue, he argued that increased representation would provide the large counties more strength for further change. "This is progress," he asserted. "This can help get the state out of the pork chop strait-jacket. This will provide new men, new troops to take up the battle in the years ahead. . . . Let's get these reinforcements and with them push forward to still better representation for all Florida."[17] Collins's effort gained the support of a majority of the state's newspapers, including several of the most influential dailies.[18] One editorialized, "The chief virtue of the compromise plan is that it would break the ice."[19]

Major opposition came from Pinellas County, which included St. Petersburg, and the Gold Coast, in the southeastern portion of the state. Several urban mayors, including Haydon Burns, of Jacksonville, and John Russel, of Fort Lauderdale, contested the proposal. The Florida Committee for Fair Representation, led by attorney Earl Faircloth, also fought the reapportionment measure. He claimed, "The people of the populous areas have seen through this scheme to retain pork chop control of the legislature." The St. Petersburg *Times* stated the position of many people who were opposed to the amendment. "The truth is," the paper charged, "the Porkchop Gang and their allies fervently want the people of

Florida to accept this gold-brick amendment for fear that they might lose some of their unjustified power in an equitable reapportionment forced on them by overwhelming public demand—or by the courts."[20]

On November 3, 1959, Floridians defeated the amendment. Collins's dream of constitutional reform died. He sadly reflected, "I just don't think the people understood." The election results were in a "crazy-quilt" pattern. The margin of defeat came from seven small northern counties, the six counties of the Gold Coast, and Pinellas County. The combination of large and small counties indicated that neither was really ready for compromise. Mayor Russel exalted, "Mr. Porkchopper, we say that your days are numbered." Harriet Gulkis, of Miami, summed up the feelings of many citizens when she asserted, "I didn't think half a loaf was better than none."[21]

A few months later, Collins said, "somewhere along the line, in some way, some remedy is going to have to come. And if the Legislature does not provide the remedy itself, I think it will be just a matter of time before the courts are going to step in and find a way to furnish relief."[22] His prediction proved to be accurate. In 1962 the U.S. Supreme Court ruled in the case of *Baker* v. *Carr* that Tennessee had to reapportion its legislature to reflect population changes. Two years later, *Wesberry* v. *Sanders* established the principle of "one man, one vote." Also in 1964 the Court ruled in *Reynolds* v. *Sims* that geographical diversity could not be considered in reapportioning legislative seats. Justice Hugo Black later told Collins that Florida's inability to resolve the reapportionment problem affected the Court's decisions.[23]

The constitutional reform effort initiated by Collins was to influence Florida directly in the mid-1960s. Under court pressure, the legislature passed a reapportionment measure in 1966 that provided a more equitable system. Nevertheless, the U.S. Supreme Court, in *Swann* v. *Adams* (1967), found the Florida law unconstitutional. Under the Court's direction, the legislature devised an acceptable apportionment scheme. After that divisive issue was resolved, a new Florida constitution was ratified in 1968.[24]

Collins's failure to obtain constitutional revision during his years as governor left a major goal unfulfilled. In fact, though, reapportionment presented an insoluble problem for the state. The constitutional method prescribed for redistributing legislative seats required the small-county lawmakers voluntarily to surrender political power.[25] Long-standing social, psychological, and political grievances insured that the Porkchoppers and their agrarian constituents would not concede control. The reapportionment issue incorporated a conflict between fundamental values and traditions. Collins's effort at moral suasion produced no effect because both sides laid claim to moral right. Ultimately, only an outside agency—such as the U.S. Supreme Court—could have forced the change.

Collins could not have exerted any more pressure on the Porkchoppers without completely alienating them from his administration. He refused to take that step. Never concentrating his administration's energies on a single issue, he submitted numerous reform measures to the legislature that allowed antagonists to oppose a major proposal but to accept others. Opponents never sustained a solid front against his whole program. As a result, he lost some spectacular fights, but quietly won many victories.[26] One reporter believed that, by not putting undue pressure on the Porkchoppers when he pushed for reapportionment, Collins gained their support for measures they would not otherwise have accepted.[27] Although race and reapportionment attracted headlines, without fanfare he accomplished reforms that had created tumult in earlier administrations.[28]

Considering the bitter divisions created by the reapportionment and racial conflicts, Collins's reform record was remarkable. The 1957 session, for example, was one of the most active in the state's history. Major laws included the introduction of water resources control, the establishment of a labor conciliation board, the creation of a Department of Corrections to run the state prison system, the funding of a study to propose reorganization of the Department of Agriculture, the establishment of a central purchasing system, the formulation of a revised road code, increased appropriations for county health units and indigent hospitalization, and a 10-percent increase in old-age benefits. "Few governors have been able to look back on a Legislature with as much satisfaction," one columnist wrote.[29]

Collins also achieved a revision of the Ninety-Day Divorce Law. It had been enacted in the depression years to entice more people to the state. Collins had objected to the measure as a representative and senator and continued his opposition as governor. In his first address to the legislature, he called for reform of the provision. During the 1955 session, the senate voted thirty-three to three to institute a one-year residency law, but the house Judiciary Committee defeated the proposal. Critics claimed that lawyers, who constituted a majority on the committee, were reluctant to revise a law that brought them a continuing and profitable flow of business.[30]

The governor told the 1957 legislature, "It is wrong for Florida, with the great stake we have in maintaining the finest possible moral atmosphere, to hold out quick and easy severance of marriage ties among our attractions and businesses."[31] The house Judiciary Committee again blocked the one-year residency bill. Newspapers throughout the state attacked the lawyers for sacrificing moral principle to insure legal business.[32] The public pressure forced the committee to reconsider and compromise on a six-month residency proposal. The measure passed with large majorities in both legislative houses. Although Collins had wanted the one-year law, he demonstrated his willingness to accept the best measure possible. He signed the bill on May 3, 1957.[33]

The Collins administration also made significant progress in education. He continued the efforts he had begun as a legislator to improve teachers' salaries. In 1955 the legislature voted a two-hundred-dollar raise, but two years later the pay scale was still a hotly contested issue. Although supporting an increase, the governor disagreed with the demands of the Florida Education Association. He labeled the organization's goals "unrealistic and unsound." Eventually, Collins, educators, and legislators compromised to provide the teachers with a substantial raise.[34]

Higher education presented special challenges. The state expected college enrollment to triple by 1970. Attorney General Ervin spoke for one faction, which predicted the problem would "work itself out" without large expenditures. Groups seeking state funds, such as the road lobby, agreed with him. Collins, education leaders, and many legislators advocated a more positive program.[35]

Collins was forced to balance his own design for higher education with political realities. He believed an expansion of the public junior college system offered the best opportunity to meet the challenge. Under his administration, the number of such colleges increased from five to twenty-four. In contrast, he wavered in his support for university expansion. He wanted the state to improve the quality of the existing institutions (the University of Florida, FSU, and FAMU) while counting on junior colleges to absorb the bulk of added enrollments. Yet, the populous areas exerted intense pressure for new universities in their communities. In the end, Collins advocated initiating some university construction along with fostering the growth of the junior colleges. He led in the planning, building, and opening (in September 1960) of the University of South Florida, at Tampa. He also gained legislative authorization to begin planning for universities in Palm Beach County (Florida Atlantic University) and in Escambia County (the University of West Florida).[36]

In the midst of the 1957 legislative session, an extradition case momentarily deflected attention from educational, constitutional, and racial issues. Melvin and Frances Ellis and their daughter Hildy McCoy Ellis were the central figures. The Brookline, Massachusetts, couple had legally adopted Hildy on March 2, 1951, ten days after her birth. Marjorie McCoy, the child's natural mother, agreed to the adoption. As was customary, McCoy, a Roman Catholic, knew neither the adoptive parents' names nor their religious affiliation. Within a few months, she discovered that Hildy had been placed with Jewish parents. She consulted with her priest, who encouraged her to seek the child's return. If she gained custody, she planned to place her daughter for adoption through a Catholic agency.[37]

Initiating court proceedings, McCoy cited a Massachusetts law that provided, "when practicable," an adopted child was to be matched with parents of the same faith. The Ellises contested the legal action, but offered to compromise by rearing Hildy in the Catholic faith. McCoy rejected the proposal, and the court found in her favor. The Ellises appealed the decision, selling their home and dry cleaning business to pay legal costs. In 1955 the Massachusetts Supreme Court ordered them to give up Hildy.[38]

Instead, the Ellises fled the state. They lived in seven different cities from Maine to Florida, finally settling in Miami, where Melvin Ellis worked as a clothing salesman. On March 15, 1957, he purchased a new car, which required a routine registration check. Officials discovered that in September 1956 Massachusetts authorities had issued fugitive warrants for the Ellises that charged them with kidnapping Hildy. Initially, Frances and Hildy Ellis went into hiding, but Melvin Ellis announced, "I don't care if I go to jail. . . . We're not running anymore." They decided to fight the extradition request.[39]

The Ellises' determined efforts to keep Hildy and the religious basis for the case attracted nationwide interest in the extradition hearings. One newspaper reported that Collins received nearly thirteen thousand telegrams supporting the Ellises and about one hundred favoring extradition. On May 23 the Ellises and J. Blake Thaxter, an assistant district attorney from Dedham, Massachusetts, presented their respective positions to Collins in a capitol committee hearing room. Although admitting that the Ellises were good parents, Thaxter emphasized, "These people are guilty of the crime of kidnapping." Frances Ellis contended that she and her husband had committed only "the crime of loving a child." She also claimed psychologists had determined that separating Hildy from her parents would cause her "irreparable harm."[40]

After the hearing, Collins went to his office, where he reviewed the testimony and wrote out his decision on the case. At five o'clock that afternoon, he read his statement before the reporters and network radio and television personnel who jammed the hearing room. The Ellises sat directly across the table from the governor.[41] Collins labeled the criminal charge "synthetic" and concluded that "no crime of kidnapping in a proper sense is involved." Hildy's future, not legalities, he insisted, constituted his primary concern.

> In this [he continued] the rights of the Ellises and the rights of the natural mother are necessarily involved. The controlling question,

however, must be the welfare of the child, and I think simple right
and justice require that Hildy McCoy's present home life should not
be disturbed. It has been argued that the natural mother has the
right to have Hildy reared in the environment of her own faith. This
is a right I respect, but it must yield to more fundamental rights.
The great and good God of all of us, regardless of faith, grants to
every child to be born first the right to be wanted, and secondly the
right to be loved. Hildy's mother has denied both of these rights to
her. . . . It was the Ellises in truth and in fact who have been the
persons through whom God has assured to Hildy these first two
rights as one of His children. It was the Ellises who wanted Hildy to
be born. . . . It was the Ellises also who have given of themselves to
Hildy, as only parents can understand, thereby fulfilling Hildy's
right to be loved. . . . I sincerely hope that this child can now be
allowed to continue to grow and develop in the only home, and with
the only mother and father, she has ever known.[42]

When Collins finished, a front-row observer sobbed, "Thank
God," and spontaneous applause burst out. "There were few
entirely dry eyes," a newsman wrote. Although the governor
gaveled the meeting to order, maintaining that applause was
inappropriate at an official proceeding, one reporter noted, "Governor Collins' eyes seemed suspiciously bright behind his glasses."
He received more than nine thousand letters and telegrams complimenting his decision and the sentiments in his statement.[43] The
Hildy Ellis case brought him nationwide recognition.

Collins's leadership role in the National Governors' Conference
also added to his stature. At their May 21, 1958, Miami Beach
conference, the governors chose him as chairman of their organization. He believed the credit he received as host for the enjoyable
and productive meeting influenced his selection. Furthermore,
the South's "moderate" governors—most importantly Luther
Hodges of North Carolina—championed him for the office. During
his term, Collins urged the governors to expand the organization's
interests into foreign affairs. The conference he chaired convened
in San Juan, Puerto Rico, the first meeting held outside the
continental United States. He centered the program on improving
relations with Latin America.[44]

In a demonstration of the governors' growing concern with

foreign affairs, Collins led a delegation from the conference's Executive Committee on a trip to the Soviet Union. Private foundations sponsored the tour.[45] The goal was to compare the functions of American state governments with the administration of the Soviet republics. The governors first spoke to national leaders in Moscow and then traveled to most of the provincial capitals. At each stop, they visited agricultural and industrial sites, met with local citizens, and exchanged ideas with regional governmental officials.[46]

In 1959 cold war tensions were at their height, and, for many Americans, friendship with the Soviet Union was difficult to comprehend. Indeed, two governors on the Executive Committee deemed the trip to be so politically dangerous that they declined the invitation.[47] The cordiality of the Russian people came as a revelation to Collins. "I was frankly surprised over the instinctive, spontaneous, friendly reception that we got from the rank and file of the people," he admitted.[48]

An incident in Leningrad illustrated the favorable response the governors received. Collins knew that Soviet authorities had denied the Reverend Billy Graham's request to speak at a Baptist church in Leningrad. Out of curiosity, Collins asked to see it. His Soviet hosts balked, but he finally persuaded them to let the governors attend a Sunday service there.[49]

The church was a modest, tin-roofed structure on the city's outskirts. Inside, it resembled any rural Baptist church in Leon County, Florida. Elderly women composed the bulk of the congregation. Collins wanted to sit in back and observe the services, but officials escorted the governors to a front pew. The minister welcomed them and asked if one of the group would please speak to the assembly. None of them was prepared to do so. Collins peered down the pew and asked, "Who's a Baptist?" The governors quickly identified their loyalty to other denominations and agreed that, as chairman, Collins should be their spokesman. As he walked to the pulpit, he realized, "Good gracious Collins, you're getting to do something Billy Graham couldn't do." He decided to make the most of his opportunity.

Through an interpreter, Collins thanked the congregation for its friendly welcome. Telling the Russians of his respect for their contributions to Allied victory during the Second World War, he described their suffering and perseverance under German attack as one of the most courageous acts in history. He then pointed out the similarities between their church service and the ones held in the United States. They shared traditions and beliefs that went beyond differences in political ideology. National boundaries, Collins declared, should not keep Christians from being "brothers, sisters, friends." Responding warmly, the congregation waved white handkerchiefs to applaud his words. He invited the Russians to visit the United States, where he assured them they would be greeted by the same sort of Christian friendship he had experienced that day.

The emotional message left many in the audience with tears streaming down their faces. The minister asked the congregation to sing "God Be with You till We Meet Again." As the governors left the church, Russians on all sides reached out to greet them. The memory of "those hardened but sweet old faces," lined by years of toil and war, always remained with Collins. It was one of the most dramatic scenes he ever experienced.[50]

In Moscow, the governors met with Soviet Premier Nikita Khrushchev in his Kremlin office. Bringing up the subject of press censorship, Collins told Khrushchev that the absence of American newspapers had prevented him from keeping up with baseball scores. Khrushchev pointed out that Collins could have had newspapers mailed to him. "But," the premier added, "I realize your question has a different meaning; that's not what you had on your mind." He could allow the distribution of American newspapers, Khrushchev said, but he resented their tone of criticism toward the Soviet Union. He did not believe their sale would turn the Soviet people from communism. "We have been able to prove to our people the advantage of our system," he claimed.[51] Collins later told newspersons he did not believe a free press would threaten the Soviet Union. He perceived "no apparent weakness or crack in the armor of their governmental control."[52]

Collins thought Khrushchev and other Soviet leaders approached politics in a manner similar to the way the St. Louis Cardinals' "Gas House Gang" had played baseball: loud, brusque, and willing to take any measures to win. He described how at times Khrushchev appeared to be furious, pounding on the table to stress his points. Yet, whenever he realized the Americans were becoming angry, he would shift to a softer, more considerate tone. If the governors replied with sharply stated arguments that incorporated emphatic arm gestures, Collins said, then Khrushchev appeared more willing to accept the credibility of their viewpoint.[53]

On his return, Collins gave reporters an evaluation of Soviet life devoid of cold war clichés. He reminded them of Russia's history of peasant poverty and war. Under the Communists' regimented governmental system, he contended, the Soviet Union had made remarkable strides in agriculture, science, and industry. The Russians were proud of their advances. "I don't think the Russian people have ever had it as good as they have it now," he asserted, "and I saw no indication, whatever, of dissatisfaction with their form of government, or the form of their economy." In fact, he argued, "we could well reevaluate our own way of life." He added, "You can't help but become conscious of the fact that much that we put a great deal of emphasis upon is superficial, and that we could well eliminate a lot of that superficiality to our benefit."[54] The Russian tour gave Collins new perspectives on world affairs and added to his stature as a national leader.

During his second administration, Collins continued his efforts to enhance Florida's economic growth. On October 8, 1957, he told the New York Sales Executive Club that the state was booming because "industry wants to go where people want to live" and that Florida was "a businessman's dream." In April 1960 he led state businessmen on an industrial tour of Chicago, Cleveland, New York, Boston, and Philadelphia. His initiatives attracted new industries, such as Martin-Marietta, at Orlando; Pratt and Whitney, at West Palm Beach; and Portland Cement, in Dade County. By the conclusion of his term, Florida led all states in new industrial development.[55]

The tours boosted not only the economy, but also the governor. Twenty-four reporters greeted him upon his arrival in Chicago, the first stop on his 1960 tour. Inevitably, opponents accused him of using the northern forays to advance his political career. He claimed, "I have only one sole and single motivation for making [the 1960] trip, and that is to help Florida grow—by adding to its industrial potential and development." He denied that the media response resulted from an interest in his future. "They did not come out to hear me; they came out to hear about Florida. I was not trying to sell myself; I was trying to sell Florida," he said.[56] Whatever his goals, the effect was to enhance his national standing. By 1960 commentators viewed him as a leader among the nation's governors.

9

The Collins Plan:
The Racial Crisis, 1958–1959

During 1958 and 1959 the racial crisis would continue to preoccupy Collins and other Americans. The Little Rock impasse led him to reevaluate the integration issue. He decided that the *Brown* decision, itself, had not created the crisis. Instead, the methods used for implementing the ruling had made conflict inevitable. Following the Little Rock episode, Collins sought support for a plan that was designed to avoid violence by establishing new methods for carrying out the Supreme Court's ruling.

In a May 1958 *Look* magazine article entitled "How It Looks from the South," Collins provided an enlightening analysis of his own prejudices, fears, and goals in the racial crisis. He first discussed the role of blacks in southern society. They had not been treated equally, he admitted. Yet, he charged, "to listen to some reformers talk all the Negro needs in the South is to break down the lines of segregation. Nothing could be more ridiculous." Most importantly, blacks needed better health, education, moral, and housing standards in order to improve their talents and gain the respect of whites. Blacks, he claimed, had made major strides before the *Brown* decision, but white hostility to the ruling had interrupted the progress. "Now there are ugly scars on the former good feelings between the races in the South." Since the *Brown* ruling, Collins pointed out, "the voice of extremism has grown loud and the voice of moderation has been reduced to a feeble murmur." He believed "the great majority of silent Southern people" favored segregation and that "deeply entrenched attitudes" made the issue "more fundamental than law." Instead of forced integration, the governor wrote, "the battle for progress should be directed toward improving Negro achievements and toward changing [whites'] attitudes."

Collins then turned to a defense of his moderate segregationist position:

> In Florida, we have no integration in our public schools. And, since I have encouraged our people to regard the Constitution, as interpreted by the Supreme Court, as the law of the land, I have been accused of dealing in words, not deeds. I respond that there are times when words are deeds. I regard integration in and for itself as no proper goal. But developing a healthy climate for racial tolerance is a very high goal. In Florida, we have achieved a far more wholesome climate of opinion than we would have if we had plunged into desegregation at all costs. . . . One of my critics says that, on the racial issue, I am playing the middle against both ends. He is right, and I am convinced that unless we reinforce the middle ground, it will become a no man's land across which the extremists will fight. . . . As a moderate, I am determined that in Florida: 1) law and order shall prevail; 2) segregation of the races in public schools and recreational facilities will continue in any community where its abandonment would cause deep and dangerous hostility; 3) any integration at any time shall be keyed to the achievement standards of colored and white; 4) harmonious, friendly biracial meetings and discussions shall be encouraged.

Collins realized that his goals would be criticized for not emphasizing "justice," presumably meaning immediate desegregation. However, he argued, "In the quest for right, there are times when wisdom must restrain the pace of unfettered justice until it can catch up and walk hand in hand with it."[1]

Collins's words revealed the enduring influence of southern racial traditions on his thinking. Paternalistic racial views suffused his analysis. He held to the myth of an "era of good feelings" in southern race relations prior to the Supreme Court's intervention; he believed that blacks' inferior standards had made segregation necessary and motivated whites to oppose any change. Instead of immediate integration, he called on whites to renew their assistance in raising blacks' standards to a level that would make desegregation acceptable.

Collins based his evaluation on faulty premises. The myth of racial harmony resulted not from mutual respect, but from a carefully maintained code of racial decorum. Paternalistic assistance by whites, in fact, had worked to insure the continuation of the blacks' second-class citizenship. Like most whites, Collins failed to realize that the lower standards of employment, housing, health, and education among black people were the result of, not the cause of, their imposed status in southern society. Furthermore, the presumptions based on a half century of southern living kept Collins from perceiving the underlying moral issue of individual dignity. Only the failure of his plan would prompt him to question the fundamental precepts of his heritage.

In the *Look* article, Collins applied his racial perceptions to the crisis that was embroiling the South after the Little Rock confrontation. President Eisenhower and Governor Faubus had to share blame in the incident: "the Governor, for using his police powers affirmatively to prevent enforcement of a judicial order; the President, for not anticipating the explosiveness of the situation and moving early to head it off." Yet, an underlying problem concerning the implementation of the *Brown* decision had made such a conflict inevitable, Collins argued. The Supreme Court based its ruling on the Fourteenth Amendment to the U.S. Constitution, which required "equal protection of the laws." Collins noted that the amendment's wording concluded, "The Congress shall have power to enforce, by appropriate legislation, the provisions of this article." Congress had not acted on the *Brown* decision, though. As a result, "the courts now are placed in the unnatural, and I believe untenable, position of acting in executive and legislative, as well as judicial capacities." The governor called on Congress to accept the responsibility for devising a plan to implement the *Brown* decision.

Such a congressional plan would need to account for what Collins deemed the realities confronting forced integration. The *Brown* ruling did not require total integration, he asserted, but demanded that no state use racial criteria to deny a person entrance to a public school. On this basis, he asked, "Is it our aim to force admission of a student, regardless of how many tanks, troops and bayonets it takes? Do we seriously propose to garrison hundreds of Southern schoolyards? Surely not." He advocated the formulation of a plan which recognized that:

1) conditions and opportunities vary from community to community and state to state;

2) power should be granted to guard against improvident integration as well as to facilitate integration where feasible;

3) people of each state should be secure in the knowledge that decisions affecting their state will be developed by citizens of that state and will be enforced by them.

As an example of the thinking he favored, Collins suggested the consideration of a plan under which the Congress would create state civil rights commissions. The president could appoint the members upon recommendations by the governors. Collins believed implementation devices could be formulated that would insure local responsibility and avoid conflicts between federal and state power such as had occurred at Little Rock.[2]

Collins later enlarged upon his design and sought adherents for his plan of congressional action. At an August 21, 1958, news conference, he observed, "I think that we desperately need at this time some bold, creative, constructive leadership if we are going to avoid some very serious and perilous conditions. . . . The important thing now is for somebody to come forward with a constructive plan." He briefly outlined his rationale for congressional intervention and concluded, "We have got to find a way to avoid the application of raw force when it is contrary to the deep-seated will of the people."[3]

In September 1958 Collins chaired the Southern Governors' Conference, at Lexington, Kentucky. Before the meeting, Faubus had closed the public schools in Little Rock and had initiated plans for a private corporation to administer a new educational system. Public and press attention centered on Faubus, as it had at the Sea Island conference the year before. Massive resisters appeared to be determined to uphold segregation or destroy the South's public schools. Collins admitted to reporters, "Tragically, I see little hope of pulling out of this crisis short of national catastrophe, if we continue to follow the present pattern of events."[4]

As chairman, Collins delivered a brief opening speech to the conference. Traditionally the governors had avoided the racial issue in their discussions because of the diverse opinions held in the sixteen states represented. In his address, though, Collins submitted, "I cannot live easily with my conscience if I completely side-step [the racial issue]." He insisted, "I think the American people throughout the land should begin by recognizing some realities, for if a way out is to be found, while it must contain idealism, it must be basically realistic as well." Firstly, "the great majority of white Southerners and a considerable number in the North are bitterly opposed to sending their children to schools with Negro children." Secondly, the *Brown* decision would not be changed, and defiance of it would only undermine law and order. Recognizing these facts, Collins contended, the nation could devise a means to carry out the Supreme Court's ruling.[5]

Next sketching out his plan for congressional action, Collins asserted that "the conditions we face require more flexibility of administration, more discretion and adaption [*sic*] than the courts are by nature and rule permitted." Congress's failure to legislate implementation procedures constituted the "central difficulty." Collins did not request specific action from the southern governors because he considered integration to be a national problem. Instead, he planned to ask the Executive Committee of the National Governors' Conference to sponsor a meeting of governors, congressional leaders, and the president or his representatives to study plans for carrying out integration. Collins concluded:

> There are those who will contend that the approach by congressional action will facilitate desegregation. There will also be those who will contend that it will impede and prevent desegregation. Indeed, it will likely do both. I do not suggest it to appease or satisfy anyone, but rather to provide a possible workable basis for resolving a problem with the application of reason and with respect for law.[6]

Reaction to the speech varied. One newsman reported, "Observers of the national political scene here interpreted Collins' shrewdly timed move yesterday as another step in what is viewed as his bid to win a place on the national Democratic ticket in 1960."[7] Repeated charges of political ambition forced him to disclaim any future goals for elective office. The governors' responses were predictably mixed. McKeldin, of Maryland, a liberal, contended, "We do not need an act of Congress to spell out for us what the decision of the supreme court has made so clear—that a citizen is a citizen." Faubus thought the plan offered "possibilities" and saw nothing in it that conflicted with his views. North Carolina's Hodges liked the emphasis on a national approach, and Underwood, of West Virginia, offered his support for the idea. Resisters such as Griffin, of Georgia, and Timmerman, of South Carolina, were not impressed. Timmerman declared, "In the final analysis, the suggestion offers no solution."[8]

During the ensuing months, Collins formalized what came to be called the "Collins Plan."[9] He urged Congress to authorize "educational adjustment commissions," which would exercise original jurisdiction in school desegregation cases. In each state, the president would appoint members to the commission upon the recommendation of the governor. The commissioners would be empowered to assist local school authorities, investigate complaints, establish advisory committees, and supervise research projects. They could resolve desegregation disputes, but their decisions would be subject to appeal in the federal courts.[10]

Collins expected "extreme opposition from both sides to this plan." He also admitted, "I think more and more people are on one extreme side of the issue or the other. The ranks of those who want to be truthful and fair and reasonable and honorable seem to be thinning out very rapidly." Yet, he saw "a great number of people in the middle in this matter who are seeking to find a constructive solution," and he thought his concept would "give them the vehicle by which this whole matter can be resolved." For the moderates, "the plan would provide for congressional action which would facilitate desegregation where, when and how it was feasible. But further, and of great importance, the plan also provides for safeguards and protection against the improvident coercion of integration anywhere. And this is what gives the plan strength."[11]

The Collins Plan gained few adherents. He discarded the idea of a national conference when he was "firmly advised" that President

Eisenhower had no interest in it. In 1959, the governor sought congressional support for his proposal. "The reaction that I got from the congressmen was that [integration] was a rather hot issue and that they were unwilling specifically to line themselves up as favoring [the Collins Plan]," he reported. The next year, he urged the Advisory Council of the national Democratic party to consider his concept. The council studied and discussed it, but did not formally accept it.[12]

The Collins Plan failed to gain acceptance because it did not provide a viable alternative in the integration impasse. A majority of Americans considered a "moderate," compromise solution to be unacceptable politically and morally. Advocates of integration had gained the federal judiciary as a political ally. They would not accept a power shift to Congress, which their adversaries controlled. Furthermore, they could not approve a plan that, in effect, made integration a local option decision (because communities expressing sufficient opposition would remain segregated). Resisters also found the concept to be politically unacceptable. They could not accede to partial integration implemented by the federal government—whether the Supreme Court or Congress—without denying the validity of the states' rights theory, their fundamental political concept. Moreover, the Little Rock confrontation had benefited them by polarizing southern opinion and solidifying segregationist sentiment. They wanted no alternative that would depreciate their growing strength.

The Collins Plan also did not acknowledge the ethical issues involved. Both sides claimed moral right. Opponents believed integration threatened not only their political and social institutions, but also the nation's moral fiber. Convinced that "race mixing" would dilute whites' moral superiority, they could accept no compromise on principle. On the other hand, those seeking integration had won a moral, as well as legal, victory in the *Brown* decision. Accepting token integration would compromise that triumph. Moreover, their nonviolent strategy juxtaposed against the riotous response of many whites had enhanced the moral credence of their cause. Increasing numbers of Americans were reconsidering the rectitude of their racial precepts. The Collins Plan would have mitigated the integrationists' claim on the nation's conscience. In sum, he based his plan on faulty premises that rendered it unacceptable. He had not confronted the moral issues that made the civil rights movement a fundamental test for the country's citizens and institutions.

Consistent with his plan's philosophy, Collins did not use state powers to press openly for school desegregation. At the college level, token integration occurred at the University of Florida graduate school. To block the entrance of Virgil D. Hawkins, the Board of Control had raised the law school's admission requirements. George H. Starke, of Orlando, a black Air Force veteran and a graduate of Morehouse College, in Atlanta, then applied for admission. He met the higher test standards required by the Board of Control and, on September 15, 1958, entered the University of Florida Law School without incident. In January 1959 Collins urged that graduate programs at FAMU be moved to the other state universities. By eliminating repetition in graduate programs, he argued, money would be saved. Of course, the proposal would also have eliminated segregated graduate education. House Speaker-designate Thomas Beasley asserted that Floridians would pay "whatever is necessary to maintain segregation." Facing threats of resistance, Collins chose not to force the issue of desegregated graduate education.[13]

Referring to elementary and secondary schools, Collins insisted, "under our laws the admission of pupils is a local matter." Nevertheless, he met twice in the autumn of 1958 with selected county school officials to urge consideration of some integration. In part, he later maintained, his recognition of integration's inevitability prompted his action. At the time, he emphasized the necessity for token integration to strengthen the legal standing of Florida's Pupil Assignment Law. He pointed out, "The United States Supreme Court has held very positively that if laws like ours are so administered as to be an absolute and complete bar to any integration they will not be upheld." Local officials argued that even token integration would result in community disruption and refused to act unless under direct court orders. Collins conceded that he knew of no community in the state where "the climate of opinion" would allow integration "without deep violent resistance and antagonism."[14]

Only the Dade County School Board offered Collins any hope for token integration. Although segregationists predominated on it, the members recognized the threat posed by NAACP legal actions under the Pupil Assignment Law. Describing the act, Phil Meyer, a Miami *Herald* reporter, noted, "In effect, it permits the School Board to keep a Negro out of a white school if it can find some reason for keeping him out other than the fact that he is a Negro." In one case, he observed, the Dade County School Board could find no reasonable excuse to deny blacks admission. The action involved the application of four of them for entrance to Orchard Villa Elementary School. In October 1958 the board authorized Superintendent Joe Hall to carry out a study on the practicability of admittance. Collins supported the move, arguing, "The student-assignment act especially anticipates that boards will give consideration to sociological and psychological factors, and certainly they cannot intelligently consider those factors without determining the facts existing in the community affected."[15]

The Orchard Villa Elementary School became a test for the validity of the Pupil Assignment Law. The neighborhood was in a period of transition; whites were leaving and blacks were moving in. When the board announced the study, an Orchard Villa teacher commented, "there are so many whites moving out that by next year almost all of them may be gone." According to the survey, only about fifty white parents would send their children to an integrated institution. Yet, the black applicants lived near the school and were academically qualified. Dr. Robert S. Butler, a board member, emphasized that they met the criteria under the Pupil Assignment Law. Hall recommended admission on the basis of his study. On Wednesday, February 18, 1959, the board unanimously voted to admit the four black students to Orchard Villa beginning in the September term. "Without this action," Butler explained, "the Pupil Assignment Law wouldn't be worth the paper it's written on." The Miami *Herald* pointed out that months of preparation had preceded the ruling. Nevertheless, the journal reported, the final decision had been made in a secret meeting between Collins and board members held on Monday at a Miami hotel.[16]

Collins insisted that the "action which the board took was its own action, independently arrived at and pursuing a good-faith effort to comply and conform with the student assignment law." He admitted meeting with two board members, Dr. Butler and Jane Roberts. However, he said, they did not consult with him; they only informed him of the impending ruling. Describing the move as "a good-faith local decision," he offered his support for it. He contrasted the problems encountered by the massive resistance movement in states like Virginia to North Carolina's success with token integration. He also mentioned the latter state's economic attainments. Florida, too, had much to gain in industrial development, "and I know . . . that if we go off into a period of racial antagonism and friction our state will have much to lose by it." He concluded, "there can be no justification whatever for any violent reaction or anything that would be a discredit to the county or to the state."[17]

Other state leaders expressed little enthusiasm for the decision. Reverend Lowry, the state NAACP president, stressed the tokenism in the ruling and urged blacks to "press toward total compliance." G. E. Graves, a NAACP attorney, expressed satisfaction, but admitted, "it's nothing to be jubilant about." Senate President-designate Dewey Johnson, of Quincy, charged that the board had violated the state's constitutional requirement for segregated schools, and house Speaker-designate Thomas D. Beasley, of Walton, declared, "It's an outrage." Sumter Lowry contended that Collins had "violated his oath of office by advocating any integration whatever in the schools." Even Senator Pope, of St. Augustine, one of Collins's staunchest allies, said, "I do not feel any school board should accept integration unless forced to under court order." Attorney General Ervin asserted that the decision emphasized the need for a Parent Option Plan.[18] According to one newsperson, "Gov. LeRoy Collins and his race relations committee appeared to be the only ones in favor of the School Board action."[19]

When the 1959 legislature met a few weeks after the Orchard Villa decision, Collins faced a strong force of lawmakers who wanted to strengthen segregation codes. In his opening address, he urged the legislators to resist the lure of the massive resistance movement. "Never, never, never set up any plan or device by which our public schools can be closed," he pleaded. During the session, he and his allies blocked extremist legislation. Of the thirty-seven race-related bills introduced, only three became law. One allowed segregation of students by sex, another exempted students in integrated schools from compulsory attendance requirements, and a third strengthened the Pupil Assignment Law. Bills that failed to pass included measures furthering the "last resort" school-closing plan, allowing tax credits for contributions to private schools, providing state aid to private schools, and making teaching in integrated schools a criminal offense. Following the session, Collins praised the legislature for its restraint. "Perhaps its biggest accomplishment was in what it did not do," he suggested.[20]

On September 8, 1959, the four black children integrated the Orchard Villa Elementary School.[21] Only eight whites registered. No incidents marred the day, though segregationists Fred Hockett, of Miami, and J. B. Stoner, of Louisville, Kentucky, engaged a group of black bystanders in a heated argument. Within the next few weeks, six additional whites entered the school and more than a hundred blacks applied for admission. On October 7 the school board assigned 379 blacks to the school and replaced the white staff with a black principal and teachers. Soon Orchard Villa was an all-black school in an all-black neighborhood.[22]

Collins could have pressed more firmly for public school integration. Yet, as the *Look* article illustrated, he did not believe that complete integration was a viable or attractive goal. Instead, he reflected the desire of the business progressives for well-measured change. At least in part, he wanted law and order because disruptions interfered with economic progress. Moreover, he entertained the respect of a "hominy husker" for the values of public education. If establishing complete integration would result in violence and school closing, then he opposed the action. Furthermore, as an astute politician, he realized that advancing too far on integration would cost him his reform constituency. He deemed governmental and economic gains to be vital for *all* citizens.

Throughout his administration, Collins searched for an alternative to confrontation. In reaction to the *Brown* decision, he urged restraint and legal opposition. During the Tallahassee bus boycott, he called on white people to recognize the legitimacy of black demands and to accept some nonschool integration. In the midst of the Little Rock crisis, he challenged the massive resisters and adopted a policy of legal implementation represented by the Collins Plan's tokenism. He had accepted the ethical standards of business progressivism and southern racial customs. Yet, he was not bound by them. Each crisis brought a reappraisal. Each crisis brought intellectual and emotional growth. Each crisis brought new efforts to provide leadership. During the last year of Collins's administration, a racial crisis that began in the Upper South and then spread to Florida again provoked new thinking and led him to issue a final challenge to his white constituents.

10

Moral, Simple Justice:
The Racial Crisis, 1960

In 1960 young southerners began a "sit-in" movement to test Dixie's segregationist traditions. The protests initiated an era of civil disobedience from those who were seeking change and violent resistance from those who were determined to preserve racial customs. Collins would again strive to provide leadership, calling on whites to recognize the immorality of their racial codes. His influence had waned, though. Although his racial views gained national respect, they sapped his strength in Florida. The 1960 gubernatorial primary, held within months of the first sit-ins, demonstrated that six years of crisis had diminished his political stature.

The sit-in movement began in Greensboro, North Carolina, on February 1, 1960, when four black college students ordered coffee at a whites-only F. W. Woolworth lunch counter. When the waitress refused to serve them, the men remained seated until the store closed. The next morning, they resumed their sit-in. Although the Congress of Racial Equality (CORE) had used the technique as early as 1942, most young blacks viewed it as a new and imaginative device for nonviolent protest. Within days, demonstrations spread into every southern and border state. During the next twelve months, more than fifty thousand southerners took part in the protests. White officials reacted by jailing more than 3,600 demonstrators. Some resisters responded with violence. In

Houston, Texas, for example, a group of whites randomly selected a black man, hanged him from a tree by his feet, beat him with chains, and carved "KKK" on his chest and stomach. Despite white resistance, merchants integrated lunch counters in 126 cities by the end of the year. Just as importantly, the sit-in movement shifted the focus of black protest from the courts to the streets.[1]

Florida, which had remained relatively quiescent during the preceding two years, exploded as activists staged sit-ins at Tampa, Daytona Beach, Sarasota, St. Petersburg, St. Augustine, Deland, Jacksonville, and Tallahassee. In some instances, whites responded with violence. Although the demonstrations were widespread, the attention of the state, and later the nation, centered on the capital city. When the Greensboro sit-in touched off sympathy demonstrations across the South, Tallahasseans under the leadership of CORE acted quickly. On February 13 and February 20, black students sat-in at the Woolworth lunch counter. Police arrested eleven demonstrators during the second protest. Sit-ins at McCrory's dime store on March 5 resulted in more arrests.[2]

During the following week, CORE organized and trained students for an expanded test of the city's segregation traditions. On Saturday morning, March 12, a group of white students seated themselves at the Woolworth's lunch counter. When blacks entered and were refused service, the whites, as planned, offered them their coffee. A force of policemen led by Mayor George Taff arrested the demonstrators for "engaging in riotous conduct" and "unlawful assembly." At 12:30 three black students attempted another sit-in. A group of white men "pushed them around" and forced them to leave. Approximately a hundred FAMU students then held a march to protest the earlier arrests. When they demonstrated in front of McCrory's, police took seventeen into custody.[3]

The remaining protesters moved north on Monroe Street toward Woolworth's. A group of thirty-five club-wielding whites blocked the march in a park between the police station and the post office. Homer Barrs, operator of a soda fountain in a local drugstore and executive director of Florida's Citizens' Councils, led the counterdemonstrators. The two groups stopped about six feet from each other and hurled insults. The police refused to intervene. After

several tense minutes, the blacks retreated and returned to the
FAMU campus. Later in the day, they reorganized and several
hundred began a march downtown. Police intercepted it with tear
gas and arrested six demonstrators. Collins then stepped in and
ordered state police to restrict FAMU students to campus.[4]

The governor's initial reaction to the sit-in movement reflected
the legalistic precepts of his racial views. In early March, he
charged, "I think these demonstrations, when carried on contrary
to the requests of management, are illegal, dangerous and should
be discontinued." If a black person resented a store's policies,
Collins argued, "certainly he is within his rights to refuse to
patronize it altogether." Violent confrontations, especially, disturbed the governor. "I hate to see demonstrations of this kind at
any time," he said. "Demonstrations lead to disorder and, of
course, disorder leads to danger to the general welfare." During
the March 12 Tallahassee conflict, he ordered authorities to dis-
perse all groups of people who became "extremely agitated."
"Nobody has any right at any time, anywhere, regardless of his
race or color or creed," he proclaimed, "to persist in any demonstration which will likely result in violence and disorder imperiling
the peace and welfare of a community."[5] His continued emphasis
on law and order offered blacks little hope for support from the
executive mansion.

Tension escalated in Tallahassee following the March 12 mass
protest. On March 18 eight youths, including William H. Larkin,
the FAMU student body president-elect, went to jail rather than
pay a three-hundred-dollar fine for participating in the February
20 demonstration. In a statement endorsed by other black leaders,
the Reverend Charles A. Hunter, of the Trinity Presbyterian
Church, attacked the students' incarceration and observed, "we
may soon join them." He promised that on Saturday, March 19,
the black community would take some action to dramatize its
opposition. In an effort to calm the situation, officials restricted
FSU and FAMU students to campus and censored the *Flambeau*,
the FSU student paper, which had strongly supported the sit-ins.
At Collins's request, black leaders agreed to call off the Saturday
demonstration and to delay further action until after he had an
opportunity to speak on the issue.[6]

Collins had decided to use his most powerful weapon to defuse the sit-in crisis. He would appeal directly to the people by way of television, a tool he had used effectively in the past. His staff arranged for a statewide network to carry the speech, which would originate from a Jacksonville television studio on Sunday, March 20.[7] Rejecting the idea of a written transcript, Collins decided to deliver an impromptu talk that would express his true sentiments. He knew what he wanted to say.[8] He arrived at the studio shortly before the 5:30 telecast time. Excitement filled the air as the station crew bustled about preparing for the speech. The men expressed friendliness and pleasure with their roles in the important occasion.[9]

Collins began by acknowledging the intensity of the divisions on the sit-in issue. He understood the risks of speaking out. Yet, he pledged: "As long as I am in this office, I will say what I think is right." He continued, "I will not have on my conscience a feeling that at any time the people needed my help, I ducked or dodged or looked the other way in order to follow the easy course." Beyond that, "I think the people of this state expect their governor to have convictions, and I think the people of this state when their governor has convictions about a matter expect him to express those convictions directly to them."[10]

Confirming his belief in the legal rights of all citizens, Collins vowed to protect the businessmen's prerogative to select the patrons they served as well as the right of others to demonstrate. Yet, if a demonstration incited public disorder, then it was unlawful. "We are going to have law and order in this state," he pledged.[11] But he did not stop with a legalistic analysis. Instead, he challenged his constituents to recognize new insights he had gained from his constant reflection on the racial dilemma.[12]

"We are foolish if we just think about resolving this thing on a legal basis," the governor contended. The racial issue also involved certain "moral rights" and "principles of brotherhood." If a businessman invited the public to come into his store and trade, then he lacked any moral right to single out one department, such as a lunch counter, that he would not allow blacks to patronize. "Now he has the legal right to do that," Collins conceded, "but I still don't think he can square that right with moral, simple justice."[13]

Were the South's racial traditions moral? Many southerners recognized that racial strife damaged the nation, Collins observed, but they argued "this could be eliminated if the colored people would just stay in their place." He responded:

> Now friends, that's not a Christian point of view. That's not a democratic point of view. That's not a realistic point of view. We can never stop Americans from struggling to be free. We can never stop Americans from hoping and praying that someday in someway this ideal that is imbedded in our Declaration of Independence . . . that all men are created equal, that somehow will be a reality and not just an illusory distant goal.

To guide the state during the racial crisis, Collins announced the appointment of a biracial committee that would be chaired by Cody Fowler, of Tampa, former president of the American Bar Association. The governor then urged every community to form its own biracial committee to resolve racial grievances. For the state to progress, solutions to the racial problems needed to be found. "Citizens, please do not fail this great challenge," the governor implored.[14]

The station crew gave Collins his first reaction to the speech. The conviviality had disappeared. The cameramen, director, and other personnel seemed stunned. They met the governor's searching glances with icy stares. Collins left the studio without a word being spoken.[15]

Conservatives angrily condemned the speech. "I don't think he has supplied the answer to any of the current problems," Mayor Taff, of Tallahassee, complained. The city commission rejected Collins's proposal for a biracial committee. Senator Johnson and Representative Beasley agreed that the governor had hurt, rather than helped, the racial situation. "It substantiated what I've thought all the time," Johnson said. "He's a strict integrationist and will sell his soul to prove it for the benefit of his national political ambitions." Mayor Haydon Burns, of Jacksonville, who favored "separate but equal lunchroom facilities," also found no value in the speech. State Senator Fred O. Dickinson, of West Palm Beach, dissented and placed the blame for the disruptions on "out-of-state radicals who have started this racial strife and should be exposed for exactly what they are." State Representative Ray Mattox, of Winter Haven, charged Collins with "encouraging mob violence."[16] The editors of the St. Petersburg *Independent* added: "Unless the governor got carried away with his own oratory or ambitions, his talk of moral obligations makes less than no sense at all."[17]

Many southerners criticized Collins's speech and questioned his motives. A South Carolina newspaper charged that, by injecting morality into the racial controversy, he had "confused the issue" and warned he was "treading on dangerous ground." An Alabama journal accused him of selling out the South to enhance his vice-presidential prospects. U.S. Senator Lister Hill, of Alabama, maintained that Collins's comments on morality did not apply to his state. Hill joined his colleagues Strom Thurmond and Olin D. Johnston, of South Carolina, in issuing a statement disputing Collins's analysis. Outside agitators and Communist schoolteachers had instigated the demonstrations, they contended.[18] The governor's speech changed few minds among the resisters.

Blacks generally welcomed Collins's words, though some of them disputed his stand on the basis of legalities. Tallahassee's black leadership met after the address and decided to step up measures for integration, including the use of boycotts. Len Holt, of Norfolk, Virginia, general counsel for CORE, called Collins's statements "commendable," but claimed they did not go far enough. Dr. John O. Brown, head of Miami's CORE, disagreed with the governor on the illegality of sit-ins and the potential value of biracial committees. Yet, he grudgingly admitted, "Coming from a Southern governor, it's a speech to be admired." The Reverend Lowry thought, "The governor has shown that this is really a democracy in which all men can and should be treated as equals." The Reverend T. R. Gibson, Miami NAACP leader, added, "With that speech, Governor Collins became to me one of the greatest statesmen Florida has ever known." The variations in black response to the speech reflected the growing schism between the traditional guidance of the NAACP and the more radical demands of many younger blacks under the leadership of CORE.[19]

In addition to support from some elements of the black community, Collins received praise from many whites across the state and nation. The St. Louis *Post Dispatch* called him a spokesman for "Southern political sanity." The Washington *Post* wrote: "He exemplifies and expresses the best traditions—and the best hope—of the South."[20] A Miamian called a local newspaper to declare, "I haven't heard a speech like that since Franklin D. Roosevelt." William H. Roundtree, an attorney from Cocoa, Florida, congratulated Collins for his courage in stating what many thought but feared to say.[21] The Miami *Daily News* contended that the speech was remarkable for filling an entire thirty-minute television segment with common sense. The Miami *Herald* commended Collins's courage and candor, and the Bradenton *Herald* believed he provided "a pattern for sanity." The Daytona Beach *Morning Journal* submitted, "[viewers] watched him grapple with that issue courageously, and face up to the mob with it. . . . It was a speech of a man talking sense to the people. It was a speech ringing with conviction, courage, logic."[22]

The intensity of the response to the speech resulted from the fundamental issues it confronted. Collins's racial perceptions had matured. Although earlier statements had suggested his ethical concerns, he had publicly stressed legalisms. Yet, constant crises brought soul-searching. Finally, he concluded that legalities did not delimit the problem. In the sit-in speech, he shifted from analyzing legal rights under the U.S. Constitution to emphasizing moral rights under the Declaration of Independence. Rejecting the mythology of "outside agitators" and a pre-1954 "era of good feelings," he placed the southern black activists squarely in the history of America's search for human equality. The demonstrators, not the resisters, held claim to the nation's ideals and traditions.

Collins's challenge to southern values insured a heated response.[23] In 1960 many people in that part of the country held tightly to the "Lost Cause" mythology of the Civil War and Reconstruction. The region had based its social customs on such myths.[24] For a century, its politicians, intellectuals, and pastors had glorified an ordered society that was characterized by a precise class structure and social codes. Everyone had a "place" in a design that many people felt was divinely inspired. From their own view, southerners might be defeated, poor, and ill educated, but they were moral. They genuinely and paternalistically believed they cared for black people. The highly stylized code of ethical racial conduct, together with the myths of sectional history, provided the basis upon which whites affirmed their community.

By censuring segregated lunch counters as immoral, Collins implicitly challenged the ethical basis of all segregated customs. Moreover, he condemned efforts to keep blacks in "their place" as unrealistic, undemocratic, and un-Christian. Many southerners correctly perceived, either emotionally or intellectually, that his words threatened the foundations of their carefully constructed society. In defense of it, they lashed out at him. For many Floridians, the sit-in speech marked an irreparable breach with his leadership.

The sit-in speech illustrated Collins's paradoxical political position. The emphasis on the morality of integration heightened his national stature; yet, it eroded his standing in his own state. He received acclaim as the man most able to lead in the transformation of the South's traditions, which earned him national reputation and respect. This political capital, however, could not be converted into political advancement because, in gaining it, he lost his home base of support. The 1960 Democratic gubernatorial primary demonstrated the damage to his prestige in Florida.

The racial issue had bitterly divided the Democrats there. Party factionalism was not a new phenomenon. The "politics of pulverization" more often had proved to be the rule rather than the exception.[25] Although personal leadership retained its importance, the racial issue modified party alignments during the 1950s. It forced voters to support the moderates' effort to delay the inevitable or to heed the resisters' cry of "never." To an extent, the state's Democratic party was more polarized than pulverized in 1960.

The gubernatorial primary accentuated party divisions. C. Farris Bryant, who built an efficient statewide organization after his loss in Collins's 1956 sweep, led the field of ten candidates in the first primary. He appealed to south Florida with a pledge favoring fair apportionment and promised the Porkchoppers he would use all legal means to block integration. State Senator Doyle E. Carlton, Jr., of Wauchula, whose father had served as governor from 1929 to 1933, contested Bryant in the runoff election. As one of Collins's senate floor leaders, he was closely identified with the administration. Especially after the sit-in speech, though, some of his advisers thought the governor's open support would hurt their candidate's chances. In the campaign, Carlton sought a "quiet endorsement" from him, but avoided the Collins label.[26] Wanting to avoid the intraparty conflict, the governor professed neutrality.[27]

Political antagonism between Collins and former Governor Millard Caldwell added rancor to the primary campaign. Philosophical distinctions rooted in three decades of Florida politics accounted for the party leaders' estrangement. As a member of Congress during the New Deal era, Caldwell consistently disagreed with Collins on the policies of the Roosevelt administration. Although opposing Caldwell's successful gubernatorial campaign in 1944, Collins played a crucial role in the administration's most important accomplishment, the enactment of the Minimum Foundation Program. In the 1948 gubernatorial primary, Caldwell supported the unsuccessful candidacy of Collins's close associate, Daniel McCarty. Personal conflicts, though, led to Caldwell's complete alienation from McCarty's triumphant 1952 campaign.[28]

The physical proximity of Caldwell and Collins in Tallahassee exacerbated the tensions between them. Socially, Caldwell, who had moved to the capital city from Milton shortly before running for governor, did not enjoy the local status of Collins, a hometown boy. Professionally, they were associated with the city's two major, and competing, law firms. In 1950 Julius Parker, Caldwell's law partner, had challenged Collins's senatorial reelection in vain. Repeated jousts in important lawsuits added to the ill will between the firms. Politically, both ambition and philosophy separated the two men. Caldwell must have resented the epithet applied to Collins as the "Father of the Minimum Foundation Program." The former later observed, "Well, you've got to recognize the political necessities here and there. [Collins] was ambitious and he needed some help."[29]

The racial crisis and the concomitant issue of states' rights widened the philosophical breach between the two politicians. Caldwell charged that moderates were not expressing the true feeling of the South. Collins responded, "Well, there is an awful lot of immoderate feeling in the South, and I suppose he classifies himself as such. If he disparages moderate views, why, he must embrace immoderate ones."[30] One observer noted, "More and more, Caldwell leaned—socially, economically, and philosophically—to the conservatives, to the Pork Choppers. . . . Collins leaned the other way." Personal animosity slowly grew between them while each attracted elements of the state Democratic party to his leadership.[31]

In the 1960 gubernatorial primary, Bryant asked for the support of Caldwell, who believed that a Collins endorsement of Carlton would end the moderate's chances. The goal should be to force the governor to state his choice publicly, Caldwell maintained. He waited while pressure built on Collins to make an endorsement. Finally, just six days before the election, blasting both Carlton and Collins in a statewide telecast, Caldwell charged, "[Carlton] has long been soft toward integration. He is endorsed by that same combination of Miami, Tampa, and St. Petersburg newspapers, also soft on integration, [and] backed by the present administration, also soft on integration."[32]

This statement shifted the decision on the endorsement to Carlton and Collins. Actually, a few members of the former's staff had urged him to ally his campaign with the Collins administration from the beginning. Yet, an axiom in Florida politics was that voters viewed endorsements from incumbent governors as an effort to establish a "machine" and rejected the candidate on that basis. Following Caldwell's address, though, Collins heard pleas from Carlton backers across the state to become personally involved. Polls indicated that this intervention might be decisive. Because observers judged Bryant to be the front-runner, Carlton had little to lose by risking the endorsement.[33] Furthermore, the press and public had linked Collins to Carlton throughout the campaign. Even if the governor said nothing, many would consider a Carlton defeat as a rejection of him. Therefore, despite the tradition of official neutrality, an endorsement made sense for both men.

Committing the full weight of his prestige to Carlton's candidacy, the day after Caldwell's statement Collins proclaimed, "Senator Carlton is best qualified and best equipped to make this state the best governor." In an election eve speech on statewide televi-

sion, Collins said of Caldwell, "This is the voice of reaction. What
he stands for is retreat." He feared Bryant "would represent the
three R's—reaction, retreat, and regret."[34] Following the endorsements, one reporter contended that, in the minds of the voters, the
contest was between Caldwell and Collins.[35] Another analyst wrote,
"The battle lines now have been clearly drawn."[36]

The Grove, 1960. (*Courtesy, Florida State Archives*)

Bryant soundly defeated Carlton.[37] Several factors contributed to
the latter's poor showing. His hesitancy in requesting Collins's
endorsement meant that the governor's talented and experienced
campaign staff did not enter the fray until very late. Also, Bryant
had spent four years building a disciplined machine, whereas

Carlton's organization seemed to be incapable of uniting on strategy.[38] Bryant performed well on television and exhibited a sound knowledge of state government in debate. In contrast, one newsman observed, "if ever there was a political floperoo on TV, it was Carlton."[39] Another journalist concluded that Carlton was just not in Collins's league as a vote-getter.[40]

Nevertheless, the distinction between the candidates' racial views was a key issue in the primary. Profiting from his segregationist stance, Bryant charged that only the "Negro bloc vote" had enabled his opponent to enter the runoff. After the election, Collins pointed out that Bryant had expressed more moderation than many southern candidates and had supported his position of never closing public schools. Yet, Collins also admitted that the election demonstrated the popularity of a rigid stand on segregation.[41]

The election was a setback for Collins—personally, philosophically, and politically. It demonstrated the state's growing conservative sentiment since his overwhelming victory, based on moderation, in 1956. It undercut his potential for national office by clarifying his political paradox of diminishing influence in Florida. Most observers concurred with the New York *Times* evaluation that the election had been "a rude political defeat" for him.[42]

11

The Political Brier Patch:
National Politics, 1960

The year 1960 was one of political transition for Florida and the nation. In selecting a governor, Floridians chose to turn back to issues and answers that were rooted in the past and to reject Collins's commitment to moderate change. Yet, that same year, the country rallied to a call for reform. Massachusetts Senator John F. Kennedy brought a youthful vitality to the national scene that sharply contrasted with the grandfatherly conservatism of the Eisenhower years. Challenging Americans to conquer "new frontiers" at home and abroad, Kennedy initiated a decade of ascendant liberalism. For Collins, the country's turn leftward meshed with the transition in his own philosophy. By moving against the current in his state, he entered the mainstream of national politics. In the scramble for the 1960 Democratic presidential nomination, he would capitalize on his personal and political strengths to gain an influential position in the national party.

Senator Kennedy had been campaigning for the presidency since his narrow defeat for the second spot on the 1956 Democratic ticket. His assets included wealth, a personality and appearance tailored for television, and an organization so efficient observers normally characterized it as a "machine." Yet, he also suffered liabilities. He was only forty-three years old and lacked any executive background. In the spring of 1960, cold war tensions made youth and inexperience seem to be crucial inadequacies. Ken-

144

nedy's Roman Catholic faith presented an even more difficult problem. After Alfred E. Smith's troubled campaign in 1928, the impossibility of electing a Catholic president had become an article of American political dogma.[1]

Trying to exploit Kennedy's weaknesses, other candidates maintained that his nomination would result in a Democratic defeat. To convince party leaders he could win, he chose to campaign in the state primaries. Minnesota Senator Hubert H. Humphrey challenged Kennedy in the primaries until his May 10 defeat in solidly Protestant West Virginia. Thereafter, the Democrats fought a bitter internecine battle for the presidential nomination. The "Stop Kennedy" forces had to gain enough votes within the state party caucuses to deny him a first-ballot victory at the national convention. Senator Stuart Symington, of Missouri, initiated a campaign aimed directly at the party power brokers. The support of former President Harry S. Truman constituted his primary asset. Senate Majority Leader Lyndon B. Johnson also sought a deadlocked convention. Along with his fellow Texan and mentor, Speaker of the House of Representatives Sam Rayburn, he had many political credits that could be cashed in if a stalemate resulted in the party leadership determining the nomination.[2]

Ultimately, though, the "Stop Kennedy" movement depended on Adlai E. Stevenson, of Illinois, the party's only charismatic figure in the spring of 1960 (the national infatuation with the "Kennedy style" lay in the future). Stevenson, the party's 1952 and 1956 presidential nominee, could count on a nationwide reservoir of devoted followers. Declining to campaign, however, he emphasized that he would accept the nomination if the party wanted him. George Ball, one of his friends, and Oklahoma Senator A. S. Mike Monroney headed a "Draft Stevenson" movement that became "almost explosive" because of the international crises in early 1960. In spite of the pressure on him as the party's foremost foreign policy spokesman, Stevenson refused to seek the nomination. Without an active candidate, his backers joined in the "Stop Kennedy" coalition by providing volunteers and money for Humphrey's primary campaigns. Kennedy, angered by the strategy, exerted intensive pressure on party leaders to support his candidacy or be left with little influence after his victory.[3]

The intraparty clash affected all Democrats. Loyal Stevenson backers, for example, pilloried intellectuals, such as the historian Arthur M. Schlesinger, Jr., for switching to Kennedy. California Governor Edmund G. Brown so badly bungled the conflicting pressures that some observers thought his political career had ended.[4] Florida's Senator George A. Smathers, a close friend of Kennedy, Symington, and Johnson, suffered a "triple ordeal" during the months leading up to the nomination. Finally, he supported Johnson, the most conservative candidate, though the decision isolated him personally and politically from Kennedy.[5]

On January 12, 1960, Speaker Rayburn resigned as permanent chairman of the Democratic National Convention. After chairing three successive conventions, he retired in order to head the Johnson campaign. The most important of the convention officers, the permanent chairman presided over the adoption of the platform and the nomination of the candidates. Specific duties included maintaining order, recognizing speakers, and ruling on parliamentary procedures.[6] Rayburn's resignation forced the Democrats to fill the powerful office in the midst of a heated party conflict.

Early in the year, reporters began mentioning Collins for a possible role at the convention. Initially, rumors suggested he might be the keynote speaker. Speculation soon shifted, though, to the possibility he might replace Rayburn as permanent chairman.[7] During the ensuing months, Collins performed a remarkable political feat by convincing the competing factions that he would be an attractive, neutral, and competent convention chairman.

Collins first persuaded Democratic National Chairman Paul M. Butler of his worth. The outspoken South Bend, Indiana, lawyer was a controversial leader. Critics accused him of seeking to nominate liberals and expel conservatives from the party. Stevenson opposed his initial appointment in 1954 and sought his ouster to no avail two years later. Butler's liberal civil rights stance and his stated belief that a southerner could not be nominated for the presidency alienated Dixie. His controversial statements led Truman to charge, "the business of a chairman is to keep the party together, not tear it apart." Butler's early and fervent support of Kennedy further angered many Democrats, North and South. In

March 1960 he predicted that Kennedy would be nominated on an early convention ballot. Rayburn called the remark "very distressing," and Humphrey suggested the chairman had outlived his usefulness.[8]

Despite the criticism, Butler exercised considerable power within the party. During his term, he retained control of the Democratic National Committee and formed strong ties with the party functionaries at the state and regional levels. Perhaps recognizing the national chairman's key influence, Collins maintained a cordial relationship with him throughout the raging controversies. Butler selected Collins as the first southern governor to serve on the Democratic Advisory Council, a group of leaders who helped guide the party during the years between presidential campaigns. In 1960 the thirty-one-member council included Butler, Humphrey, Kennedy, Stevenson, Symington, and Truman. Although admitting that Butler sometimes caused needless acrimony, Collins also noted, "I do not know of anyone who tries to serve the Party more loyally, or any more faithfully than Mr. Butler does." Butler urged the party to choose Collins as permanent chairman of the convention.[9]

Some of Butler's most bitter opponents also supported Collins for the permanent chairmanship. Collins's friendship with the Symington-Truman faction withstood an early faux pas by the candidate. During a January 1960 visit to Florida, Symington said he would welcome either Collins or Smathers as a vice-presidential running mate, but he felt the senator's foreign policy background made him a better choice. When newspersons interpreted the remark as a rebuke of Collins, Symington immediately wrote the governor and claimed his statement had been reported inaccurately. Collins assured Symington he had taken no offense.[10]

On February 26, 1960, Collins met for five hours with Truman in the home of Monroe County Sheriff John Spottswood at Key West, Florida.[11] The press speculated variously that Truman and Collins discussed a convention office, the vice-presidential nomination, or a diplomatic post. Collins later explained that they spent most of the day talking about Truman's presidential experiences. He admitted, "there was a casual reference to [a convention office], but there was no specific planning regarding it, or anything of that sort." In a letter to Collins, however, Truman intimated that the conversation had been more than casual. "I am hoping, in spite of Paul Butler, that you will make the Key Note speech," the former president wrote.[12] The reference to Butler implied that, during the Key West conference, Collins's association with the national chairman had not been clarified.

By 1960 mutual hostility characterized the Truman-Stevenson relationship. Disputed campaign strategy in 1952 had initiated the split, and Truman's opposition to Stevenson's nomination four years later had intensified the division. Stevenson's indecisiveness, Truman feared, "would make him ineffectual as a President." Referring to Truman's charges concerning the 1952 and 1956 elections, Stevenson rejoined, "I respect President Truman—if not his memory of events."[13] Despite this open enmity between the men, Collins managed to retain the respect of both.

Truman may have been unaware of Collins's esteem for Stevenson. Correspondence, marked "personal and confidential," between Collins and Herbert M. Davidson, editor of the Daytona Beach *Morning Journal,* clarified the governor's view. In a February 7, 1960, editorial, Davidson called on the Democrats to nominate a Stevenson-Kennedy ticket. He wrote Collins, suggesting that the governor lead a Florida convention delegation pledged to Stevenson. "I will have some voice in the selection of these delegates," Collins replied, "and high on my list will be several I know will share my own feeling of high respect and regards for Adlai Stevenson." Reflecting on recent conversations with Stevenson, Collins added, "He will give no overt encouragement whatever to any draft movement, and frankly I think it is going to be very difficult to rally support for him if he maintains this attitude."[14]

Although not expressing publicly his choice for the nomination, Collins apparently made his support evident to Stevenson. In a congratulatory telegram following Collins's selection as permanent chairman, Stevenson asserted, "Hooray. But I know that this is a day of mixed feelings for you." Stevenson ostensibly believed the neutral office would prevent Collins from supporting his candidacy. The latter confirmed this supposition in a letter to the former nominee. "My only regret is that this now prevents me from exercising any partisan effort on behalf of the man I have told you I am convinced is still the most qualified one in either party for the presidency," he wrote.[15] Presumably, neither Truman nor Butler was aware of Collins's plan to undertake a "partisan effort" for Stevenson.

Although Collins managed to retain an image of neutrality, commentators judged his main rival for the chairmanship, Louisiana Congressman Hale Boggs, to be a partisan candidate. Boggs emerged as Rayburn's choice for the post.[16] The congressman's close identification with the Johnson-Rayburn faction contrasted sharply with Collins's support, which was based on a coalition of contending candidates.

In addition to neutrality, Collins added political, religious, and sectional balance to the convention offices. The Committee on Arrangements, consisting of fourteen members under Butler's leadership, was responsible for choosing the officers. Connecticut Congressman Chester Bowles had earlier been picked to chair the Platform Committee. When Rayburn resigned, the Committee on Arrangements enjoyed an opportunity to provide balance by selecting a governor and a senator for the other two major offices (permanent chairman and temporary chairman, or keynote speaker). The committee decided to choose a senator for keynote speaker. This left Collins, as the only governor being given serious consideration, the front-runner for the permanent chairmanship.[17]

The religious issue also aided Collins. He was Protestant, and Boggs was Catholic. At previous conventions, religious affiliation would not have been an important factor. Yet, Kennedy's Catholic faith had been an issue in the early primaries, and the problems encountered in the 1928 campaign lingered in the minds of Democrats. The Committee on Arrangements thought the permanent chairman should be Protestant to demonstrate the party's religious balance.[18]

The troubled relations between the Democratic party and the "Solid South" likewise contributed to Collins's selection. The conflict on the platform's civil rights plank at the 1948 convention had begun a decade of increasing disaffection from the national party on the part of southern Democrats. Although the party retained its strength at the state and local level, southerners had increasingly demonstrated their independence in presidential elections. In 1948 South Carolina Governor Strom Thurmond, the States' Rights (Dixiecrat) candidate, carried South Carolina, Alabama, Louisiana, and Mississippi. Four years later, Eisenhower, the Republican candidate, won the electoral votes of Florida, Tennessee, Texas, and Virginia. Despite the *Brown* decision, which occurred during his first term, Eisenhower held the votes of these four states and added Louisiana in 1956. Democratic leaders believed southern electoral votes might be decisive four years later. Rayburn had been selected for permanent chairman, in part, because of his commitment to party unity.[19] Democrats wanted a similar leader to be the new chairman.

Both Collins and Boggs provided regional balance. Northern liberals, though, opposed the Louisiana congressman because he had signed the Southern Manifesto and had voted against an extension of the 1957 Civil Rights Act. In contrast, northerners viewed Collins as a leading moderate on the racial issue. The May 21, 1960, announcement of the Washington Interfaith Committee that he would receive its National Interfaith Award underscored the respect accorded his record. The committee cited him as a "dedicated bridge-builder of better understanding between ethnic and racial groups." His civil rights stance was a decisive factor in his selection as permanent chairman.[20]

Collins, moreover, repeatedly affirmed his party loyalty. At a February 27, 1960, fund-raising dinner in Miami, he assured Truman, Butler, and other visiting dignitaries that he would strive to keep the South in the Democratic fold. "To run out on the party would be not only a shameful betrayal of our heritage, but of our future as well," he said. When some southern governors held a meeting in March to discuss the possibility of a third party, they did not invite him. He explained to the press, "I understand that the basis for my exclusion was that I was a loyal Democrat, and I regard that rather as a compliment." A week later, he predicted that Florida Democrats would not bolt the party. At any rate, he added, "If there is any desertion going on, I am not going to be a party to it."[21]

The Democratic leadership viewed Collins as a valuable party asset who might bridge the ideological chasm between the northern and southern wings of the party.[22] Their design was ill founded.

As one columnist pointed out, Collins did not rate equally with Boggs in the hearts of southerners.[23] Commenting on the possibility of himself as a bridge, Collins conceded, "There's more hope than assurance in that view. I know that my own feelings differ rather substantially from the attitudes of many [convention] delegates from the South—in fact, this divergence is present in my own state."[24] Nevertheless, the party leaders needed a southerner to provide regional balance at the convention and thought Collins was the most acceptable candidate.

Collins's demonstrated competence as chairman of the Southern Governors' Conference and National Governors' Conference constituted a final factor in his selection as permanent chairman. Democratic conventions had a history of being raucous affairs. The intensity of the presidential campaign and the threatened floor fight on the platform's civil rights plank promised to make the 1960 party meeting even more disorderly than usual. The chairmanship required competency. Members of the Committee on Arrangements told Collins that their belief in his ability to handle the challenge determined his selection.[25]

On May 24, 1960, the Committee on Arrangements met at the Biltmore Hotel in New York to choose the convention officers. National committeewoman Peggy Ehrman of Gainesville, Florida, nominated Collins for the permanent chairmanship and Mary Cunningham of Rulo, Nebraska, seconded the nomination. His wide lead on the first ballot convinced the committee to make the choice unanimous. Ironically, on that same day, Florida Democrats denied Ehrman's bid for reelection to the national committee and defeated "Collins's candidate," Doyle Carlton, in his campaign for governor.[26]

Following his selection as permanent chairman, Collins met with party leaders to seek their views on the convention. In Washington, he talked for forty-five minutes with Rayburn and Missouri Congressman Clarence Cannon, the party parliamentarian. They discussed procedures and potential problems. Reporters "practically mobbed" Collins at a press conference after the meeting with questions centering on the vice-presidential nomination. Collins insisted that the neutrality required of a convention chairman virtually ruled him out of consideration for the office.[27]

Senator Kennedy mentioned a special problem in his meeting with Collins. In 1956 Kennedy had nearly won the vice-presidential nomination. Senator Estes Kefauver of Tennessee led on the first ballot, but, before vote shifts on the second ballot, a Kennedy upset seemed certain. As the delegations clamored for recognition, Kennedy appeared to enjoy enough support to insure his nomination. Yet, the first states recognized by Rayburn changed their votes from lesser candidates to Kefauver. Humphrey resolved the nomination by releasing his delegates to the Tennessee senator. Kennedy believed the initial shifts to Kefauver had created a "bandwagon effect," which denied him the nomination. The senator now feared a combination of favorite sons and legitimate candidates would again keep him from gaining a majority on the first ballot. In this eventuality, recognition of states for vote changes after the first roll call could be crucial. Kennedy requested a ruling that would prohibit any candidate from receiving a series of vote shifts by design. Collins decided, if the Rules Committee did not state a policy to insure fairness, then he would.[28]

Between the time of Collins's appointment and the opening of the convention, an intraparty brouhaha of major dimensions occurred. The "Stop Kennedy" forces accused the party leadership of "rigging" the convention in favor of the Massachusetts senator. A Republican official had first made the charge in March 1960, stating that Butler was "trying to 'rig' the Democratic Convention."[29] During the spring, Kennedy's primary victories and successes in state caucuses brought him nearly enough votes to insure his nomination. Frustration and anger intensified in all camps. In May, Johnson supporters renewed the accusation that Butler had fixed the convention. They pointed out, for example, that Bowles, Kennedy's foreign policy adviser, chaired the platform committee. Although voicing discontent, they hesitated to instigate a public controversy because of the stature of Kennedy's leaders.[30]

Former President Truman felt no constraint. On July 2, nine days before the convention began, he called a news conference to explain his resignation as a delegate. "I have no desire whatever," he said, "to be a party to proceedings that are taking on the aspects of a prearranged affair." He accused the Kennedy campaign staff of pressuring delegates into preconvention commitments. He asked

Kennedy, "Senator, are you certain that you're quite ready for the country or the country is ready for you?" Truman called for a nominee possessing the broadest possible maturity and experience. His list of ten qualified Democrats excluded Kennedy and Stevenson, but included Collins. After censuring the party leadership, Truman concluded, "I don't like a fixed convention."[31]

Most Democratic leaders denied Truman's charge. Butler labeled the statement that he would unfairly favor Kennedy at the convention a "complete falsehood." Symington saw no indication of rigging. W. Averell Harriman, Truman's 1956 choice for the nomination, believed the convention would be "entirely open." Kennedy thought Truman regarded "an open convention as one which studies all the candidates, reviews their records, and then takes his advice."[32]

Collins tried to minimize the damage caused by the "rigging" charge. Talking to Truman by telephone before the news conference, he sought a reconsideration. He later urged the former president to attend the convention "for the best interests of the Democratic party." On the July 3 segment of the news program "Meet the Press," Collins portrayed the incident as a typical Democratic brawl. Speaking of Truman, he suggested: "I rather think he's enjoying it. He certainly seemed in his press conference the other day to be enjoying it." Collins rejected the rigging charge. "It could not be rigged unless the permanent chairman was a party to the rigging and there has been nothing like that," he argued.[33] After the convention, he brushed aside the accusation as an attempt to undermine Kennedy's strength. Collins defined rigging as "what the losers say when the winners have the votes."[34]

Johnson used the rigging allegation in his effort to block Kennedy's nomination. Following Truman's news conference, Johnson noted, "I don't think it's any secret that the national chairman [Butler] . . . has been somewhat active in Senator Kennedy's camp." After his arrival at the convention, Johnson renewed the controversy. "Is this convention open," he asked, "or has the outcome been determined somewhere in a back room, with the result only now being announced to the delegates?"[35]

Senator Johnson's exploitation of the issue created a problem for Collins within the Florida convention delegation. Collins had wanted it to be selected in an open primary, one in which all the candidates participated. But, because Symington and Johnson were foregoing the primaries and Stevenson was not an active candidate, Florida Democrats were denied the opportunity to express their preference at the ballot box. State leaders decided to nominate a favorite-son candidate, Collins explained, "because we had those early indications of disfavor of candidates for participating in the preferential primary." In the summer of 1959, a three-way telephone conversation between Collins, Smathers, and Senator Spessard L. Holland broached the selection of a favorite-son candidate. Each disclaimed interest, but Holland suggested Smathers would be the best choice in recognition of his service as chairman of the Democratic Senatorial Campaign Committee. The three men made no final decision. Shortly thereafter, Collins left for his tour of the Soviet Union. Prior to his departure, he said he thought the choice of Smathers was a fine idea.[36] During the autumn of 1959, Democrats assumed Smathers would be the favorite-son candidate.

The role of favorite son posed potential problems for Smathers. Kennedy wanted to run in the Florida primary. His family owned a winter home in Palm Beach and he had often visited the state. Believing he could win its delegates in a primary election, he pressured Smathers to withdraw as a favorite son. The "Stop Kennedy" forces insisted that Smathers hold Florida's votes on the first ballot.[37] The favorite-son candidacy apparently had evolved into a political quandary for Smathers.

In a January 7, 1960, press conference, reporters questioned Collins on the favorite-son issue. One pointed out that this strategy, in effect, kept candidates such as Kennedy from entering the primary. "Senator Smathers has certainly said, and I have said also, and others too," Collins responded, "that if they all come in and we can get a representative group of these candidates participating, that would no longer make the 'favorite son' idea an appropriate one." There seemed little hope of obtaining a large group of candidates, he added. A column three days later in the Miami Herald created a furor among the state's Democrats. John L. Boyles wrote that the choice of Smathers as the favorite son was made while Collins was visiting the Soviet Union. With Smathers heading the delegation, Boyles contended, Collins and his advisers feared the governor would possess little influence.[38]

Smathers immediately requested a clarification from Collins concerning the column, which he characterized as "filled with misperceptions." Smathers asserted he had never sought the favorite-son designation and offered to step aside if the governor desired the role. At his next press conference, the latter affirmed his participation with Smathers and Holland in determining the candidate. He had supported Smathers because the senator had a chance to be on the national ticket and deserved the recognition for his service to the state; and the choice would insure an uncommitted delegation. Since then, Smathers had predicted that no southerner would be on the Democratic ticket and had come to consider the favorite-son designation an imposition rather than a compliment. If neither the favorite-son nor open-primary strategies proved to be possible, Collins suggested the selection of a slate of outstanding Floridians as uninstructed delegates. He emphasized his support for Smathers if the senator still wanted to be the favorite son and added that under no circumstances would he accept the position. Collins believed he was not being antagonistic to Smathers but was helping him resolve his dilemma.[39]

Shortly after Collins's news conference, the state Democratic Executive Committee met at Orlando and endorsed Smathers's favorite-son candidacy. Although Collins supported the decision, the vote appeared to be a setback for him. Smathers advised him by wire that he considered his explanation of the issue "an eminently fair presentation." Collins released the telegram and expressed the hope that it "put at rest some unfounded deductions" of a rift between the two men.[40]

In February 1960 a committee of Democratic leaders chose a slate of delegates for the Smathers favorite-son candidacy. John Perry represented Collins at the private meeting in Miami. Most of those picked for the delegation supported Johnson. Angry Kennedy adherents charged that the committee chose no delegates who were committed to their candidate. The committee selected Collins and included some of his backers, such as Brailey Odham, of Sanford. Although Congressman Robert Sikes, of Crestview, and former Governor Caldwell also served in the delegation, the

Miami *Herald* at first judged Collins to be "the head of the convention team."[41]

After his selection as a delegate, Collins suggested bringing each of the candidates to Florida for informal meetings with delegates. He believed the idea would give citizens a better understanding of the contenders, would make the party's choice more democratic, and would attract the national media to the state. The concept would also have resulted in a more independent delegation. Moreover, it would have concentrated attention on the governor as the probable host for the meetings, and would have brought in the national media at a time when he was being considered for a convention post and the vice-presidency. His plan increased the division among party leaders. Without doubt recognizing the potential value of the project for Collins, Caldwell rejected his proposal to invite the candidates "for some persuasive doubletalk." Furthermore, Caldwell urged the delegates to choose either Sikes or Holland, rather than Collins, for their chairman. The success of Collins's idea became a test of his strength in the delegation.[42]

Collins tried for three months to organize the meetings. Although only three of the delegates expressly disapproved the idea, the exigencies of the presidential campaign worked against the plan. Kennedy and Humphrey initially agreed to participate, but the latter withdrew after his defeat in the West Virginia primary. Symington and Johnson stated their regrets that congressional duties kept them from taking part. Stevenson liked the idea, but refused to attend because he was not an announced candidate. Furthermore, during these months the sit-in crisis and the gubernatorial primary deepened the divisions among the state's Democrats. Finally, when the national party selected Collins to be the permanent chairman of the convention, he resigned as a delegate. The plan for conferences with the candidates proved to be unfeasible. After Collins accepted the convention post, Smathers announced his choice of Sikes as chairman of the Florida delegation.[43]

The controversies over the makeup and strategies of the delegation, in the end, left the governor with little authority over his state's convention representatives. Although poised for national leadership, he confronted the reality of waning influence in the Florida Democratic party.

12

A Wild Horse to Ride:

The 1960 Democratic Convention

On July 11, 1960, the Democratic National Convention opened at Los Angeles in an "ill tempered" atmosphere.[1] The heated primaries, the personality and political clashes among party leaders, and the "rigging" controversy insured that Collins would encounter vituperation and disorder. "It is a wild horse he has been chosen to ride," one newspaper observed.[2] The Florida delegation was especially rancorous. Well-publicized dissension within the state caucus aired the intraparty divisions that had undermined Collins's political strength in Florida.

Several factors at the convention angered conservative Floridians. The failure to slow Kennedy's momentum for the nomination frustrated Johnson's advocates. Moreover, the conservatives were appalled by the party platform's "ultra-liberal" civil rights plank. The platform called for an end to racial discrimination in voting, housing, and employment. It pledged that a Democratic administration would enforce the Supreme Court's decision on school desegregation and called on every affected school district to submit a plan for compliance by 1963. Referring to the sit-in movement, the platform proclaimed, "The peaceful demonstrations for first-class citizenship which have recently taken place in many parts of this country are a signal to all of us to make good, at long last, the guarantees of the American Constitution." The New York *Times* contended that the civil rights plank was the strongest in Demo-

157

cratic history. Holland, a platform committee member, told Florida's delegates, "the hearings were dominated entirely by what I would call the left wing groups—ADA [Americans for Democratic Action], NAACP, and Farmers' Union."[3] Many Floridians believed the committee had been stacked in favor of the liberal civil rights view.

Butler's effort to limit demonstrations following the nomination of favorite-son candidates also irritated the delegates. The move would have shortened the Wednesday session and provided a more attractive television offering. The Floridians, though, were determined to stage a demonstration for Smathers, who, himself, accused Butler of "behaving like a dictator." Sikes blasted "Butler's group," but added, "I don't know anybody that's going to stop us when we get started."[4]

Butler's decision on ticket distribution further provoked the Florida delegates. Johnson and Stevenson adherents charged him with manipulating the distribution of gallery tickets in Kennedy's favor. The strict enforcement of ticket policies resulted in sparse attendance at the Monday night session. Notwithstanding the empty seats, Floridians were unable to obtain additional tickets for the Tuesday session, when Collins would speak, or for the Wednesday session, when Smathers would be nominated. After two frustrating days, national committeeman Jerry Carter, who was responsible for procuring tickets, devised a plan for those who would participate in Smathers's demonstration. He told the state caucus, "If you ever get inside the door, . . . before they get you back to the door to march you outside, all break up and go every different direction just as fast as you can." The Floridians greeted this suggestion with rebel yells and laughter.[5]

The ticket and demonstration policies, the liberal civil rights plank, and the success of the Kennedy campaign convinced many Florida delegates that the convention indeed was fixed. In the Tuesday caucus, they decided to express their anger dramatically. William Chappell, of Ocala, Speaker-elect of the house of representatives, introduced a resolution calling for a telegram to Truman inviting "the old war horse" to come and help "unrig the riggers." The telegram would have been an affront not only to Butler, but also to Collins, because he had said no rigging would occur without his cooperation. Odham made a motion that the word "rigging" be expunged to prevent embarrassment for Collins. Caldwell then moved that the Odham motion be tabled, thus retaining the original wording of the resolution.[6] The venomous exchanges brought to the surface the enmity within the state's Democratic party in 1960.

Several members of the delegation intervened to restore a semblance of harmony. President J. Ollie Edmunds of Stetson University prevailed on Caldwell to withdraw his motion. William C. Lantaff, of Miami, reminded the delegates that the resolution would implicate Collins in the rigging. "I think that we should be very cautious in adopting a resolution which the press would pick up as a great split between the Florida delegation and the permanent chairman," he argued. Chappell agreed to reword his resolution. Sikes relieved the tension by suggesting the delegation plan a demonstration to follow Collins's introduction to the convention.[7]

The conservatives were quieted but not convinced. On Tuesday evening, Caldwell termed the convention "a hag-ridden, Butler rigged, left wing dominated fiasco" and claimed that Collins was "a tool of the rigger."[8] One newsman concluded, "Yesterday the Florida delegation by and large just wasn't in the same century with the governor of the state."[9] Sikes presented the resolution to party officials, who suggested that an invitation be sent to Truman from all the delegates at the convention. Collins called Truman, read him the resolution, and expressed his hope that the former president would come to Los Angeles.[10] Although the former was spared public embarrassment, the maneuvers of the Florida delegation demonstrated to the knowledgeable politicians at the convention that Collins did not control his state's Democratic party.

When the convention delegates entered the Los Angeles Sports Arena on Monday evening, they were forced to make their way through a picket line of Stevenson supporters encircling the building. The placard-carrying marchers' chant of "We want Stevenson!" echoed throughout the Sports Arena. His followers dominated the Democratic party in Los Angeles. No other city could have better served the purpose of the "Draft Stevenson" movement. He had wavered but never given his full support to those working in his behalf. When the convention opened, his

advocates realized that only a strong show of popular demand
would convince him to run and, at the same time, halt the
Kennedy drive for a first-ballot sweep.[11] Throughout the convention, the necessity for the Stevensonians to demonstrate a ground
swell of support for their candidate created problems for Collins.

On Monday evening, Collins watched as Idaho's Senator Frank
Church, the temporary chairman and keynote speaker, tried to
control the convention. Collins was "really shocked by the disorder."[12] His turn came on Tuesday. Church introduced him as "a
man of high principle and purpose—and a dedicated and loyal
Democrat." Floridians led a demonstration proclaiming the state's
pride in its governor. Two members of the delegation, Caldwell
and Bryant, conspicuously remained seated. Church had requested that the aisles be cleared, but order had not been established when Collins accepted the gavel. The Florida demonstration
added to the confusion. Despite the governor's pleas, the turbu-
lence on the floor continued. He decided to carry on with his
speech despite the hubbub.[13]

Collins first reminded the delegates that serious business had
brought them to Los Angeles. America confronted an era of crisis.
He attacked the Republicans for not providing leadership. "We
know that Americans can do anything," he contended. "It is their
leaders who have failed to point the way." Lamenting the passing
of a time "when the word, 'America' was magic throughout the
world," he urged the delegates to proclaim the nation's commitment "to wage war on the very causes of war: colonialism, poverty,
hunger, disease, ignorance, and prejudice." He added, "If this be
assaulted by the selfish as a 'do-good' policy, we will ask in reply,
since when in America is it wrong to do good." The conclusion
called on the delegates to make the convention the kind "which
will make you . . . proud to say in the limitless years ahead: 'I
was there.' "[14]

Although the effort left Collins dissatisfied, journalists praised
the speech. One reporter called it "an old fashioned political
speech full of sonorous, rolling phrases," and another judged it the
best of the convention.[15] The editors of a Daytona Beach newspaper
were "struck with the earnestness and the moral tone of the
Governor's remarks." They complimented "his perceptive grasp of

the tremendous task confronting the party, the next President and America." The Tampa *Times* believed Collins "had some important things to say—and he said them well."[16] Despite the accolades, he admitted, "Addressing a national political convention is a very discouraging experience." The tumult on the floor had disrupted his continuity and slowed his delivery. He repeatedly was forced to stop and ask the delegates to be seated. According to one report, "only a hastily penned note from the national chairman, telling him that the speech was projecting well on national television, persuaded Collins to continue." If it had not been for that audience, he conceded, "I would have stopped without delivering the last half of my speech."[17]

Other interruptions were also distracting. Two minutes after he began, a cheer from the Texas delegation greeted the entrance of Speaker Rayburn. Collins paused to introduce the former chairman to the convention and asked him to stand for an ovation. Then, midway through the speech, Eleanor Roosevelt entered the hall. The delegates welcomed her with tremendous applause, again bringing Collins's address to a halt. Following the convention, she wrote to him, "I do hope you realize that because of the noise I did not know you were speaking. Had I the faintest idea that my entrance was going to attract attention which would interfere with your speech, I would never have come in when I did." Each day of the convention, her appearances resulted in disruption. One Ohio television viewer plaintively asked Collins, "Can you stop Eleanor from changing seats?" Collins later said that she should have given the convention managers an opportunity to prepare for her arrivals.[18] Whether by design or accident, the attention given Roosevelt, a fervent Stevensonian, helped keep the "Draft Stevenson" movement before the convention.

Shortly after Collins's speech, Stevenson, himself, entered the Sports Arena to take his seat as a delegate from Illinois. The hall erupted in a dramatic display of affection for the party's titular leader. During this emotional demonstration, Collins virtually lost control of the convention. He decided the only way to quiet the delegates was for Stevenson to address the assembly. Because his request could not be heard over the microphone, Collins sent an aide to ask Stevenson to speak. When he declined, saying it would

not be "proper," Collins insisted that only a speech could restore
order to the convention. Stevenson agreed to talk briefly. "After
getting in and out of the Biltmore Hotel and the hall," he quipped,
"I decided that I know who you are going to nominate, it will be
the last survivor."[19] After his remarks, Collins resumed the convention business. His insistence that Stevenson speak to the delegates
was a timely improvisation.

During the four days Collins chaired the convention, maintaining order proved to be his most difficult problem. Extending
himself physically, he broke three pounding boards with a large
gavel in his attempts to quiet the delegates. A New York City
television viewer wired Collins, "The delegates seem to be a herd
of non-descript cattle in our living room." Their lack of attention
during the national anthem particularly concerned some viewers.
One considered the sight "very distressing." When the television
networks received numerous complaints about the noise and disorder, commentators blamed the Sports Arena's acoustics. Yet, when
Eleanor Roosevelt spoke at the Wednesday session, "the entire
arena hushed."[20]

The noise resulted not from acoustical problems, but from a
combination of factors that made the convention unusually dramatic. Collins later pointed out that, for the first time since 1948,
the Democratic nominee would not need to face the seemingly
unbeatable Eisenhower. As a result, an aura of optimism suffused
the convention and gave the delegates "enormous enthusiasm" for
their role in selecting a candidate. Collins also noted the frustration
of the forces who were trying to block Kennedy; he went to Los
Angeles with approximately 600 of the 761 votes necessary for
nomination. The battle for a first-ballot victory required intense
lobbying. Each candidate had crews of workers on the convention
floor to procure and maintain delegate votes. Moreover, when
Collins finally managed to seat the delegates in fair order, news
media personnel roamed the aisles and created pockets of confusion scattered about the floor. Collins later concluded, "The convention in Los Angeles was beyond the possibility of orderly
management."[21]

Party leaders feared that a debate on the platform's civil rights
plank might lead to further disruption. Their concern proved

groundless. Southerners presented a minority plank protesting the party's "ultra-liberal" civil rights stance. Accusing "radicals" of trying "to drive the States of the South from the Democratic Party," it defended states' rights, condemned the sit-in demonstrators, and warned that the majority plank would result in the party's defeat. For the most part, the delegates defused the southerners' anger by giving them a courteous reception. Holland, though, received some boos when he attacked the Fair Employment Practices Commission as a proposal of "well meaning socialistic reformers." He quieted the delegates with a reminder that millions of Democrats in the South were watching and listening. In a voice vote on the minority report, the shouts of those in favor seemed louder, but Collins ruled that the amendment was defeated. Southerners did not dispute the decision, realizing they would have been overwhelmingly defeated in a roll-call vote.[22] Their reluctant acceptance of the platform spared Collins the complications inherent in a walkout.

On Wednesday the Democrats nominated their presidential candidate. Because the Rules Committee had not broached the issue, Collins determined a procedure for changing votes at the end of the first roll call. He said the chair would first be informed of those states wishing to make a change and would then call them in the order they initially balloted. The ruling insured fairness because if a series of states did change to the same candidate, it would be the result of happenstance, not design. Collins also tried to impress the need for decorum on the delegates. "I urge you, and I demand of you, that we have better attention," he entreated. They ignored the edict on order, just as they disregarded a ruling limiting demonstrations to ten minutes. A six-hour marathon of nominations resulted.[23]

Johnson was the first nominee placed before the convention. Despite Collins's call for order, Johnson's adherents demonstrated through the aisles for more than twenty minutes. Sixty-seven minutes elapsed before the final cheer and seconding speech concluded. Just as Collins regained control, he realized to his dismay that he was rising. He had pressed the wrong button, activating the small elevator used to keep all speakers at a common height. When his knees reached microphone level, technicians

finally found the right button and lowered the platform. Collins ruefully explained, "They have my elevator here going the wrong way."[24]

The supporters of Kennedy, Smathers, and Symington repeated the ritual of nominations, demonstrations, and seconds—each group taking more than the allotted time. Milling crowds made the aisles virtually impassable. Pounding the gavel, Collins called again and again for order. The next two candidates, governors Herschel C. Loveless, of Iowa, and George Docking, of Kansas, withdrew in favor of Kennedy following their nominations.[25] It was then time for the nomination of Stevenson—one of the most electrifying and unmanageable moments in convention history. He finally had announced for the presidency on Wednesday. The viability of his candidacy lasted only a few hours. Hope ended when Mayor Richard J. Daley, of Chicago, informed him that the Illinois delegation solidly backed Kennedy. Without the support of his home state, Stevenson lost any chance for the nomination.

Democratic party notables at the Los Angeles Memorial Coliseum, July 15, 1960 (*left to right*): Senator Eugene McCarthy, Senator Edmund Muskie, Senator A. S. ("Mike") Monroney, Congressman Hale Boggs, Lady Bird Johnson, Governor Collins, Senator John F. Kennedy, Senator Lyndon B. Johnson, House Speaker Samuel Rayburn (partially hidden), Congressman James Roosevelt, Senator Hubert Humphrey (partially hidden), Governor Adlai Stevenson, Senator Stuart Symington (partially hidden), and Edward G. Robinson. (*Courtesy, United Press International*)

Nevertheless, his advocates believed an outpouring of popular will might even then sway the convention. Although allotted only thirty-five tickets, the Stevensonians had used ruse and subterfuge to pack the gallery with nearly four thousand of their faithful. A wild roar greeted Senator Eugene J. McCarthy, of Minnesota, when he strode to the podium to nominate Stevenson.[26]

McCarthy made a memorable speech. He implored the delegates, "Do not reject this man who made us all proud to be called

Democrats. . . . Do not, I say to you, do not leave this prophet without honor in his own party." His words set off the "nearest thing to hysteria" the convention had seen. Collins futilely tried for nearly half an hour to achieve order. Finally, in exasperation, he declared, "Nobody can be nominated President of the United States if we are going to conduct ourselves like a bunch of hoodlums."[27] This forceful language brought cheers from the delegates and boos from the demonstrators. Knowing Stevenson could not be nominated, the delegates were committed to other candidates. One observer noted, "this sound and fury did not signify votes."[28]

When the balloting began, most people judged that the outcome was uncertain. No one knew Kennedy's exact strength, and many doubted he could hold his delegates on a second ballot. Robert F. Kennedy, his brother and campaign manager, later admitted, "We had to win on the first ballot." They did. The nomination released the tensions that had gripped the convention for three days. Governor James T. Blair, of Missouri, moved that the convention make the selection unanimous. The delegates concurred in Collins's call for a vote of acclamation.[29]

Critics disputed two of Collins's rulings. His decision on acclamation infuriated some southerners who did not want to be associated with the vote for Kennedy. The Mississippi delegation was especially embittered. Senators James O. Eastland and John C. Stennis "pulled Collins off the platform" and pleaded with him to announce their delegation's change from Governor Ross Barnett, their favorite-son candidate, to Johnson. Collins refused. Although recognizing that the acclamation vote denied favorite-son delegations an opportunity to express their actual preferences, he believed the ruling expressed the overwhelming sentiment of the convention.[30] His plan for vote changes, though academic in light of Kennedy's majority, also prompted some concern. Before and after the convention, a few suspected that Collins in some way designed the procedure to favor one candidate over another. He insisted his decision simply would have insured fairness.[31]

Some commentators had speculated that Collins would be selected for vice-president, but, on Thursday, Kennedy chose Johnson as his running mate. Consideration of Collins went back to 1956, when Sikes had nominated him for vice-president, though just as a courtesy.[32] Following his Sea Island speech in 1957, Collins was accorded more serious consideration. In May 1960 the New York *Times* mentioned his possible selection and reported that some of his friends were active in his behalf. At the time, he disclaimed active candidacy, but said he would willingly accept the nomination. He later stressed that no discussions or planning took place to gain the post. Nevertheless, just before the convention, an Atlanta newspaper reported that "insiders" included him as a front-runner. If Kennedy chose a southerner as vice-president, the newspaper wrote, then Collins would be his choice.[33]

Collins would have been an asset to the national ticket. The television coverage of the convention made him a recognized political figure throughout the country.[34] In the 1956 election, he had proven his ability to attract voters. Moreover, as a southern civil rights moderate, he would have added balance to the ticket. Basically, the same factors that made him a logical choice for convention chairman would have made him an attractive national candidate.

Collins's status had changed substantially, though, since his selection as chairman. The political paradox of gaining national stature while losing support in his home state had become evident. The Bryant-Caldwell faction had demonstrated his weakness in the gubernatorial primary and in the state's convention delegation. The conservatives had tapped the deep vein of resister sentiment in Florida and, to an extent, left him isolated "beyond the horizon of the people." He realized the problem. If he could have obtained the cooperation of the state's Democrats, he later revealed, he would have encouraged a move for the vice-presidency. Speaking to Collins after the convention, Robert Kennedy expressed his preference for him over Johnson. However, Kennedy explained, Collins's lack of influence in his own delegation constituted an insurmountable problem.[35]

Florida Democratic politics only partially explained the slight consideration given Collins for the vice-presidency. Other factors contributed. The Kennedys' primary concern was the presidential nomination. They used hints of potential vice-presidential choices to gain support for the senator's candidacy.[36] A disgruntled Stevenson leader maintained, "If they called a meeting of all the people to

whom they've promised the Vice-Presidency, they couldn't find a
room in Los Angeles large enough to hold it in."[37]

Even presuming the Kennedys' sincerity, the presence of Lyndon Johnson insured that Collins would not be offered the nomination. First, Johnson brought the same balance to the national ticket
and, as the South's leading political figure, he had to be offered the
nomination before anyone else from his region. He needed to be
given "first refusal," Kennedy aide Theodore C. Sorensen later
pointed out. Second, Johnson accepted. His decision to relinquish
the powers of Senate majority leader for the relative obscurity of
the vice-presidency surprised most observers. Robert Kennedy
later said his brother felt obligated to tender Johnson the nomination, *but he never dreamt that there was a chance in the world
that he would accept it.*" Collins expressed the view prevalent at
the convention: "I was personally surprised that Senator Johnson
was willing to accept Senator Kennedy's invitation to serve as our
vice-presidential nominee."[38] At any rate, this decision closed out
all other candidates for the position.

The Democrats held their Friday session outdoors at the Los
Angeles Coliseum. While Collins introduced Stevenson, a helicopter hovered overhead, pulling a banner that proclaimed the merits
of the Republican party. To the delight of the Democrats, Collins
observed, "It is a typical Republican performance. They are going
round and round and they are beating the air but they are going no
place." When Stevenson began to speak, a high school band,
costumed as Indians, entered the coliseum. As it blared out a
welcome to Stevenson, some of its members used machines to
send puffs of smoke skyward. Turning to Collins, Stevenson asked
him "what in the hell" was going on. Collins replied he did not
know because he had never learned to read smoke signals. When
officials finally silenced the band, Stevenson commented, "I am
sure the helicopter is Republican, but I don't know about the
Indians." Stevenson introduced Kennedy, who accepted the nomination and called for pioneers on a "New Frontier." Collins then
declared the thirty-third National Democratic Convention adjourned.[39]

Although the rancorous campaign for the presidential nomination made the convention extraordinarily difficult to chair, Collins

received universal acclaim for his performance.[40] "Governor LeRoy Collins of Florida was an excellent choice for chairman," according to one columnist, who added, "He is handsome and imposing on television and his voice and sentiment hit the right note."[41] Others remarked about his attractive television personality.[42] A New Jersey woman believed: "The Democrats really goofed. If they had put Governor LeRoy Collins of Florida up for President, there isn't a female regardless of age or political affiliation who wouldn't vote for him. What a doll!"[43]

Newspaper editorials from across the nation added to the plaudits. Collins had displayed qualities of timing, fairness, goodwill, and fortitude "in abundance," the New York *Times* wrote. The Chicago *Tribune*, a Republican journal, stated that Collins was one figure whose reputation was enhanced by the convention. A Tennessee newspaper evaluated him as "eminently fair and even handed." In Florida, the Daytona Beach *Evening News* judged that he had "performed with firmness tempered with graciousness," and the Lakeland *Ledger* stressed his "polish, firmness, and fairness." The editors of the Tampa *Times* suggested, "LeRoy Collins introduced a new flavor to convention management. He acted with dignity and expected dignity in return. He was courteous and demanded courtesy. In short, the delegates got as good a lesson in the manners of a Southern gentleman as could be had anywhere and under any conditions."[44]

The political "pros" also complimented Collins. Congressman Cannon, citing Collins's "faultless conduct of the convention," termed him "one of the most expert parliamentarians I have ever known." Illinois Senator Paul H. Douglas called him a "magnificent chairman"; James A. Farley acclaimed his "super job"; and Illinois Congressman Roman C. Pucinski suggested that he should be the party's 1968 presidential candidate. Former President Truman complimented him on "one of the best jobs I have ever seen." Even Vice-President and Mrs. Richard M. Nixon sent their congratulations. "As a matter of fact," they added, "our only regret is that you happen to be a member of the opposition party rather than our own!"[45]

At a news conference following his return to Florida, Collins suggested changes in convention procedures based on his experi-

ences in Los Angeles. First, he believed the disruptive influence of
the news media should be removed from the convention floor. He
also urged the elimination of public participation in demonstrations. Such staged performances had become degrading spectacles
rather than meaningful shows of strength, he charged. Finally, he
wanted only those directly involved to be allowed into the convention. Television now gave the general public access to the convention. Collins called for an end to the "circus atmosphere," which
distracted from the convention's serious business.[46]

Despite the problems, Collins relished the challenge of the
chairmanship. "It was a most interesting experience," he recalled.
"I never did feel that I was a complete stranger to the job. I
enjoyed the work."[47] In responding to letters of congratulation, he
wrote, "After returning to my duties here, I had a glimpse of
heaven one night in a dream, and in a great auditorium there—
imagine it—the aisles were completely clear!"[48]

Following the convention, the pace of Collins's activities slowed.
Political intrigues lacked the intensity of prior months. Almost as
an anticlimax, ceremonial functions, speaking engagements, and
plans for the future filled the governor's days. Yet, duties remained. During the final weeks of his term, Collins carried out
administrative routine, worked for the election of a Democratic
president, and defended his moderate stance in the racial crisis.

Using sit-in tactics, civil rights advocates continued to pressure
for change in segregation customs. Although four Florida communities quietly integrated lunch counters, demonstrations in Jacksonville flared into violence.[49] The population of the seaport city on
the St. Johns River was 199,000, which included more than
110,000 blacks. Testing the force of segregation, activists initiated
sit-ins at the F. W. Woolworth's and Grant's lunch counters on
August 13, 1960. Hot, humid days contributed to growing tensions
as demonstrators disrupted the normal flow of business. On Friday, August 26, a number of name-calling incidents preceded a
hair-pulling altercation between a white woman and a black
woman. During the resulting scuffle, two white women were
knocked to the sidewalk and a plate-glass window at Woolworth's
was broken.[50]

On Saturday morning, approximately 150 white men, armed

with baseball bats as well as ax handles and carrying Confederate flags, gathered in a small city park near the picketed stores.[51] At 11:35 A.M., the group learned that demonstrators had entered Grant's department store. It began marching toward the establishment and assaulted black bystanders along the way. When the demonstrators attempted to walk away from the scene, the whites attacked and a melee ensued. Some blacks retreated to "Little Harlem," ten blocks away, and then returned to the conflict with reinforcements. The violence continued for one-and-a-half hours. Finally, police, armed with riot guns, dispersed the crowd, which had grown to three thousand, including shoppers and onlookers. Fights, shootings, arson, and clashes between police and blacks spread throughout the city. The Ku Klux Klan held meetings in two nearby towns and burned a cross in a suburban neighborhood. Violence peaked on Saturday and Sunday nights and tapered off during the next week; more than seventy people had been injured and 150 arrested.[52]

Black leaders called on President Eisenhower and the Department of Justice to investigate the actions of local authorities. They also suspended sit-ins and began an economic boycott of downtown merchants. The Jacksonville Ministerial Alliance announced plans to form a biracial committee to open communications between the city's blacks and whites. The Reverend Martin Luther King, Jr., cautioned against a violent response to white attacks. "It is urgent for Negroes to keep to a plan of non-violence," he advised. "The Jacksonville incident makes it more urgent than ever."[53]

In the wake of that violence, conservatives challenged Collins's moderate policies. Mayor Haydon Burns blamed the "poorest element of both races." Admitting he had repeatedly refused merchants' requests to order lunch counter integration, he said, "The merchants are trying to duck the decision by going to city officials and asking them to make the decision for them." Burns criticized Collins's concept of biracial commissions and refused to recognize the panel set up by the Ministerial Association. "The record of these committees in other cities is that they invariably result in decisions to integrate," he explained.[54] Democratic gubernatorial-nominee Bryant implied that Collins could have prevented the violence by anticipating the crisis. Governor Faubus, of

Arkansas, also welcomed the opportunity for a jab. The Jacksonville violence indicated that "the moderate governor there hasn't
control of the situation." He gloated, "They have had more hell
there in three days than we have had in three years, make that 30
years."[55]

Collins initially reacted by placing the National Guard on
standby alert. Without a local request for assistance, though, he
took no direct action. In response to Faubus's charges, he observed, "I see no useful purpose in comparing our shames."
Placing primary blame for the conflict on Jacksonville's citizens and
officials, he emphasized their refusal to establish a biracial committee. "Basically, everyone should recognize that the maintenance of
law and order and the development of good human relations is
primarily a local responsibility, and where breakdowns occur there
have been local failures that have caused that breakdown," he
contended.[56]

The governor's concerns, though, went beyond the assessment
of individual blame. The problem "certainly has its base in racial
intolerance," he believed. He emphasized the Jacksonville black
community's poor housing standards and limited recreational facilities. To those who blamed black and white "trash" for the problem,
he replied, "You cannot try to sweep the trash under the slums and
expect to avoid difficulties, because slums breed difficulties, slums
breed crime, vice, and disorder. They always have, and they
always will." Similar conditions existed throughout Florida and the
United States. Indeed, Collins warned, "It is not just in the cities
of the South, but Detroit and Chicago and New York, and all of the
great cities of America have basic elements that will produce the
same thing that happened in Jacksonville." Wise leadership would
be needed to solve the nation's deeply rooted racial problems.[57]

In a September speech to the Executives' Club, of Chicago,
Collins expounded on his views of leadership. His generation's
failure to provide national guidance concerned him. "We have
been largely a generation of followers—in the main, followers of
paths of least resistance," he submitted. The South especially
distressed him. "I want to speak to you of the South I love so
deeply that while I sing its praises and laud its virtues," he said, "I
cannot be blind to its shortcomings." Southern leaders had not met

the issues "squarely and with courage." He claimed, "Too many strong names—strong men—honored men—with past records glittering with accomplishment, have failed the South in its time of great need." As a result, though the region made dramatic economic advances, "our political progress has not kept pace with the rate of other progress."

Collins did not consider the want of guidance in days of crisis a cause for despair. He believed leaders would emerge in the South and in the nation:

> Great leadership never comes in the quiet and sweetness of early morning when all things seem good and clean with newness and promise.
> Rather, it comes as the shadows lengthen on dark and stormy days—days ruled by wrong, tormented by fear.
> For without wrong there is no urge to do right.
> Without sickness there is no will to search for cures.
> Without oppression there is no longing for liberation.
> Great leadership does not come *to* the people; it comes *from* the people.

In conclusion, Collins referred to the motto of the Episcopal Seminary, at the University of the South, in Sewanee, Tennessee: "Seek the truth, come whence it may, cost what it will." He declared, "The truth is, we have been failing. The further truth is, we have every reason to be hopeful for the future if we set ourselves to the task."[58]

During the presidential campaign of 1960, Collins made clear his belief that John Kennedy could provide leadership for the nation. The latter asked him to serve as chairman of the Democratic National Committee's Speaker's Bureau. He accepted and on September 19 opened offices in Washington, D.C. He was responsible for assigning speakers to party rallies and dinners across the country. He also planned to deliver campaign speeches nationwide.[59]

Although taking an active national role, Collins played only a small part in Kennedy's Florida campaign. In August Collins wrote to Sheriff John Spottswood, "This Democratic campaign in Florida could not look worse than it does right now."[60] Because the gover-

nor entertained little hope for a party victory in the state, he may
have believed his efforts would be more productive in other
regions. Intraparty rivalries also contributed. The Caldwell-Bryant
faction controlled Kennedy's campaign, Collins maintained. One
Collins adherent complained to Robert Kennedy that Bryant, "who
neither supports the nominees nor the party platform, has assumed
command of the Florida Democratic campaign organization and he
is frank to admit that he will do nothing in behalf of the national
ticket." Collins assured his supporter, "I have said these same
things to [the Kennedys] over and over again."[61]

Collins resented suggestions that Kennedy had asked him to
avoid a conspicuous role in Florida politics. "Senator Kennedy has
been very anxious for me to campaign for him anywhere I could
campaign," he insisted. He decided to work outside the state
because "everybody knows where I stand in Florida—how I feel
about this ticket." Although not taking an active role, Collins spoke
out against the state supporting a third-party candidate or an
independent elector plan. "When the party ship is in a storm I
don't believe in seeking to 'aid' it by chopping a hole in its bottom,"
he said. Amidst implications that he had lost his constituents'
respect, an appearance with vice-presidential nominee Lyndon
Johnson in Tallahassee provided him some solace. Reporters noted
that the Floridians gave him the warmest applause of the day. The
reception provided him strong satisfaction, he conceded, "and, I
was extremely grateful for it."[62]

On October 10, 1960, Collins's work for the Democratic party
ended when he was appointed as president of the National Association of Broadcasters (NAB), effective after his gubernatorial term
ended in January 1961. The NAB, a trade association that included
more than two thousand radio and television stations, set standards
for the industry, and represented its members' interests before
Congress and federal agencies. Collins's reputation as "Florida's
super salesman" influenced his selection by the board of directors.
Furthermore, his performance at the Democratic convention had
impressed the communications industry. When he accepted the
three-year appointment, he recognized the association's nonparti-
san posture by announcing his withdrawal from party politics.[63] A
prescient Florida newsman noted, "If the broadcasting industry

has a conscience, it can expect to have it needled by the leader it has just chosen. . . . It will find Collins pushing it along as fast as the law and his job allows." Describing the governor as "the nemesis of the stand-patter," the journalist concluded, "while Collins will become the powerful association's spokesman, he is unlikely to become its blind mouthpiece."[64]

During the last month of his governorship, Collins accepted a final opportunity to speak on the racial issue. In an address accepting the Leonard Abess Human Relations Award of the Anti-Defamation League of B'nai B'rith, he remarked:

> I am convinced that the antidote to intolerance and bigotry and prejudice, is people—people learning about people who are different from themselves—learning about them as individuals—learning that they have common hopes and fears, common concerns and aspirations—and learning that the people we have classified under a single label are as different from one another as those we have long identified as our own "kind" differ among themselves.

Collins then once more called on southerners to accept new ideas. "Meaningful progress in race relations takes place when people decide in their own minds that the attitudes of yesterday are not adequate for the realities of today," he said. Black Americans sought fundamental changes:

> They long to be treated equally before the law, and not have their worth measured solely by the color of their skin. And this is a goal the Constitution of the United States holds assurance they can achieve. The struggle toward it is no more their responsibility than ours if we accept the idea of the brotherhood of man and the dignity of the individual under the fatherhood of God.[65]

Since the 1954 campaign, Collins's racial perspective had shifted markedly. During his gubernatorial years, Floridians confronted profound challenges to their traditions. He recognized new realities and, by 1960, welcomed them. Yet, most people in the state retained ties to the past. Accepting conservative guidance, they resisted change in racial customs. During the next few years, the civil rights revolution would intensify its pressure on American society. While serving in Washington, D.C., Collins would encounter new people and ideas that would provoke further revisions in his thinking. Meanwhile, the conservative tide in Florida would swell. When Collins returned to mount a final statewide campaign, the philosophical schism between him and his constituents would prove to be unbreachable.

13

National Service:

1961–1966

In January 1961 Collins moved to Washington, D.C., where he would live and work for nearly six years. A decade of challenge was dawning. During that time, America met cold war tests in Cuba, Berlin, and Vietnam, it accepted the liberals' agenda for creating a "Great Society" without poverty; and it wrote into law equality of opportunity for blacks. Yet, by 1966, the national consensus had dissolved. Instead, conflict seemed the norm: conservatives versus liberals, blacks versus whites, urbanites versus suburbanites, young versus old, rich versus poor, feminists versus traditionalists, and Doves versus Hawks. During this turbulent era, Collins served as NAB president (1961–64), as director of the Community Relations Service (1964–65), and as undersecretary of commerce (1965–66). The time in Washington provided him with an opportunity to acquire an understanding of the new American nation that was emerging from years of social revolution.

Controversy surrounded Collins's tenure as NAB president.[1] According to him, a large number of broadcasters—though a minority—thought that maximizing profits was their sole responsibility. Collins, on the other hand, believed that "the public interest was involved." He questioned the broadcasters' reliance on ratings, the paucity of cultural offerings, and the volume of violent programming. His call for an end to televised cigarette advertising caused an even bigger stir. The tobacco companies' youth-oriented selling techniques especially concerned him. Many broadcasters bitterly disputed his opposition to advertising that brought the industry millions of dollars each year. Some also criticized his wide-ranging speaking schedule, which often concerned subjects unrelated to his NAB duties. Despite the antagonism, the broadcasters renewed his contract in 1963.[2]

Later that year, Collins again came under fire. In a December 3, 1963, speech to the Greater Columbia Chamber of Commerce, in South Carolina, he returned to the theme of leadership. President Kennedy's assassination several days earlier had underscored Collins's distress with America's violence, extremism, and lack of positive guidance. He emphasized the national scope of his concerns. Yet, as a fellow southerner, he spoke of the region's distinctive problems.

Facing an audience that included conservative U.S. Senator Strom Thurmond, he charged:

> We have allowed the extremists to speak for the South. . . . The very ones against whom we in the South have had to struggle in our towns and in our state capitals for much of the progress we have made. . . . And all the while, too many of the rest of us have remained cravenly silent or lamely defensive while Dixie battle cries have been employed to incite sick souls to violence—egged on by the rabble-rouser's call to "stand up and fight!"
>
> It is little wonder that other Americans fail to regard us on occasions as being in the mainstream of American life and citizenship.
>
> And I ask you tonight, how long are the majority of southerners going to allow themselves to be caricatured before the nation by these claghorns? How many Sunday school children have to be dynamited to death? How many Negro leaders have to be shot in the back? How many Governors have to be shot in the chest? How many Presidents have to be assassinated?

Southerners must recognize the futility of defending outmoded institutions and traditions. "Any rational man who looks out at the horizon and sees the South of the future segregated is simply seeing a mirage," he proclaimed. "I say to you, tonight, that above all else it is the moral duty of our generation to plow under racial injustice everywhere in the United States."[3]

Collins's unflinching denouncement of extremism resulted in rancor and confusion. Ignoring his national emphasis, many people concluded that he had accused southerners of causing the presidential assassination. Inaccurate press reports contributed to the misunderstanding. An Associated Press story, which was not corrected for nearly two weeks, reported Collins as "blaming the climate of violence in the South for President Kennedy's assassination." In Florida, a headline in the Orlando *Sentinel* read, "Governor Collins Libels South." Excerpts of the speech used in the article left the impression that he believed the region should accept responsibility for the violence afflicting the nation. The uproar led to an emergency NAB meeting, at which the board of directors by a vote of twenty-five to eighteen confirmed his right to express his personal opinion. Nevertheless, the constant criticism affected him. "While I felt I could stand my ground," he later admitted, "I was getting a little discouraged."[4]

In 1964 President Lyndon B. Johnson asked Collins to head the Community Relations Service (CRS).[5] Congress had created it in Title X of the Civil Rights Act of 1964 to foster peaceful compliance with the law. Conservative southerners insisted that the agency be established to help with education and understanding. Johnson, as Senate majority leader and as president, had advocated a federal office that would utilize moderate southerners in conciliating racial conflicts. He took an active role in the CRS's formation and staffing. Congress placed the agency under the Commerce Department because it dealt with owners of such public accommodations facilities as motels, restaurants, and theaters. Secretary of Commerce Luther Hodges, former governor of North Carolina and a close friend of Collins, recommended him as the ideal man to direct the CRS.[6]

Although he represented the class of moderate southerners on whom Johnson based his strategy, Collins hesitated to accept the post. The NAB presidency paid four times more. Even with a severance settlement, the move would require substantial financial sacrifice. However, Collins's leadership had created tensions within the NAB. Although his position was secure, the pressures of the office were extreme. Collins realized the CRS post would be equally demanding, yet welcomed the opportunity for change.

Besides, he recalled, "President Johnson was the most persuasive man I've ever known." Johnson told him, "At this time, in the history of this country, *this* is the number one job I've got to offer." Collins also viewed a presidential request almost like a military command. Moreover, he understood the importance of the office and wanted to serve the country in a time of crisis. Accepting the challenge, he agreed to lead the new agency for a year.[7]

The confirmation hearings led to a confrontation with Senator Thurmond, who still resented the Columbia Chamber of Commerce speech. Grilling Collins in the Commerce Committee hearings, Thurmond tried to expose him as a traitor to the South. On the day of the confirmation vote, Thurmond and Senator Ralph Yarborough, a liberal Texan and Collins supporter, scuffled outside the committee room. Thurmond won the physical combat, but lost the committee vote 16–1. The Senate then overwhelmingly (53–8) agreed to the confirmation.[8]

Collins recruited persons with varied backgrounds and ideas. "We have a man for every occasion," a staff member noted in jest: "We have an Uncle Tom, a black nationalist, a Mr. Charlie, and a fuzzy white liberal."[9] Inevitably, contact with such a diverse group influenced Collins's racial perceptions. Before his CRS duties, he later pointed out, "I had done things for [blacks] but I had not done things with them." Not only did he work closely with black staff members, but he also conferred with leaders of the NAACP, CORE, the Southern Christian Leadership Conference (SCLC), and the Student Nonviolent Coordinating Committee (SNCC). He listened as intellectual blacks (conservatives, moderates, and radicals) presented their views on American society. Only after the CRS experiences did he begin to view blacks as individuals rather than as a separate caste, he remembered. In a 1965 speech, he chided southerners who professed dismay over black ingratitude for everything the whites had done for "their Negroes." He labeled such views as "condescending, patronizing paternalism" and called for blacks to be made partners in decision making.[10]

Collins and the CRS undertook an energetic program to further compliance with the Civil Rights Act. According to Title X, the CRS was "to provide assistance to communities and persons therein in resolving disputes, disagreements, or difficulties relating to discriminatory practices based on race, color, or national origin." To gain local leaders' confidence and cooperation, the law required that the agency's activities "be conducted in confidence and without publicity." From October 1, 1964, to June 30, 1965, the CRS worked to ameliorate problems in 120 communities in twenty-eight states.[11]

A 1965 crisis in Selma, Alabama, constituted the severest test for the strategy of the agency. The SNCC brought the civil rights movement to Selma in the spring of 1963. During the next year and a half, the community experienced a series of bitter demonstrations that resulted in the jailing of hundreds of people. In January 1965 the Reverend Martin Luther King, Jr., added the strength of the SCLC to the Selma movement. He anticipated that nonviolent demonstrations would elicit official repression and thus draw national attention to the suffrage issue. He stressed, "Just as the Civil Rights Act of 1964 was written in Birmingham, we hope that the new federal voting legislation will be written here in Selma." Throughout the spring, tension permeated the city of 28,775, perched on a high bluff on the north bank of the Alabama River. Dallas County's black citizens became adamant in their demands for voting rights, economic opportunity, and integration.[12]

County Sheriff James G. Clark served as the foil in King's design. Clark, at the age of forty-three, was a tall, heavyset man whose stomach sagged over his belt. He wore "a grey and brown military-style uniform, complete with an officer's billed hat shiny with gold braid." A billy club and battery-operated cattle prod hung from his belt. He opposed any compromise on segregation. Backed by a volunteer posse, he insisted on a hard-line policy toward demonstrators. One observer noted, "When it came to dealing with these 'agitators,' the sheriff seemed to go more than a little crazy."[13]

Alabama Governor George C. Wallace and Colonel Albert J. Lingo, state director of public safety, cooperated with the local authorities in suppressing demonstrations. Lingo, a former small-town businessman and policeman, had been appointed by Wallace in return for loyal political support. The reputation of Lingo's force for violence against blacks matched that of Clark's posse. As Lingo remarked, "We don't believe in making arrests. It's better to break them up."[14]

The conflict in Selma created an aura of hostility that spread across Alabama's black belt. Violence followed. On February 17 a state trooper killed a black youth during a demonstration in Marion, a Perry County community thirty miles northwest of Selma. To protest the slaying, civil rights leaders decided to march fifty miles along U.S. Route 80 from Selma to the state capitol, in Montgomery. On Sunday, March 7, some 650 blacks set out from Brown's Chapel AME Church. Just across Edmund Pettus Bridge, an impressive structure of concrete and steel spanning the Alabama River, state troopers blocked the march. They attacked the blacks with clubs, tear gas, and smoke bombs. As the terrified marchers scrambled back across the bridge, Clark's mounted posse joined the assault, wielding bullwhips, ropes, and lengths of rubber tubing wrapped with barbed wire. Before the bedlam ended, seventeen blacks had been hospitalized and sixty-seven others treated for injuries.[15]

The assault incensed the nation. King announced that the march would be completed on Tuesday, March 9, and called on the nation's church leaders to join him. In response, more than 450 clergymen and hundreds of sympathizers began a pilgrimage to Selma. Governor Wallace recognized that violence harmed the segregationists' cause, but refused to sanction the demonstration. Some knowledgeable citizens of Selma believed that, if the civil rights advocates marched, "there would be many people dead by nightfall."[16]

Pressure mounted on President Johnson to intervene. He decided to use the incident to fulfill a campaign pledge for a law guaranteeing all Americans the opportunity to vote. He realized the nation's anger would dissipate quickly; immediate action was essential. Yet, he understood, as perhaps few northerners in those emotional days could have, that a large reservoir of moderate opinion existed in the South. He knew that many white southerners opposed extralegal or violent responses to blacks' demands. To retain the support of the moderates, he did not want to intrude without a request from the state for assistance. He refused to make Wallace "a states' rights martyr."[17]

Trying to convince the Reverend King to postpone Tuesday's march in order to avoid a repeat of Sunday's violence, Johnson assured him that, if he delayed the march, the administration's voting rights bill would be completed by the weekend. Moreover, a federal judge had issued an injunction barring the demonstration until hearings could be held. Nonetheless, the multitude gathered in Selma pressured King to carry through. At four o'clock Tuesday morning, he advised the administration that he would defy the court and march.[18] Bloodshed seemed certain. Johnson's plan to postpone the march appeared to have failed. Violence would not only bring criticism for not protecting the marchers but would also necessitate federal intervention, which would undermine the support of southern moderates for his voting rights bill. At this crucial moment, he turned to Collins, asking him to try to head off the confrontation.[19]

In the predawn darkness of March 9, 1965, Collins flew to Craig Air Force Base, near Selma, in one of the smaller, two-engine jets available for presidential use. He proceeded immediately to the Federal Building, in downtown Selma, where he conferred with John M. Doar, assistant attorney general in charge of the Justice Department's Civil Rights Division. The court injunction prohibiting the march placed Doar, as a representative of the Justice Department, in a difficult position. He could not support any alternative to obedience to the court. Collins, though, who enjoyed semi-independent status under the Commerce Department, could seek a compromise. The concept of a partial march evolved during a discussion the two men held on the minimum demands of both sides. They sought a strategy that would allow both the marchers and state officials to claim victory. Bearing the outline of a plan in mind, Collins and Doar went to talk directly to the Reverend King.[20]

King was staying at the home of Dr. Sullivan Jackson, a black dentist. When the federal officials arrived, they found several black leaders in the living room, where discussions had been going on most of the night. King emerged from a bedroom still wearing his pajamas. Pleading with him to abide by the court injunction, Collins and Doar emphasized the "explosive situation" in Selma. The Reverend Fred Shuttlesworth, a King associate, argued that, instead of asking blacks not to march, Collins should urge the state troopers not to be brutal. Collins sympathized but warned that a repeat of Sunday's events would be a tragedy for the entire nation. King insisted that his conscience required him to march. Moreover, he argued, many people were so emotionally committed they would carry through whether he led them or not.[21]

Collins and Doar realized the futility of further discussing the postponement of the march. Doar withdrew from the conversation because he could approve no action that contravened the injunction. Collins, though, suggested a compromise. Would King accept a symbolic victory? The demonstrators could walk across Edmund Pettus Bridge, confront the troopers, hold a prayer service, and then return to Selma. This stratagem would allow blacks to express their indignation while avoiding direct conflict with the troopers. King replied, "I cannot agree to do anything because I don't know what I can get my people to do, but if you will get Sheriff Clark and Lingo to agree to something like that, I will try."[22]

The Collins-King meeting created considerable controversy. Militants later criticized the latter's willingness to cooperate with federal authorities. He described as "a perversion of the facts" the charge that he made a deal with the government "to throttle the indignation" of the demonstrators.[23] The dispute may have resulted from a question of semantics. What constituted a "deal"? King certainly at no point guaranteed he would turn the march around. Collins, though, sought an agreement to try, and King did try.

Time was short. Collins set out to find Clark and Lingo. A sense of foreboding blanketed the silent Selma streets as he drove across town. Five hundred troopers, more than two-thirds of the state's force, were in the city. As the time for the march neared, they began to take positions in the center and at the corners of each block. Across Edmund Pettus Bridge, whites congregated along Route 80 in anticipation of a repeat of Sunday's spectacle. About 150 newspersons from around the world had assembled to record the event. At the King's Bend intersection, the first stoplight across the bridge, more than a hundred troopers had begun to form their barricade.[24]

Collins found Clark and Lingo organizing their forces. Instead of his customary uniform, Clark wore a dark business suit, a narrow

striped tie, a black hat, and sunglasses. Lingo was also attired in a
business suit, but incongruously wore a white trooper's helmet,
which was a bit oversized and rested just above his eyes. They
agreed to meet with Collins in a nearby office, at the rear of the
Lehman Pontiac Company.[25]

Clark and Lingo initially seemed antagonistic. Collins, though,
urged them to accept a settlement that would provide a face-saving
victory for both sides. Edmund Pettus Bridge had become a
symbol for the civil rights advocates, he explained; blacks believed
they had the right to cross it without being attacked on the other
side. If Clark and Lingo allowed the demonstrators to cross,
confront the troopers, and conduct a twenty-minute prayer meeting, they might then return to the church. But, for the plan to
succeed, the state forces would need to refrain from moving into
the marchers as they had on Sunday. The plan would give both
sides a symbolic victory, Collins pointed out, because the blacks
would cross the bridge and the state officials would block the
march, which was their avowed purpose.[26]

Clark and Lingo expressed an interest in the proposal, but
refused to make a commitment. Instead, Lingo asked Collins to
step out into the hallway while he made a phone call. Collins
complied, assuming that Lingo was talking to Governor Wallace.
After a few minutes, Lingo summoned him back into the office and
told him that they would try the arrangement. Clark drew a map
tracing a route from Brown's Chapel that he adamantly insisted the
marchers follow. Collins never understood the sheriff's concern
with the map, but he lacked time to press the point.[27] A man who
witnessed the conference remembered, "Colonel Lingo said the
state did not want violence and there would be none if the
marchers turned back at the designated point."[28] Bearing this
assurance, Collins rushed back across the bridge to seek out King.

At about 2:15 P.M., while Collins had conferred with Clark and
Lingo, King spoke to the crowd of 2,500 gathered at Brown's
Chapel. "I have no alternative but to lead a march from this spot to
carry our grievances to the seat of government," he proclaimed. "I
have made my choice. I have got to march." Few people carried
supplies for a long march as they moved out behind 450 clergymen. The demonstrators assumed they were headed for a confron-

tation with the state forces, and all remembered the bloody culmination of Sunday's drama. "In all frankness, we knew we would not get to Montgomery," King recalled. "We knew we would not get past the troopers." At an intersection near the church, some twenty hecklers hurled jeers and curses at King, though most of the whites lining the streets looked on silently. The marchers appeared to be grim yet resolute. Then, tentatively at first, but growing into a ringing affirmation of faith, they joined in singing the movement's familiar marching song, "Ain't Gonna Let Nobody Turn Me Around."[29]

Fired by his hope that he held the key to the crisis, Governor Collins fell in beside King as the front ranks moved through Selma. He showed him Clark's rough sketch and explained the agreement. King restated his concern that he could not stop the marchers, but accepted the plan, providing the troopers gave them time for prayer and did not attempt to push them back. Despite grave doubts, he concluded, "I'll do my best." Collins promised to stand in the line with the troopers and try to see that all of them kept their word. "We'll all do the best we can," he added. "I think everything will be all right."[30]

Collins again scurried across Edmund Pettus Bridge. A double line of troopers now crossed Route 80, and whites filled the parking lots alongside the road. Informing Clark and Lingo that King had accepted the proposal, Collins assured them the plan would work, though they remained skeptical. Collins insisted on standing with the front rank of troopers in order to be near the confrontation. One newsperson observing the scene reported, "Collins was with state and county forces at the head of the column of whites and had there been the kind of difficulty which occurred Sunday he would have been in the middle of it."[31] The group gathered on Route 80 waited nervously for the marchers to appear.

Tension gripped Selma, Washington, and indeed, the nation as King led the ecumenical and interracial march toward the bridge. The line, stretching back nearly a mile, walked up Sylvan Street to Water Avenue, and then along the Alabama River to Broad Street. At the foot of the bridge, Chief Deputy United States Marshal H. Stanley Fountain read the court order banning the demonstration. King stated his determination to continue, and the marshal stepped aside. The front ranks turned sharply left and began to cross the elevated bridge. The singing ceased as the marchers reached the crest and saw the "human wall" that blocked their path. King led his silent followers down Route 80 toward Montgomery. For those standing at the King's Bend intersection, the tightly bunched procession appeared to be pouring across the bridge in a tidal wave. Collins would always remember the sight of the black and white mass that filled the highway and edged closer to him and the troopers.[32]

"What happened next was a little play that Collins worked out on the spot," one observer commented.[33] Major John Cloud stood in front of the troopers. He waited until the marchers were within fifty feet and then yelled through a bullhorn: "You are ordered to stop and stand where you are. This march will not continue." King replied, "We have a right to march. There is also a right to march to Montgomery." Cloud repeated the order. Doar, observing the proceedings from an upper-story window of the Federal Building, gave a moment-by-moment telephone account to Attorney General Nicholas Katzenbach, in Washington. As King and Cloud talked, Doar reported, "They're up to the barricade." At 2:56 P.M. Katzenbach informed presidential aide Bill Moyers, at the White House, "We're right at the critical moment. I'll keep you posted."[34]

On Route 80 the confrontation had reached an impasse. At least one person, though, sensed the restrained rhetoric in the encounter. He wrote, "Like characters in a play, King and Cloud spoke their lines and went through their motions. If it was not rehearsed, it could have been. Passion fled the scene; they were all mechanical men filling their inevitable roles."[35] Collins, the author of the scene, looked on anxiously to be certain they followed the script.

Testing Collins's plan, King asked if they could pray. "You can have your prayer, and then you must return to your church," Cloud insisted. King asked the Reverend Ralph Abernathy to lead the devotions, and the line stretching back to the crest of the bridge knelt down. Abernathy prayed: "We come to present our bodies as a living sacrifice. We don't have much to offer but we do have our bodies, and we lay them on the altar today." Other national religious figures also offered prayers. When the marchers rose from their knees, they joined in singing the anthem of the civil rights movement, "We Shall Overcome." The service had lasted for fifteen minutes.[36]

Cloud then made a surprising move. He shouted, "Troopers, withdraw!" They stepped aside. Later, commentators would contend that Wallace had ordered the maneuver to expose King's lack of militancy to black radicals. A state official at the scene told a federal officer standing nearby that the order came directly from Wallace's office, where he was directing the events by telephone.[37] Whatever the purpose of the action, it threatened Collins's plan. Route 80 to Montgomery now lay open before the marchers. Doar reported the startling turn of events to Katzenbach. All awaited King's decision. Then Doar exclaimed, "King is walking back this way. He's asking the marchers to turn back." Katzenbach quickly informed the White House, "King has turned around."[38] The demonstrators followed him. Collins had succeeded.

As King led the front ranks back across the bridge, those behind them walked to the point where the leaders had been and then turned around. Most of the marchers were satisfied. After preparing themselves to face death, they had confronted the troopers and returned unharmed. They had demonstrated their determination to protest repression. Moreover, King pledged to complete the march to Montgomery, even if troopers or legal obstacles delayed his plans.[39]

After the demonstrators turned back, Collins talked with reporters, though he refused to answer questions in detail, citing the statute that required his agency's activities to be confidential. Also, President Johnson wanted the federal role deemphasized. Collins accentuated the contributions of local officials in avoiding the conflict. "I think good people on both sides were anxious to avoid violence," he concluded. "I am delighted that all the people involved today used good judgment and good sense."[40]

Privately congratulating Collins, the president said that had he not defused the Selma crisis "the ditches would have been knee-deep in blood." To underscore his contribution, Collins and his wife were invited to share the presidential box with the first family as Johnson called on Congress to pass a voting rights bill. When the act was passed in the summer of 1965—with the support of thirty-seven southerners in the House of Representatives—he presented Collins with one of the pens he used to sign the measure into law.[41]

On Wednesday, March 17, the federal court ruled that King could carry through with the march to Montgomery and directed the state to provide protection. When Wallace informed Johnson that his state could not afford to escort the demonstrators, the president federalized the Alabama National Guard for the purpose. Thus, his plan to avoid intrusion, unless requested by the state, had succeeded. That Alabamians themselves served in the force protecting the march, Johnson argued, "made all the difference in the world."[42] Collins's achievement in heading off violence in Selma had helped make possible the success of the strategy.

Collins also played a role in the march to Montgomery that began on March 21, two weeks after the bloody attack at Edmund Pettus Bridge. Officials feared the demonstrators would be met

Collins and Selma march leaders (*left to right*): Reverend Andrew Young, Collins, Reverend Martin Luther King, Coretta Scott King, and Reverend Ralph Abernathy. (*Courtesy, Associated Press*)

with violence when they entered the capital. Collins went to Montgomery, where he worked out plans with local leaders to avoid conflict. He then conferred with King while walking along the march route and gained his cooperation. Newspersons photographed the scene, which appeared in papers throughout the country.[43]

The national attention given Collins's effort in Selma evoked the pride of many in his home state. The Miami *Herald* exalted the state's "man of moderation." "There was plenty of face that needed saving on the streets of Selma," the editors wrote, "but it was managed." The Tallahassee *Democrat* reported that Collins was being pushed for a cabinet post. However, it quoted "one friend" of his who perceived the mixed feelings of many. "There wasn't another southerner who could do what Roy's doing for the President," he observed. "Yet he may have hurt his political career in Florida—for the time being anyway."[44]

Collins's role in Selma confused many of his former constituents. The photograph of him talking to King contributed to the misunderstanding. The Pensacola *Journal*, for example, captioned the picture, "Collins Marches with King." The Miami *Herald* proclaimed, "Former Florida Governor LeRoy Collins Joins Marchers," and the Orlando *Sentinel* stated, "LeRoy Collins . . . Joins Civil Rights Marchers." The Tallahassee *Democrat* did note that he walked only about a mile. None pointed out that he was engaged in official government business.[45]

The news coverage convinced some Floridians that Collins had worked with King to organize and carry out the march to Montgomery. A former supporter from Gainesville wrote, "I wish you [would] disassociate yourself from King."[46] A Tampa woman emphasized "the dirt, filth, and immorality that have been connected with the demonstrations and march from Selma to Montgomery." She thought, "It is hard to picture anyone as fastidious as our former Governor of Florida allowing himself to become associated with a group of hoodlums."[47] The restrictions against the Community Relations Service publicizing its actions kept Collins from clearly explaining the events in Selma to the people of his state.[48]

After a year at that agency, Collins was appointed as undersecretary of commerce. As the department's second in command, he performed extensive administrative tasks. He also accepted responsibility for the Economic Development Administration, for various areas of labor-management relations, and for the effort to increase American exports. In August 1965 Johnson asked him to help calm the rioting in the Watts section of Los Angeles. Although basic economic, political, and social issues caused the disruptions, governmental ineptitude added to the blacks' anger. Federal antipoverty funds had been cut off because of an administrative dispute among city, state, and national officials. Collins broke the nine-month deadlock with a compromise satisfactory to all sides. The New York *Times* termed his accomplishment a "psychological coup in an effort to smooth community relations in the wake of the five-day race riot."[49]

The Watts riot signified the emergence of a new era in the movement for racial justice. The Civil Rights Act of 1964 and the Voting Rights Act of 1965 had not solved the fundamental social and economic problems confronting black Americans. Urban disruptions suggested that they had lost faith in the efficacy of the interracial, nonviolent civil rights movement.[50] When the focus shifted to the northern cities and suburbs, advocates of change met a reaction equal in virulence to the South's defense of its traditions. Years of turmoil followed.

Collins possessed the experience and insight to provide guidance in the crisis. While in Washington, he gained a better understanding of national issues and a broader perspective on the South's status in the federal system. Yet, administrative positions did not satisfy his desire for leadership. He wanted a more influential office. After six years of national service, he returned to Florida and sought election to the U.S. Senate.

14

Back Home Again:
The 1968 Senatorial Campaign and After

On January 3, 1966, U.S. Senator George Smathers, of Florida, announced that he would not seek reelection in 1968. Ten months later, Collins resigned his position at the Department of Commerce and moved to Tampa, where he joined the law firm of Fowler, White, Gillen, Humpkey, and Trenan. He had decided to run for Smathers's Senate seat.[1] "The people of the state had been so very good to me in so many ways, they seemed to feel so good about my service as governor, that I just thought it was a natural thing for me to do," he later explained. Before the campaign, polls indicated a generally favorable reaction toward him among the state's voters.[2] Despite the optimistic forecasts, he would become involved in what one newsman termed as a "classic political nightmare."[3]

During the years Collins served in Washington, conservatism had gained momentum in Florida. A wave of new residents, including many retirees who held Republican allegiances, combined with the right wing of the Democratic party to form a solid conservative majority. When the Democrats nominated a liberal gubernatorial candidate in 1966, Floridians elected their first Republican governor since Reconstruction.[4] President Johnson's civil rights and welfare reforms angered conservatives, and urban riots—including those in seven Florida cities in 1967—intensified their disgust. In 1968 they used the code words "law and order" to

192

express displeasure with civil rights militance, urban disorders, and demonstrations opposing the Vietnam War. For many voters, Collins's national service tied him irrevocably to the Johnson administration's policies and problems.[5]

Under the leadership of Attorney General Earl Faircloth, the conservative Democrats challenged Collins's senatorial nomination. Faircloth ran a hard-hitting, racially oriented campaign that emphasized the need for "law and order." A campaign poster that pictured a burning city was captioned "STOP RIOTS—ELECT FAIRCLOTH—A CONSERVATIVE." One advertisement implored whites, "Don't let the bloc vote control your Senator." Also delving into the former governor's past to establish his racial liberalism, Faircloth attacked the 1960 "sit-in speech" in which Collins had questioned the moral basis of segregation. Another advertisement condemned Collins's Columbia, South Carolina, speech. It quoted from the distorted Orlando *Sentinel* article and labeled his words as vicious, violent, and libelous.[6]

Most importantly, Faircloth benefited from the "Selma issue." Collins's role in the Alabama crisis had never been clarified for Floridians. In 1968 many of them believed he had been an active participant in the march. Some conservatives presented the newspaper photograph of him and King discussing plans for entering Montgomery as evidence that Collins helped lead the march.[7] A Tampa voter wrote, "I can't help but observe how hard LeRoy Collins is trying to shake off the ultra-liberal label he sought and earned when he joined Lyndon's race-mixing campaign. . . . This included his famous picture marching on Selma with Martin Luther King at Lyndon's command."[8]

An editorial in the Mayo *Free Press* illustrated the political use of the Selma issue. Under a photograph in which arrows pointed to Collins and King, the account quoted from a purported contemporary newspaper article on the incident:

> Former Governor, LeRoy Collins, acted as President Lyndon B. Johnson's personal representative during the invasion of Alabama. . . . According to Sheriff James G. Clark, of Selma, Collins made the arrangements for the infamous Selma to Montgomery March, and participated in it along with numerous reds, pinks, and degenerates. The Selma to Montgomery March has been called one

of the "filthiest, most disgraceful events ever to occur in a civilized society."

The newspaper commented, "Note this picture carefully. Then make up you [sic] mind if you want to vote for Collins next Tuesday."[9]

Although Collins narrowly defeated Faircloth in the primary, the intraparty battle left a legacy of disabling problems.[10] The racial issue, especially Selma, had been fixed in the minds of many voters. "It was said in the campaign that I was at Selma. The people assumed from this simple statement that I was leading the march. . . . This was proof positive that I was an evil 'liberal,' " Collins explained.[11] He could not convince some voters otherwise. The heated primary also cost most of the money he had planned to hold back for the general election. Moreover, he led a badly divided party. As one newsman pointed out, "a large faction of Florida's Democratic Party establishment quietly withdrew its support and money as November neared."[12]

Edward J. Gurney, the Republican nominee, capitalized on the acrimony that had been created within the Democratic party. The Miami *Herald* described the fifty-four-year-old congressman from Winter Park as "an elderly version of the all-American boy" and as a "clean cut, smooth talking, ex-war hero." Gurney did not emphasize the Selma issue because it had been clearly established in the primary. Instead, he stressed his support for "law and order"; characterized Collins as "liberal LeRoy"; and bound him tightly to Johnson's welfare, race, and war policies. Collins tried but failed to separate himself from the federal civil rights program by running as an "independent Democrat" and by opposing "open housing" legislation. Gurney urged military escalation in Vietnam and warned that the administration was falling into a "Communist Peace Trap." When Collins called for "deAmericanization" of the war, the Republican implicitly questioned his opponent's patriotism. He termed Collins "dovish" and mentioned his 1959 tour of the Soviet Union. "I'm not talking about pink or anything like that," Gurney maintained, "but the governor spent six weeks in Russia as governor."[13]

Along with the racial and war issues, organizational and financial

Collins speaking to B'nai B'rith meeting at Temple Miami in November 1967. (*Courtesy, Governor Collins*)

problems troubled the Collins campaign. Differences on strategy finally compelled him to dismiss Joe Grotegut as campaign manager.[14] Money difficulties proved to be insoluble. Recognizing the intraparty divisions, the state Democratic organization provided only $13,000. The primary drained funds and discouraged potential contributors. Old friends refused to assist Collins, whom they now viewed as too liberal and, worse, a probable loser. While the symbiotic relationship of success and fund-raising plagued the Democrat's campaign, Gurney received strong financial support from Floridians and from conservatives nationwide.[15]

The trials exacted a toll on Collins. "I could not understand why people . . . who had supported and cared and seen the same goals that I saw . . . would just turn their back on me and walk off," he lamented. "Two big agonies" dampened his spirit. "The one that hurt deepest was a feeling that the people of the state knew me and my record and yet were prone to throw all this aside because of their emotional antagonism toward my efforts to bring harmony and progress in race relations," he recalled. "I had positions on tax fairness, conservation, deAmericanizing the war, but these met with little public interest." Money matters also caused anguish. "No matter how hard our finance committee tried, I had to solicit money personally. I had never done this before, and I hated it."[16] A defeatist atmosphere suffused the campaign. One historian pointed out, "The spirited, dynamic LeRoy Collins of previous campaigns and political confrontations never surfaced."[17]

Many Collins adherents counted on his legendary command of television to repair the damage caused by the primary. It did not happen. Gurney depended on two-minute commercials that projected a dynamic, glamorous image. In contrast, a half-hour documentary stressing Collins's gubernatorial record exerted little impact. Furthermore, Gurney emerged a clear victor in televised debates. He offered simple, straightforward answers; his opponent was more introspective and philosophical. Collins also appeared to be much older and dispirited. "I did not have the poise I should have had," he remembered. "I was tired. . . . I think Gurney came out best on those things. I really do."[18]

Gurney won the election by more than 200,000 votes. Collins carried only four of the state's sixty-seven counties. For the first time since his 1932 campaign for county prosecutor, he lost Leon County.[19] The defeat disheartened his disciples. "He was the white knight . . . the unbeaten and, until he tried to buck the recent conservative tide, the seemingly unbeatable leader," a columnist wrote.[20] Collins accepted responsibility. "I didn't make a real good candidate," he admitted. "A successful candidate must have a happy spirit . . . and he can't be happy unless he feels like he is succeeding." Later, he decided that "the timing just wasn't right."[21]

Following the election, the Collinses moved back to The Grove. Tallahassee in the 1970s retained little similarity to the town of Collins's boyhood. Multilane highways linked the government center to subdivisions that had overrun Leon County's farmland. By 1980 Tallahasseans numbered 81,548, and the county as a whole had a population of 148,655.[22] Early in the decade, businesses vacated downtown buildings and moved to shopping malls on the city's outskirts. Later, the downtown area experienced a resurgence as professionals and lobbyists turned the shops and homes into offices. Midway through the decade, the state constructed a twenty-two-story, high-rise capitol, which dominated the skyline.

Even more remarkable than Tallahassee's physical transformation was the change in racial customs. Except for most churches, which remained segregated by tradition, and some private clubs, which stayed segregated by choice, the city was integrated by the mid-1970s. Few people openly questioned racially mixed public schools, buses, recreational facilities, restaurants, and theaters. Discrimination remained, however. Economic, social, and political barriers kept blacks from sharing fully in the city's society. Yet, the impediments were not of a local or regional character; instead, they paralleled those confronted by all black Americans.

During the 1970s, Floridians left strident racial politics behind. The governorship of Reubin Askew, of Escambia County, who served from 1971 to 1979, resembled that of Collins. Although lacking the latter's dynamic personality, Askew projected a similar image of integrity. He also emphasized the need for the expansion of business and industry. Most importantly, he shared Collins's commitment to racial justice. Askew supported busing to end school segregation and instituted an affirmative action program to combat discrimination in state hiring.[23] Because of the Supreme Court reapportionment decisions of the 1960s, the ratification of the 1968 Florida Constitution, and the racial integration of the 1970s, many of Collins's reform dreams were realized.

When the Collinses returned to Tallahassee, they led a much quieter family life than they had during the hectic gubernatorial years. LeRoy Collins, Jr., was a Tampa business executive. Both Jane and Mary Call had married attorneys. Jane lived in Coral Gables; Mary Call, in Tallahassee. In 1973 Darby married a dentist and established her residence in Coral Gables. Eleven grandchildren were not only a source of pride, but also a youthful influence during Roy and Mary Call Collins's later years.[24]

The 1968 senatorial campaign left scars. The racial attacks, the inability to rally support, and the loss of Leon County hurt deeply. At first, Collins's old friends worried about his health. One recalled, "He was a different man."[25] Collins planned to live a more private life. Although intending to practice law, he said, "I want to be the kind of lawyer I enjoy being, not the kind that is just overwhelmed with a great deal of routine, demanding work, because I want to have some time to do many other things I have not had time to do thus far." Leisurely hours with books, music, and travel beckoned him. He especially looked forward to spending time at his Dog Island beach house, fifty miles from Tallahassee. "Man had his origins in the sea," he mused, "and I think that the sea is a good place to go for renewal."[26]

One problem lingered from the 1968 campaign: the debt that had been incurred concerned Collins. Although not legally liable for it, he felt a moral responsibility to clear the books before retiring to private life. Two mailings to supporters and a testimonial dinner reduced the debt, but left the finance committee about forty thousand dollars short of its goal. Collins vetoed any further pleas to friends. Instead, he decided to write a book, the profits from which would be used to pay off the debt. For years, he had compiled notes on Florida history. Using this file as a starting point, he dedicated several months to researching and writing a series of stories about the state's past that were designed for light reading. The book, *Forerunners Courageous: Stories of Frontier*

Florida, was published by Colcade (the Collins Campaign Deficit Committee). A friend printed the book at a nominal cost, and Collins and the committee distributed it. Reviewers and the public received it favorably. The campaign debt was paid.[27]

Physically, Collins recovered quickly from the campaign's rigors. Tall, slender, courtly in bearing, silver-haired, and soft-spoken he remained a "picture of distinction."[28] The lines deepened in his face, yet, as one reporter wrote, "When he smiles the wrinkles disappear into a sparkle that starts in his eyes and envelops his whole face."[29] During his semiretirement, he fostered an interest in jogging for physical fitness. Several mornings each week, he slipped out of The Grove before sunrise to run three to four miles through the nearby Oakland Cemetery. He loved the fact that "daylight comes to me there." Running year-round, he enjoyed the seasonal beauty of the cemetery and claimed, "The best thinking I ever do is while I am jogging."[30]

Despite plans for a more secluded life, the Collinses slowly returned to the capital city's social and professional activities. Within a few months, they began accepting invitations to public functions and parties. Collins fished, hiked, and rekindled his avid interest in Florida State University football. He joined the prestigious law firm of Ervin, Varn, Jacobs, and Odom. Because he needed a "cash flow," limiting his law practice proved to be difficult. "I've got an enormously expensive standard of living and house to run and this kind of thing," he commented. "I need to work." He and Mrs. Collins had several business investments as well as real estate holdings. He also served as director of a Miami bank, Tropicana Products Incorporated, Investors Tax Sheltered Real Estate, and Royal Palm Beach Colony Incorporated.[31]

Public service demanded much of Collins's time. In 1974 he was honorary state chairman of the Cystic Fibrosis Research Foundation, a member of the State Board of Easter Seals, and chairman of an American Bar Association committee that studied legal education. Two years later, the Leon Association for Retarded Citizens recognized his contributions by selecting him as the "Community's Outstanding Citizen."[32]

In 1979 Collins accepted a position on the Joint Legislative and Executive Commission on Postsecondary Education, which was charged with making recommendations to the 1980 legislature. A key issue studied by this body was the state's inability to integrate predominately black FAMU. Pressure had arisen to merge FAMU with FSU, located only a few blocks away, but many blacks opposed the action, which they feared would lead to FAMU's elimination. Strongly supporting FAMU's independence, Collins pointed out its value in meeting the black community's needs. Yet, he defended the importance of racial integration. "Are we going to continue to hold hands with something that is doomed to fade away?" he asked. "There are more blacks than whites who want to ignore the problem and I think there are a lot of people at Florida A and M who would like to ignore it. We're coming to a point in the state where we don't draw a color line to opportunity." He believed the government bore an obligation to seek methods for increasing integration at both FSU and FAMU.[33]

Collins also served on Florida's Constitution Revision Commission, which held the constitutionally prescribed duty of proposing changes in the 1968 charter. The chairmanship of the Declaration of Rights Committee provided him a forum to lead a movement to end the death penalty. He simply maintained, "I don't think the state has a moral right to kill."[34]

On December 8, 1977, Collins dramatically appealed to the full commission for an end to capital punishment. A newsman reported, "Former governor LeRoy Collins, a gaunt man with white hair and painful memories, begged with a shaking voice for nearly an hour today, pleading for Florida to abolish the death penalty. His pleading was in vain."[35] Collins held a list of the 196 men who had been executed in Florida, including the underlined names of the 22 whose death warrants he had signed. "The application of the death penalty is freakish," he claimed. "Its victims almost always are the mentally disturbed, the weak, the poor, who suffer grossly unequal application of the law." Despite his eloquent statement, the commission rejected the proposal by a vote of twenty-six to ten. Yet, he held faith for the future: "In time history will consign the electric chair to one of its dark closets where it now stores past records of public racks, and drawing and quartering, and decapitations and lynchings."[36]

Collins believed in progress. His faith was rooted in his twentieth-century American heritage. Like other Americans, he experienced the affirmation of national community during two world wars. He, too, acclaimed the reign of business in the 1920s and witnessed want and despair in the following decade. Franklin D. Roosevelt's bold initiatives to solve the crisis impressed on him the potential for positive governmental action. "I think of myself as being 'constructive,' " he explained. "I think it is the purpose of government to serve the needs of the people, as those needs emerge, and as the leaders of the people have the power to see those needs and to see the ways in which they can be soundly met."[37]

While participating in the American experience, Collins also fell heir to the unique traditions and institutions that defined the South. He was a "hominy husker." He accepted the principles, goals, and obligations of his familial class. As a merchant's son in a small, southern town, he followed an ethical code that stressed allegiance to the church, hard work, fair play, and honesty. The moral lessons instilled at the Trinity Methodist Church remained for a lifetime. In fact, his speeches often sounded like sermons his grandfather William Carey Collins might have delivered from the pulpit. LeRoy Collins also accepted the trust of the "hominy husker" in public education and worked for better schools throughout his career. A devotion to free enterprise was fundamental to the merchants' faith. Like any young man of his class who "made good," Collins believed explicitly in private business's capacity to provide a better life for all.

Collins, moreover, spent his formative years during a period of business progressive preeminence in Florida and the South. During the 1920s this group vanquished the "neo-populists" and initiated reforms based on "practical idealism." Although retaining the stability necessary for commercial expansion, it worked for a more equitable economic order. Collins, too, extolled a New South founded on business and industry. Yet, in seeking such reform, he encountered ideologies and institutions that were part of the state's agrarian heritage.

First, Collins, as a business progressive, believed that the South's sacred states' rights philosophy was too restrictive and unrealistic. Such thinking did not meet the test of the new nationalism being forged by the "wonders of the century." Technological innovation and economic integration bound Americans too tightly to warrant state autonomy. Furthermore, increasingly rapid technological and social change made governmental inertia unacceptable. Collins consistently warned that state governments must take responsibility for reform or surrender their right to act. Also identifying himself with the southern nationalist tradition, he commented:

> The first thing I see when I go into the governor's office is the portrait of Andrew Jackson hanging above the fireplace. Now, I believe in the kind of unity Andrew Jackson, a great Southerner, believed in. It is the same kind of unity Sam Houston, another great Southerner, believed in, and many others. I do not believe in the kind of unity that John C. Calhoun believed in, because that was the kind of unity that had as its purpose a weakening of the United States.[38]

Despite such appeals, based on the traditions of the past and the needs of the future, Collins changed few minds on the validity of states' rights.

Secondly, Collins saw a vital need for remolding governmental customs and structures. The New South advocates wanted modernized, streamlined state institutions to aid economic growth. Government and private enterprise were to be partners in prosperity. The state could provide incentives through taxes, subsidies, codes, and the exploitation of natural resources. It could also actively seek new industry. In return, business expansion would provide jobs for the state's citizens. Collins wanted reform not only because it represented good government, but also because it fostered good business.

Although instituting many changes in Florida's government, Collins failed to gain a revision of the state constitution. Institutional impediments made innovation difficult. The agrarians held tenaciously to their control of the malapportioned legislature. Social, economic, and political grievances that were based on half a century of waning influence insured rural opposition to redistricting. Moreover, the 1885 Florida constitution vested much of the executive power in the cabinet. Facing intractable foes, Collins possessed insufficient power to force change.

Thirdly, Collins encountered anachronistic racial customs. The communications revolution made Americans uncomfortably aware of the inequities in the South's segregation codes. Twentieth-century nationalism made such sectional distinctiveness unacceptable. Beginning in the Second World War and building momentum throughout the next two decades, the civil rights movement forced the nation to recognize the fact of racial injustice. National attention first focused on the South because its system of legal separation epitomized the racial discrimination in American society. The issue could not be evaded. Before the business progressives could carry out their designs for economic and governmental reform, they were compelled to seek change in the region's racial customs.

Collins responded to reform demands on the basis of his heritage. "I came up in the South, [and] as a boy and young man I grew up in an atmosphere and a climate of tolerance and friendship with black people," he recalled. "But all of this was under a basic paternalistic attitude and a system of separation. I did not feel that the paternalistic approach was wrong or that there was anything inherently unjust in it."[39] In addition to such racial customs, Collins's heritage encompassed the business progressives' practical idealism and the moral creed of the "hominy husker." He applied his legacy to the unavoidable demands of the racial crisis.

The *Brown* decision "stunned" Collins.[40] At first, he reacted to the ruling itself rather than to the problems it identified. The legal opposition and legal implementation strategies met the Supreme Court's minimum demands, while limiting the issue's impact on his reform goals and political career. Such schemes forced him to walk a fine line between compliance and defiance. "The Governor doesn't sit on the fence; he runs on it," a critic declared.[41] Yet, his "moderate" policies guided his state through a turbulent period with minimal disruptions. Massive resistance did not occur; violence was avoided; defiance was condemned; schools were not closed. In evaluating Collins's career, one historian concluded, "Perhaps what did not happen in Florida was most significant of all."[42]

Collins, though, also made positive contributions. Applying the precepts of practical idealism, he came to recognize the need for revised racial codes. Neither blacks, nor the Supreme Court, nor the majority of white Americans would accept less. Only by changing its ways could the South enter the mainstream of the nation's economic and political life. Practicality demanded it—so did morality. By the conclusion of his administration, Collins had perceived the ethical issues that made the civil rights movement a fundamental challenge to America's racial traditions. He called on the people of his state to meet the moral test. A friend declared, "I really think his lasting contribution was that of providing moral leadership that other southern states lacked at that time."[43]

Moving "beyond the horizon" of most Floridians, Collins outdistanced the constituency that sustained his political career. His early years were steeped in Tallahassee's Deep South racial traditions. His rejection of that heritage came not in a vision, but as a gradual transformation. As he questioned ideas that other southerners considered to be sacrosanct, his insight and empathy grew. Richard N. Current, in discussing Abraham Lincoln's racial perceptions, pointed out that he spent his formative years in areas where racist views prevailed. "But he did not stay there," Current continued. "The most remarkable thing about him was his tremendous power of growth. He grew in sympathy, in the breadth of his humaneness, as he grew in other aspects of the mind and spirit. In more ways than one, he succeeded in breaking through the narrow bounds of his early environment."[44]

Collins, too, demonstrated an extraordinary power of growth. Combining pragmatism, sound ethical standards, and a clear understanding of his state's destiny, he worked for reform in both the structure and the spirit of its institutions. During his gubernatorial years, the forces of reaction held steadfast. Yet, his call for business enterprise, governmental integrity, and racial justice provided a vision for Florida's future.

Notes

Chapter 1

1. W. J. Cash, *The Mind of the South* (New York: Alfred A. Knopf, 1941), p. 189.

2. David R. Colburn and Richard K. Scher, *Florida's Gubernatorial Politics in the Twentieth Century* (Tallahassee: University Presses of Florida, 1980), pp. 12–13, 220–21.

3. Wayne Flynt, *Duncan Upshaw Fletcher: Dixie's Reluctant Progressive* (Tallahassee: Florida State Univeristy Press, 1971), pp. 22–24, 36–37; Samuel Proctor, *Napoleon Bonaparte Broward: Florida's Fighting Democrat* (Gainesville: University of Florida Press, 1950), pp. 59, 61–62; Kathryn T. Abbey, "Florida versus the Principles of Populism," *Journal of Southern History* 4 (1938), pp. 464–65.

4. Abbey, "Florida versus Populism," p. 465; Flynt, *Duncan Upshaw Fletcher*, p. 42; Proctor, *Napoleon Bonaparte Broward*, pp. 59, 164, 180–82, 261–62, 308–10.

5. Bertram H. Groene, *Ante-Bellum Tallahassee* (Tallahassee: Florida Heritage Foundation, 1971), pp. 3–15; Clifton Paisley, *From Cotton to Quail: An Agricultural Chronicle of Leon County, Florida, 1860–1967* (Gainesville: University of Florida Press, 1968), pp. 1–7.

6. Paisley, *Cotton to Quail*, pp. 18, 23–31, 38.

7. Population figure from James E. Pitts, *Tallahassee Area Statistical Abstract* (Tallahassee: Tallahassee Area Chamber of Commerce, 1971), p. 11. Portions of the following discussion on Collins's early years were published in Thomas R. Wagy, "A Tallahassee Lad: The Early Years of Governor LeRoy Collins of Florida," *Apalachee* 8 (1978), pp. 82–94.

8. Hampton Dunn, *Yesterday's Tallahassee* (Miami: E. A. Seeman, 1974), pp. 34, 87, 91, 101; interview with Frank Moor, of Tallahassee, October 8, 1975; interview with Marvin H. Collins, of Tallahassee, October 8, 1975.

9. Moor interview; Marvin Collins interview, October 8, 1975; Dunn, *Yesterday's Tallahassee*, p. 97.

10. Paisley, *Cotton to Quail*, pp. 47–49; Moor interview; Tallahassee *Weekly True Democrat*, March 12, 1909.

11. Family papers in the possession of Alice Collins Wadsworth, Tallahassee. This collection includes typescripts of genealogical informa-

tion on the Collins, Herring, and Brandon families; photocopied pages from the Collins family Bible; and a photocopy of William Carey Collins's obituary as it appeared in the *Florida Annual Conference of the Southern Methodist Episcopal Church, 1900*.

12. Collins family papers; Marvin Collins interview, October 8, 1975; interview with Governor LeRoy Collins, July 22, 1982; interview with Alice Collins Wadsworth, of Tallahassee, July 22, 1982.

13. Collins family papers; Marvin Collins interview, October 8, 1975; LeRoy Collins, *Forerunners Courageous: Stories of Frontier Florida* (Tallahassee: Colcade Publishers, 1971), pp. 141–42; William Warren Rogers, "History of Greenwood Plantation" (manuscript in the author's possession).

14. Collins family papers; Marvin Collins interview, October 8, 1975.

15. Marvin Collins interview, October 8, 1975; interviews with Governor LeRoy Collins, November 19, 1975, and September 17, 1979.

16. Marvin Collins interview, October 8, 1975; Governor Collins interview, November 19, 1975; Collins, *Forerunners Courageous*, pp. 99–105.

17. "Remarks, LeRoy Collins: Sesquicentennial Program of the Trinity Methodist Church, Tallahassee, Florida, November 24, 1974," in the Governor LeRoy Collins Papers, University of South Florida, Tampa.

18. Interview with John Y. Humphress, of Tallahassee, November 5, 1975; Charlie Huisking, "LeRoy Collins: Reflections on Leadership," Sarasota *Herald-Tribune*, Florida West, November 9, 1980.

19. Governor Collins interview, November 19, 1975; Rogers, "History of Greenwood Plantation."

20. "Remarks: Trinity Methodist Church," Collins Papers.

21. Photocopied pages from the *Church Register of the Trinity/Tallahassee Methodist Episcopal Church, South, 1907*, Collins family papers.

22. Governor Collins interview, November 19, 1975; Humphress interview; Tallahassee *Democrat*, January 4, 1955.

23. Interview with Marvin H. Collins, November 4, 1975; Tallahassee *Democrat*, January 4, 1955.

24. Humphress interview.

25. Humphress interview; Governor Collins interview, September 17, 1979; *The Lion's Tale* (Tallahassee: Senior Class of Leon High School, 1927), p. 18; interview with Hazel Richards, of Tallahassee, October 6, 1975.

26. Governor Collins interview, September 17, 1979.

27. Governor Collins interview, November 19, 1975; Richards interview; Moor interview.

28. Governor Collins interview, November 19, 1975.

29. Collins, *Forerunners Courageous*, pp. 87–94.

30. *The Lion's Tale*, p. 18.

31. Interview with Allen Morris, of Tallahassee, July 13, 1977.

32. Governor Collins interview, November 19, 1975; Moor interview; Richards interview; Humphress interview.

33. Governor Collins interview, November 19, 1975; Marvin Collins interview, October 8, 1975.

34. Marvin Collins interview, November 4, 1975; Humphress interview.

35. Humphress interview.

36. Humphress interview; Governor Collins interview, November 19, 1975; interview with Mary Call Collins, November 6, 1975.

37. Governor Collins interview, November 19, 1975.

38. Governor Collins interview, November 19, 1975; Marvin Collins interview, October 8, 1975; Barb Lustig, "He's Tallahassee's Own Statesman," Tallahassee *Democrat*, September 10, 1967; *Time* 66 (December 19, 1955), p. 19.

39. Governor Collins interviews, November 19, 1975, September 17, 1979.

40. Governor Collins interview, July 22, 1982.

41. Governor Collins interview, July 22, 1982.

42. Collins, *Forerunners Courageous*, pp. 192–97; Governor Collins interview, November 19, 1975; Mary Call Collins interview; John B. McDermott, "Senator Collins, Co-Favorite in Governor Race, Turned to Politics through Romance, Chance," Miami *Herald*, December 13, 1953.

Chapter 2

1. The population of Tallahassee increased from 5,638 in 1920 to 10,700 in 1930. Pitts, *Tallahassee Area Statistical Abstract*, p. 11.

2. Moor interview; New York *Times*, January 2, 1929.

3. Moor interview; Richards interview.

4. Cash, *The Mind of the South*, pp. 221–22.

5. Gerald W. Johnson, "Greensboro, or What You Will," *The Reviewer* 4 (1923–24), p. 169, quoted in George Brown Tindall, *The Emergence of the New South, 1913–1945* (Baton Rouge: Louisiana State University Press and the Littlefield Fund for Southern History of the University of Texas, 1967), p. 99.

6. Twelve Southerners, *I'll Take My Stand: The South and the*

Agrarian Tradition (New York: Harper and Brothers, 1930); H. Brandt Ayers, "You Can't Eat Magnolias," in H. Brandt Ayers and Thomas H. Naylor, eds., *You Can't Eat Magnolias* (New York: McGraw-Hill, 1972), pp. 20–21; Cash, *The Mind of the South,* pp. 378–83; Tindall, *The New South,* pp. 577–82.

7. Ayers, "You Can't Eat Magnolias," pp. 10–11; George Brown Tindall, *The Disruption of the Solid South* (Athens: University of Georgia Press, 1972), p. 25; Tindall, *The New South,* pp. 162, 184–85; Cash, *The Mind of the South,* p. 318.

8. Tindall, *The New South,* p. 224.

9. Flynt, *Duncan Upshaw Fletcher,* pp. 43–49, 166, 188–90, 194–96.

10. Claude Pepper, quoted in ibid., p. 196.

11. Wayne Flynt, *Cracker Messiah: Governor Sidney J. Catts of Florida* (Baton Rouge: Louisiana State University Press, 1977), pp. 2–3, 24–26, 29–93, 153–58, 214–36, 339–40.

12. Ibid., pp. 247–74, 301–02, 305–26; Flynt, *Duncan Upshaw Fletcher,* pp. 127, 142.

13. Flynt, *Cracker Messiah,* pp. 254, 302–03, 316; Herbert J. Doherty, Jr., "Florida and the Presidential Election of 1928," *Florida Historical Quarterly* 26 (October 1947), p. 186.

14. Tindall, *The New South,* p. 551; Jerrell H. Shofner, "Custom, Law, and History: The Enduring Influence of Florida's 'Black Code,' " *Florida Historical Quarterly* 55 (January 1977), p. 293.

15. V. O. Key, Jr., *Southern Politics in State and Nation* (New York: Alfred A. Knopf, 1950), pp. 82, 88–91, 97–98.

16. Colburn and Scher, *Florida's Gubernatorial Politics,* pp. 2, 103–06; Morris interview, July 13, 1977; William C. Havard and Loren P. Beth, *The Politics of Mis-Representation: Rural-Urban Conflict in the Florida Legislature* (Baton Rouge: Louisiana State University Press, 1962), p. 36; Helen L. Jacobstein, *The Segregation Factor in the Florida Democratic Gubernatorial Primary of 1956* (Gainesville: University of Florida Social Science Series, no. 47, 1972), pp. 14–15; Allen Morris, comp., *The Florida Handbook, 1971–1972* (Tallahassee: Peninsular Publishing Company, 1972), p. 145.

17. Jacobstein, *Segregation Factor,* p. 15; Howard Jay Friedman, "We Need English in Schools," Tallahassee *Democrat,* February 29, 1980.

18. Governor Collins interview, November 19, 1975; Mary Call Collins interview.

19. Governor Collins interview, November 19, 1975; Humphress interview; Moor interview; Richards interview; Tallahassee *Daily Demo-*

crat, June 10, 1932. The vote totals were Atkinson 2,123 and Collins 1,855.

20. Mary Call Collins interview; Tallahassee *Daily Democrat,* June 29, 1932; Collins, *Forerunners Courageous,* p. 197; Governor Collins interview, September 17, 1979.

21. When Collins later served in the navy, the military bureaucracy insisted that he use his full name. He therefore was known as Thomas L. ("Tom") Collins while in the service. Governor Collins interview, September 17, 1979. Newspersons first became aware of his full name in 1960 when they spotted his naval discharge on the wall of his den. They surmised, incorrectly, that he must have felt the name Tom Collins would cost votes in the "dry" counties of north Florida because of the alcoholic drink of the same name. Robert W. Delaney, "Another Political First for Florida's Gov. Collins," Orlando *Sentinel,* Florida Magazine, July 10, 1960.

22. Governor Collins interview, September 17, 1979.

23. Governor Collins interview, November 19, 1975.

24. Governor Collins interview, November 19, 1975; Tallahassee *Daily Democrat,* June 6, 1934. Collins received 2,089 votes to his three opponents' combined total of 774.

25. *Journal of the House of Representatives, State of Florida,* Twenty-fifth Regular Session, 1935, p. 281; Tallahassee *Daily Democrat,* May 1, 9–10, 22, 29–31, 1935.

26. Tallahassee *Daily Democrat,* May 20, 31, June 3, 1936. The vote totals were Collins 2,976 and H. E. Bierly 1,058.

27. Interview with Malcolm B. Johnson, of Tallahassee, October 15, 1975; *Journal of the House,* Twenty-sixth Regular Session, 1937, pp. 21, 373–74; Tallahassee *Daily Democrat,* May 31, 1937.

28. Floyd T. Christian, "Dedication of LeRoy Collins Building, Tallahassee, Florida, May 2, 1967," Collins Papers; *Journal of the House,* Twenty-sixth Regular Session, 1937, p. 56; Governor Collins interview, November 19, 1975; Miami *Herald,* editorial, March 18, 1954.

29. Mary Call Collins interview; interview with Jessie Conrad, of Tallahassee, October 10, 1975; Moor interview.

30. Collins, *Forerunners Courageous,* p. 199; Mary Call Collins interview; Conrad interview; Richards interview.

31. Governor Collins interview, November 19, 1975; *Journal of the Senate, State of Florida,* Twenty-eighth Regular Session, 1941, p. 83; Moor interview; Tallahassee *Daily Democrat,* June 1, 1936.

32. Interview with Rainey Cawthon, of Tallahassee, October 14, 1975;

Governor Collins interview, November 19, 1975; Humphress interview; Moor interview; Tallahassee *Daily Democrat,* May 7, 1940.

33. Governor Collins interview, November 19, 1975; Humphress interview; Moor interview. The vote totals were Collins 3,907 and Hodges 1,927. Tallahassee *Daily Democrat,* May 5, 1940.

34. *Journal of the Senate,* Twenty-eighth Regular Session, 1941, pp. 142, 249, 316, 426; Jacksonville *Florida Times-Union,* May 1, 6–8, 16–17, 29, 1941.

35. Jacksonville *Florida Times-Union,* April 7, 23, 28, 30, May 6, 15, 19, 25, 29, 1943.

36. Cawthon interview; Terry L. Christie, "The Collins-Johns Election, 1954: A Turning Point," *Apalachee* 6 (1967), p. 8.

37. Key, *Southern Politics,* p. 95, notes a "vague liberal-conservative cleavage" in statewide elections. For example, he states that in the 1948 gubernatorial primary "Fuller Warren was thought less conservative than Dan McCarty." But David R. Colburn and Richard K. Scher, "Florida Gubernatorial Politics: The Fuller Warren Years," *Florida Historical Quarterly* 53 (April 1975), pp. 391–92, point out that peripheral issues made Warren appear to be more liberal and that actually the platforms differed very little.

38. Collins to Hortense K. Wells, Bainbridge, Georgia, October 19, 1943, Collins Papers.

39. Governor Collins interview, November 19, 1975.

40. Mary Call Collins interview; Marvin Collins interview, October 8, 1975; Conrad interview; Richards interview.

41. Governor Collins interview, November 19, 1975; Moor interview.

42. Interview with Malcolm B. Johnson, of Tallahassee, February 25, 1976; interview with Governor Millard Caldwell, of Tallahassee, July 13, 1977; Colburn and Scher, *Florida's Gubernatorial Politics,* pp. 244–45.

43. Jacksonville *Florida Times-Union,* April 30, May 3, 1947.

44. Johnson interviews, October 15, 1975, February 25, 1976; Malcolm B. Johnson, "The Governors C: A Political Epic," Tallahassee *Democrat,* May 22, 1960; Jacksonville *Florida Times-Union,* April 22, 1957.

45. Johnson interview, October 15, 1975; Johnson, "Governors C," Tallahassee *Democrat,* May 22, 1960; Jacksonville *Florida Times-Union,* April 22–23, 25, 30, May 3, 1947.

46. Jacksonville *Florida Times-Union,* May 7, 18, 1949, May 1, 4, 9, 1951, May 6, 12, 1953, June 2, 1953; Herbert Bayer, "Inside the Legislature," Jacksonville *Florida Times-Union,* May 31, 1953; Mary Call Collins interview; Johnson interview, October 15, 1975.

47. Governor Collins interview, November 19, 1975; Allen Morris, comp., *The Florida Handbook, 1959–1960* (Tallahassee: Peninsular Publishing Company, 1959), pp. 141–42.

48. Governor Collins interview, November 19, 1975; Colburn and Scher, *Florida's Gubernatorial Politics*, p. 139.

49. Herbert Bayer, "Inside the Legislature," Jacksonville *Florida Times-Union*, May 24, 1953.

50. Colburn and Scher, *Florida's Gubernatorial Politics*, p. 139.

51. Tallahassee *Democrat*, September 28, 1953.

52. Colburn and Scher, *Florida's Gubernatorial Politics*, pp. 140–44; Tampa *Morning Tribune*, December 12, 1953; Governor Collins interview, November 19, 1975.

53. Daytona Beach *Morning Journal*, November 12, 20, 1953; Governor Collins interview, November 19, 1975; Ocala *Star-Banner*, November 11, 22, 1953; Orlando *Sentinel*, November 20, 1953. In his second administration, Collins appointed McCarty to a circuit judgeship. News Release, September 6, 1957, Florida State Archives, Correspondence of Governor LeRoy Collins (hereafter cited as CGLC), Series 780, Box 335, File: News Releases, July–December 1957. In the 1960 Democratic gubernatorial primary, McCarty finished fourth in a ten-man field of candidates. Tallahassee *Democrat*, May 4, 5, 1960.

Chapter 3

1. Moor interview; Tallahassee *Democrat*, May 26, 1954.

2. Christie, "The Collins-Johns Election," p. 18.

3. Ibid., pp. 8–11; Ocala *Star-Banner*, November 11, 1953. The totals were Johns, 255,787; Collins, 222,791; and Odham, 187,782. Annie Mary Hartsfield and Elston E. Roady, *Florida Votes, 1920–1962: Selected Election Statistics* (Tallahassee: Institute of Governmental Research, Florida State University, 1963), p. 63.

4. Christie, "The Collins-Johns Election," p. 19, also interprets the election as a rural-urban confrontation.

5. Ibid., p. 14; McDermott, "Senator Collins," Miami *Herald*, December 13, 1953.

6. Christie, "The Collins-Johns Election," p. 13; Daytona Beach *Evening News*, January 15, 1954; *Time* 66 (December 19, 1955), p. 19.

7. Miami *Herald*, April 3, 1960.

8. Governor Collins interview, November 19, 1975; St. Petersburg *Times*, December 13, 1953; Jacksonville *Florida Times-Union*, May 3, 1947.

9. Morris interview, July 13, 1977; Tampa *Daily Times*, January 6, 1954; St. Petersburg *Evening Independent*, January 6, 1954; Christie, "The Collins-Johns Election," pp. 14–16; Miami *Herald*, May 13, 1954.

10. Miami *Herald*, May 14, 1954; Christie, "The Collins-Johns Election," pp. 14–15; Cawthon interview; Morris interview, July 13, 1977.

11. Miami *Herald*, editorial, May 15, 1954; Christie, "The Collins-Johns Election," pp. 15–16; Morris interview, July 13, 1977.

12. Christie, "The Collins-Johns Election," p. 17; Moor interview; Tallahassee *Democrat*, May 26, 1954. The totals were Collins 380,323 and Johns 314,198. Hartsfield and Roady, *Florida Votes*, p. 63.

13. Moor interview; Miami *Herald*, May 26, 1954; St. Petersburg *Times*, May 26, 1954. The vote totals in Leon County were Collins 8,360 and Johns 6,069. Hartsfield and Roady, *Florida Votes*, p. 63.

14. Tallahassee *Democrat*, May 26, 1954.

15. Tallahassee *Democrat*, November 2, 1954, January 4, 1955; Conrad interview.

16. Señora Cecilia Pinel de Remon and the rest of the Panamanian delegation were en route to Tallahassee when they learned of the assassination of the president of their country. They immediately returned home and thus were not present for the inauguration. Tallahassee *Democrat*, January 2, 4, 1955; Conrad interview.

17. Conrad interview.

18. "Governor LeRoy Collins: Inaugural Address, January 4, 1955," Collins Papers.

19. John L. Perry, "A Philosophy of Government," in Allen Morris, ed., *Florida Across the Threshold: The Administration of Governor LeRoy Collins, January 4, 1955–January 3, 1961* (Tallahassee, 1961), p. 6. This book is a collection of reports written by administration officials during the final weeks of Collins's governorship.

20. "Governor LeRoy Collins: Inaugural Address, January 4, 1955," Collins Papers; "Governor's Message," *Journal of the House*, Thirty-fifth Regular Session, 1955, pp. 9–10.

21. *Time* 66 (December 19, 1955), p. 21.

22. Cawthon interview.

23. "Remarks by Governor LeRoy Collins at Southern Governors' Conference, Sea Island, Georgia, September 23, 1957," Collins Papers.

24. "Governor's Message," *Journal of the House*, Thirty-fifth Regular Session, 1955, p. 15; James A. Southerland, "Government in the Sunshine," in Morris, ed., *Florida Across the Threshold*, p. 17; *Time* 66 (December 19, 1955), p. 19; "Radio Stations Carrying Monthly Report," CGLC, Box 328, File: Radio-TV, January–April 1956.

25. Morris interview, July 13, 1977; George L. Thurston, "The Governor Will See You Now," St. Petersburg *Times*, The Floridian Magazine, April 11, 1976.

26. *Time* 66 (December 19, 1955), p. 18. For a discussion of the postwar southern economy, see Charles P. Roland, *The Improbable Era: The South Since World War II* (Lexington: University Press of Kentucky, 1975), pp. 11–29.

27. *Time* 66 (December 19, 1955), pp. 18, 20; John L. Perry, "Florida's National Prestige," in Morris, ed., *Florida Across the Threshold*, p. 392; "Governor's Message," *Journal of the House*, Thirty-fifth Regular Session, 1955, p. 12; *Newsweek* 49 (January 7, 1957), p. 60.

Chapter 4

1. Interview with Governor LeRoy Collins, April 10, 1976.

2. Collins, *Forerunners Courageous*, p. 205.

3. Ibid., p. 206; Moor interview; Tallahassee *Democrat*, January 4, 1955; *Time* 66 (December 19, 1955), pp. 18–19.

4. Tallahassee *Democrat*, January 4, 5, 1955; Morris interview, July 13, 1977; Governor Collins interview, April 10, 1976.

5. Morris interview, July 13, 1977; Governor Collins interview, April 10, 1976; Johnson interview, February 25, 1976; Tallahassee *Democrat*, June 22, July 12, 1957.

6. Betty McCord, Collins's secretary during the 1953 legislative session, served as receptionist in the governor's office. Tallahassee *Democrat*, January 4, 1955; Morris interview, July 13, 1977.

7. Collins, *Forerunners Courageous*, p. 205; Perry, "Florida's National Prestige," p. 392; *Time* 66 (December 19, 1955), pp. 18–19.

8. Governor Collins interview, April 10, 1976; Morris interview, July 13, 1977; Cawthon interview; Collins, *Forerunners Courageous*, p. 205; *Time* 66 (December 19, 1955), p. 18.

9. Paisley, *Cotton to Quail*, pp. 74–98. Tallahassee's population increased from 27,237 in 1950 to 48,174 in 1960. Pitts, *Tallahassee Area Statistical Abstract*, p. 11.

10. Morris interview, July 13, 1977.

11. Interview with Allen Morris, of Tallahassee, September 24, 1979.

12. Havard and Beth, *Politics of Mis-Representation*, p. 235; interview with Governor LeRoy Collins, September 27, 1979.

13. "Governor's Message," *Journal of the House*, Thirty-fifth Regular

Session, 1955, p. 9; Douglas McQuarrie, "This State of Affairs," Ft. Lauderdale *Daily News*, June 12, 1955.

14. Fort Myers *News-Press*, July 20, 1945.

15. Manning J. Dauer and Robert G. Kelsay, "Unrepresentative States," *National Municipal Review* 46 (December 1955), pp. 572–75. See also Colburn and Scher, *Florida's Gubernatorial Politics*, pp. 172–74.

16. Tallahassee *Democrat*, January 2, 1955; Stephen Trumball, "Old Guard on Guard—Senate Clique Faces Test," Miami *Herald*, June 12, 1955; Governor Collins interview, April 10, 1976.

17. Allen Morris, comp., *The Florida Handbook, 1975–1976* (Tallahassee: Peninsular Publishing Company, 1975), pp. 174–76.

18. Havard and Beth, *Politics of Mis-Representation*, pp. 1–2; Governor Collins interview, November 19, 1975; Morris interview, July 13, 1977.

19. Governor Collins interview, November 19, 1975; *Journal of the House*, Extraordinary Session on Reapportionment, 1955, p. 48; *Time* 66 (December 19, 1955), p. 21; Frank Trippett, "Collins Hands Allies Support They've Wanted," St. Petersburg *Times*, July 2, 1955.

20. "A Proclamation by the Governor," June 3, 1955, CGLC, Box 318, File: House Messages, 1955; Havard and Beth, *Politics of Mis-Representation*, pp. 50, 54; "Excerpts from Governor Collins' monthly 'Report to the People' by television and radio, September, 1955," in Morris, ed., *Florida Across the Threshold*, p. 41.

21. *Journal of the House*, Extraordinary Session on Reapportionment, 1955, p. 114; Havard and Beth, *Politics of Mis-Representation*, p. 58; Colburn and Scher, *Florida's Gubernatorial Politics*, p. 176.

22. "Proposed Constitutional Amendments to be Voted on, November 6th, 1956," CGLC, Box 314, File: Constitution Advisory Committee, 1955; William L. Durden, "Constitutional Revision," in Morris, ed., *Florida Across the Threshold*, p. 44; "Remarks by Governor Collins to the Citizens Constitution Committee, October 8, 1956," ibid., p. 45.

23. Farris Bryant—News Release, undated, CGLC, Box 319, File: Reapportionment, 1955; News Release, September 28, 1955, CGLC, Box 318, File: News Releases, 1955.

24. Allen Morris, "Collins, a Successful Master of Art of Practical Idealism," Deland *Sun News*, May 26, 1957; Governor Collins interview, April 10, 1976.

25. McQuarrie, "This State of Affairs," Ft. Lauderdale *Daily News*, June 12, 1955; Southerland, "Government in the Sunshine," p. 20; Harvey D. Tschirgi, *The Florida Merit System: An Investigation of Performance Evaluation in Agencies of the Florida Merit System* (Talla-

hassee: Florida State University Studies, no. 47, 1966), p. 1; A Proclamation by the Governor, December 22, 1955, CGLC, Box 318, File: Merit System, 1955.

26. "The Development Commission, Excerpts from Report by B. R. Fuller, Jr., Director," in Morris, ed., *Florida Across the Threshold*, pp. 143–55; *Time* 66 (December 19, 1955), p. 18; *Newsweek* 49 (January 7, 1957), p. 60.

27. Tallahassee *Democrat*, July 23–30, 1955, February 29–March 3, 1956; Allen Morris, "Governors' Tours Produce Dividends," Tallahassee *Democrat*, March 3, 1956.

28. Morris, "Governors' Tours Produce Dividends," Tallahassee *Democrat*, March 3, 1956; Morris interview, July 13, 1977.

29. Miami *Herald*, January 10, 1956.

30. Miami *Herald*, January 11, 12, 1956; Governor Collins interview, September 27, 1979.

31. Governor Collins interview, September 27, 1979.

32. Governor Collins interview, September 27, 1979. Accompanying Collins were Senator R. B. Gautier, of Miami; W. B. Jones, of Jacksonville, Hughes's Florida attorney; Charles Ausley, of Tallahassee, Collins's former law partner; and Joe Grotegut, the governor's administrative assistant. Miami *Herald*, January 14, 1956.

33. Governor Collins interview, September 27, 1979.

34. Governor Collins interview, September 27, 1979, "Statement of Governor LeRoy Collins of Florida: Issued January 10, 1956 in Los Angeles" and "A Statement by Howard Hughes released today, Tuesday, January 10, 1956 . . . ," CGLC, Box 327, File: News Releases, January–June, 1956.

35. Governor Collins interview, September 27, 1979.

36. Governor Collins interview, September 27, 1979; Jacobstein, *Segregation Factor*, p. 44.

Chapter 5

1. Daniel M. Berman, *It Is So Ordered: The Supreme Court Rules on School Segregation* (New York: W. W. Norton, 1966), pp. 116, 126, 141.

2. For a discussion of this term, see Earl Black, *Southern Governors and Civil Rights: Racial Segregation as a Campaign Issue in the Second Reconstruction* (Cambridge, Massachusetts: Harvard University Press, 1976), pp. 14–15.

3. Joseph Aaron Tomberlin, "The Negro and Florida's System of

Education: The Aftermath of the *Brown* Case" (Ph.D. dissertation, Florida State University, 1967), p. 25; Berman, *It Is So Ordered*, p. 17; Roland, *Improbable Era*, pp. 35–36; Jacobstein, *Segregation Factor*, p. 4.

4. "Period of Thoughtful Calm," Tallahassee *Democrat*, editorial, May 20, 1954. See also Jacksonville *Florida Times-Union*, editorial, May 19, 1954; St. Petersburg *Times*, editorial, May 18, 1954; and Tampa *Morning Tribune*, editorial, May 19, 1954.

5. Colburn and Scher, *Florida's Gubernatorial Politics*, p. 224.

6. Tallahassee *Democrat*, May 16, 1954; "LeRoy Collins' Statement in Regard to the United States Supreme Court's Decision on Segregation," undated, CGLC, Box 319, File: Segregation, 1955.

7. Tomberlin, "The Negro and Education," pp. 79–100; News Release, May 31, 1955, CGLC, Box 318, File: News Releases, 1955.

8. Tomberlin, "The Negro and Education," pp. 72, 147, 151–52; "Governor's Message," *Journal of the House*, Thirty-fifth Regular Session, 1955, p. 15.

9. Collins to Herbert N. Davidson, editor of the Daytona Beach *News-Journal*, April 11, 1955, CGLC, Box 319, File: Segregation, 1955.

10. Governor Collins interviews, November 19, 1975, April 10, 1976; Jacobstein, *Segregation Factor*, p. 18.

11. Jacobstein, *Segregation Factor*, pp. 5, 8.

12. Harold C. Fleming, "The Southern Response," *New Republic* 132 (June 13, 1955), p. 7.

13. Bert Collier, "Segregation in Politics," *Current History* 31 (October 1956), p. 230.

14. Jacobstein, *Segregation Factor*, p. 3.

15. The two minor candidates were Peasley Streets, of Lake Park, and W. B. Price, of Jacksonville. Ibid., pp. 20–23.

16. Tomberlin, "The Negro and Education," p. 104.

17. Ibid., pp. 116–18; St. Petersburg *Times*, April 13, 1956; Jacobstein, *Segregation Factor*, p. 28; Jacksonville *Florida Times-Union*, March 10, 1956; Tampa *Morning Tribune*, March 10, 1956; Tallahassee *Democrat*, March 13, April 6, 1956.

18. *Time* 67 (January 30, 1956), pp. 14–15; Numan V. Bartley, *The Rise of Massive Resistance* (Baton Rouge: Louisiana State University Press, 1969), pp. 126–27, 131–34.

19. Jacobstein, *Segregation Factor*, p. 39.

20. James McLendon, "The LeRoy Collins Years," St. Petersburg *Times*, The Floridian Magazine, July 7, 1974; Jacobstein, *Segregation Factor*, pp. 51, 53–54, 57–58.

21. "Statement by Governor LeRoy Collins, February 2, 1956," CGLC, Box 328, File: Race Relations—Statements, 1956; Jacobstein, *Segregation Factor,* p. 39.

22. "Statement on Segregation," not released, CGLC, Box 328, File: Race Relations—Statements, 1956; Tallahassee *Democrat,* April 21, 1956; *Time* 67 (May 21, 1956), p. 33.

23. "Governor's Message," *Journal of the House,* Thirty-seventh Regular Session, 1959, p. 21; Governor Collins interview, April 10, 1976.

24. Orlando *Morning Sentinel,* November 7, 8, 11, December 6, 1951, February 12, 1952; Leesburg *Commercial-Ledger,* April 3, 1952; Tallahassee *Democrat,* February 16, 1956.

25. Orlando *Morning Sentinel,* November 7–14, 1951; Tallahassee *Democrat,* February 16, 1956; Jacobstein, *Segregation Factor,* pp. 28–29.

26. St. Petersburg *Times,* editorial, January 14, 1955; Bethune to Collins, February 14, 1955, CGLC, Box 317, File: Irvin, Walter Lee, February–December 1955.

27. Governor Collins interview, April 10, 1976; Tallahassee *Democrat,* February 16, 1956; Jacobstein, *Segregation Factor,* p. 29; Colburn and Scher, *Florida's Gubernatorial Politics,* p. 123.

28. L. A. Grayson, Judge, Criminal Court of Record, Hillsborough County, Tampa, to Collins, December 30, 1955, CGLC, Box 326, File: Irvin, Walter Lee, 1956; Charles E. Bache, Oklawaha, Florida, to Collins, December 20, 1955, CGLC, Box 317, File: Irvin, Walter Lee, February–December 1955; Jacobstein, *Segregation Factor,* p. 29.

29. Malcolm B. Johnson, "A Scent of Racial Pettifoggery Rises," Tallahassee *Democrat,* February 19, 1956.

30. Tallahassee *Democrat,* February 16, 24, 1956.

31. "Statement by Governor Collins with reference to calling of Grand Jury in Walter Lee Irvin commutation case," February 16, 1956, CGLC, Box 326, File: Irvin, Walter Lee, 1956.

32. John C. Heidenreich, Charlottesville, Virginia, to Collins, February 24, 1956, ibid.

33. R. A. Hawthorne, Punta Gorda, Florida, to Collins, undated, ibid.

34. Telegram from Dr. W. H. Collie, West Palm Beach, to Collins, February 17, 1956, ibid.; telegram from E. D. Koelman, chairman, Roosevelt Democratic Club, Jacksonville, February 25, 1956, ibid.

35. Pat Ford, West Palm Beach, to Collins, February 17, 1956, ibid.

36. "In the Circuit Court of the Fifth Judicial Circuit in and for Lake County, Florida, Fall Term, A.D., 1955. Presentment of the Grand Jury to Honorable T. G. Futch, Judge of the Above Entitled Court," pp. 10,

15, CGLC, Box 317, File: Lake County—Correspondence, 1955; Talla-hassee *Democrat,* February 24, March 13, 1956; Jacobstein, *Segregation Factor,* p. 30.

37. Governor Collins interview, April 10, 1976; Tallahassee *Democrat,* February 22, 1956; Bob Delaney, "State of the State," Tallahassee *Democrat,* March 4, 1956; Jacobstein, *Segregation Factor,* p. 30.

38. Delaney, "State of the State," Tallahassee *Democrat,* March 4, 1956. See also Johnson, "Scent of Racial Pettifoggery Rises," Tallahassee *Democrat,* February 19, 1956; Jacobstein, *Segregation Factor,* p. 29.

39. Jacobstein, *Segregation Factor,* pp. 30–31.

40. John J. Blair, executive secretary, Advisory Committee on Race Relations, to Judge L. L. Fabisinski, Pensacola, June 12, 1956, CGLC, Box 328, File: Race Relations, May–December, 1956; Tomberlin, "The Negro and Education," pp. 154–58; Tallahassee *Democrat,* March 12, 13, 1956; Tampa *Morning Tribune,* March 13, 1956.

41. "Statement by Governor LeRoy Collins to Conference on Segrega-tion," March 21, 1956, CGLC, Box 328, File: Race Relations—State-ments, 1956; Tomberlin, "The Negro and Education," pp. 121–24; Tallahassee *Democrat,* March 13, 22, 1956; Tampa *Morning Tribune,* March 13, 1956. Those attending the conference included cabinet mem-bers, Board of Control members, the presidents of the University of Florida and Florida State University (FSU), the president of the senate, the Speaker of the house, the chairmen of the senate and house Educa-tion Committees, and the president of the State Association of County School Superintendents. The president of FAMU was invited, but de-clined to attend, citing a prior appointment. Tallahassee *Democrat,* March 22, 1956.

42. "A Resolution: Adopted by the Conference on Integration . . . ," CGLC, Box 328, File: Race Relations—Statements, 1956; Tallahassee *Democrat,* March 22, 1956; Collins to Eisenhower, March 22, 1956, CGLC, Box 328, File: Race Relations, January–April 1956; Eisenhower to Collins, March 31, 1956, ibid.

43. "A Resolution: Adopted by the Conference on Integration . . . ," CGLC, Box 328, File: Race Relations—Statements, 1956; Tomberlin, "The Negro and Education," p. 164. Other committee members were Millard B. Smith, of Titusville; M. Luther Mershon, of Miami; Cody Fowler, of Tampa; and Rivers H. Buford, J. Lewis Hall, and John T. Wigginton, all of Tallahassee. Collins to Fabisinski, April 17, 1956, CGLC, Box 328, File: Race Relations—Statements, 1956.

44. Jacobstein, *Segregation Factor,* p. 35.

45. Ibid., pp. 31–32; Tallahassee *Democrat,* March 16, 18, 1956.

46. Jacobstein, *Segregation Factor*, p. 32.

47. Ibid., p. 45; Tallahassee *Democrat*, February 7, 1956; "Report on Press Conference in Office of the Governor of Florida, LeRoy Collins, Monday, April 9, 1956," CGLC, Box 327, File: News Releases, January–June 1956.

48. Bryant was endorsed by his hometown newspaper, the Ocala *Star-Banner*. Jacobstein, *Segregation Factor*, pp. 41, 63; McLendon, "The LeRoy Collins Years," St. Petersburg *Times*, The Floridian Magazine, July 7, 1974.

49. Jacobstein, *Segregation Factor*, p. 42. Correspondence concerning Leyshon appears throughout the CGLC and the Collins Papers. See, for example, John L. Perry to Maurice E. Fitzgerald, research director, Democratic State Committee, New York, May 31, 1960, CGLC, Box 365, File: Democratic National Committee, April 1960.

50. Hartsfield and Roady, *Florida Votes*, p. 61; Tomberlin, "The Negro and Education," pp. 141–42; Jacobstein, *Segregation Factor*, pp. 70–73; Donald R. Matthews and James W. Prothro, *Negroes and the New South Politics* (New York: Harcourt, Brace, and World, 1966), p. 148; *Time* 61 (May 21, 1956), p. 33.

51. Jacobstein, *Segregation Factor*, pp. 70, 72; Tomberlin, "The Negro and Education," pp. 142–43.

Chapter 6

1. "Governor's Message—Extraordinary Session of the Florida Legislature, July 23, 1956," *Journal of the House*, Special Session, 1956, p. 7; "Excerpts from Report of Saul A. Silverman, Staff Assistant to the Fowler Commission on Race Relations," in Morris, ed., *Florida Across the Threshold*, pp. 55–58; "A Report of the Special Committee . . . , July 16, 1956," pp. 2–3, CGLC, Box 328, File: Race Relations, May–December 1956.

2. David R. Colburn and Richard K. Scher, "Race Relations and Florida Gubernatorial Politics since the *Brown* Decision," *Florida Historical Quarterly* 55 (October 1976), p. 156; Governor Collins interview, April 10, 1976; Bradenton *Herald*, July 24, 1956; Malcolm B. Johnson, "Under the Dome," Tallahassee *Democrat*, August 2, 1956; Miami *Herald*, August 2, 1956.

3. Ft. Lauderdale *News*, August 2, 1956; John B. McDermott, "Politics in Florida," Miami *Herald*, August 5, 1956.

4. Charles U. Smith and Lewis M. Killian, *The Tallahassee Bus*

Protest (New York: Anti-Defamation League of B'nai B'rith, 1958), p. 7; Tampa *Morning Tribune,* December 30, 1956.

5. Stephen B. Oates, *Let the Trumpet Sound: The Life of Martin Luther King, Jr.* (New York: Harper and Row, 1982), pp. 64–112.

6. Smith and Killian, *Tallahassee Bus Protest,* pp. 7–10; Tallahassee *Democrat,* January 1, 1957; News Release, July 2, 1956, CGLC, Box 328, File: Race Relations—Statements, 1956.

7. Smith and Killian, *Tallahassee Bus Protest,* pp. 11–12; Tampa *Morning Tribune,* December 30, 1956.

8. William E. Leuchtenburg, *A Troubled Feast: American Society Since 1945* (Boston: Little, Brown, 1973), p. 97; Smith and Killian, *Tallahassee Bus Protest,* pp. 12–13; Tampa *Morning Tribune,* December 30, 1956.

9. Tampa *Morning Tribune,* December 30, 1956.

10. Miami *Daily News,* January 1, 1957; Tampa *Morning Tribune,* December 30, 1956.

11. Tallahassee *Democrat,* January 1, 1957.

12. News Release, January 1, 1957, CGLC, Box 335, File: News Releases, January–June 1957; "Proclamation, State of Florida, Executive Department, Tallahassee," January 1, 1957, ibid.; Orlando *Sentinel,* January 2, 1957; St. Petersburg *Times,* January 1, 1957. For examples of the editorial response, see Lakeland *Ledger,* January 2, 1957; Miami *Daily News,* January 2, 1957; St. Petersburg *Times,* January 3, 1957; Tallahassee *Democrat,* January 2, 1957; Tampa *Morning Tribune,* January 3, 1957; and St. Petersburg *Evening Independent,* January 3, 1957.

13. Tallahassee *Democrat,* January 3, 8, 1957; [Tallahassee City] Ordinance 741, CGLC, Box 336, File: Race Relations, 1957.

14. "Statement by Governor LeRoy Collins," January 11, 1957, CGLC, Box 335, File: News Releases, January–June 1957; "Statement by Governor LeRoy Collins," January 17, 1957, CGLC, Box 336, File: Race Relations, 1957; Tallahassee *Democrat,* January 17, 18, 1957; Smith and Killian, *Tallahassee Bus Protest,* p. 14.

15. "Brief Summary of Tallahassee Bus Situation," undated, CGLC, Box 335, File: News Releases, January–June 1957; Jacobstein, *Segregation Factor,* p. 76.

16. Cawthon interview; Conrad interview; Richards interview.

17. Governor Collins interview, April 10, 1976.

18. Tallahassee *Democrat,* January 8, 1957; Governor Collins interview, April 10, 1976; Moor interview.

19. "Governor LeRoy Collins: Inaugural Address, January 8, 1957," Collins Papers.

20. St. Petersburg *Times*, editorial, January 9, 1957; Tallahassee *Democrat*, January 8, 1957; *Newsweek* 49 (January 21, 1957), p. 31; Pensacola *Journal*, editorial, January 9, 1957; Ocala *Star Banner*, editorial, January 9, 1957. See also editorials in the Lakeland *Ledger*, January 8, 1957; Orlando *Sentinel*, January 9, 1957; Tampa *Morning Tribune*, January 9, 1957; St. Petersburg *Times*, January 9, 1957; Miami *Herald*, January 9, 1957; Daytona Beach *Evening News*, January 8, 1957; Fort Walton Beach *Playground News*, January 10, 1957; Bradenton *Herald*, January 8, 1957; and Sarasota *Herald-Tribune*, January 9, 1957. Although making no comment, the Palatka *Daily News*, January 16, 1957, printed on its editorial page Sumter Lowry's statement describing Collins's address as "a complete surrender to the forces of Integration."

21. Miami *Herald*, editorial, January 9, 1957; Bradenton *Herald*, January 8, 1957; Tallahassee *Democrat*, January 8, 1957.

22. Sarasota *Herald-Tribune*, January 9, 1957; Tallahassee *Democrat*, January 8, 1957.

23. Editorials pointing out the paradox of support for the Supreme Court but opposition to school integration appeared in the Pensacola *Journal*, January 9, 1957; Daytona Beach *Evening News*, January 8, 1957; St. Petersburg *Times*, January 9, 1957; and Miami *Herald*, January 9, 1957.

24. Bradenton *Herald*, January 8, 1957. See, for example, editorials in the Fort Walton Beach *Playground News*, January 10, 1957; Tallahassee *Democrat*, January 8, 1957; Sarasota *Herald-Tribune*, January 9, 1957; and Orlando *Sentinel*, January 9, 1957.

25. Pensacola *Journal*, editorial, January 9, 1957.

26. Bradenton *Herald*, editorial, January 8, 1957.

Chapter 7

1. Emmet John Hughes, *The Ordeal of Power: A Political Memoir of the Eisenhower Years* (New York: Atheneum, 1963), p. 242, argues that Eisenhower had his "own private, abiding dissent from the Supreme Court action." For an example of Eisenhower's reluctance to support the Court's decision, see "Presidential News Conference, September 3, 1957," in Robert L. Branyan and Lawrence H. Larsen, eds., *The Eisenhower Administration, 1956–1961: A Documentary History* (2 vols.; New York: Random House, 1971), vol. II, p. 1119.

2. Leuchtenburg, *Troubled Feast*, p. 94. Quote from "The Southern

Manifesto," in Francis M. Wilhoit, *The Politics of Massive Resistance* (New York: George Braziller, 1973), p. 287.

3. Bartley, *Rise of Resistance*, pp. 117, 195; Wilhoit, *Politics of Resistance*, pp. 56–99, 111.

4. Bartley, *Rise of Resistance*, pp. 192, 195; Wilhoit, *Politics of Resistance*, p. 111.

5. Roland, *Improbable Era*, p. 38; Bartley, *Rise of Resistance*, pp. 126–49.

6. Jacobstein, *Segregation Factor*, p. 74.

7. Governor Collins interview, April 10, 1976. By 1958 eleven of the sixteen southern states had desegregated their graduate schools. "Statement by Governor LeRoy Collins," June 18, 1958, CGLC, Box 340, File: News Releases, January–June 1958.

8. Jacobstein, *Segregation Factor*, p. 10; Tomberlin, "The Negro and Education," pp. 184–85.

9. Tampa *Morning Tribune*, April 21, 1957; Governor Collins interview, April 10, 1976; Tomberlin, "The Negro and Education," pp. 185–86; "Statement by Governor, Re: Sustaining of 'Last Resort' Bill Veto," June 7, 1957, CGLC, Box 335, File: News Releases, January–June 1957.

10. Tallahassee *Democrat*, April 5, 1957; Tomberlin, "The Negro and Education," p. 186.

11. Tampa *Morning Tribune*, April 19, 1957.

12. "Statement by Governor Collins Re Interposition," April 18, 1957, CGLC, Box 335, File: News Releases, January–June 1957; St. Petersburg *Times*, April 21, 1957.

13. House Concurrent Resolution 174 (1957), *Acts, Resolutions, and Memorials, 1957*, Record Group 156, Series 222, Florida State Archives.

14. Governor Collins interview, April 10, 1976; Martin Dyckman, "LeRoy Collins—Back Home with Dignity," St. Petersburg *Times*, The Floridian Magazine, March 15, 1970.

15. Much of the following discussion on Collins and the Little Rock conflict was published in Thomas R. Wagy, "Governor LeRoy Collins of Florida and the Little Rock Crisis of 1957," *Arkansas Historical Quarterly* 38 (Summer 1979), pp. 99–115.

16. Quote from Robert Sherrill, *Gothic Politics in the Deep South: Stars of the New Confederacy* (New York: Grossman, 1968), p. 116. See also Bartley, *Rise of Resistance*, pp. 260–61; and Wilhoit, *Politics of Resistance*, p. 177.

17. Bartley, *Rise of Resistance*, pp. 252–65; Tampa *Morning Tribune*,

September 8, 1957; Wilhoit, *Politics of Resistance,* pp. 181–82. Ironically, an Associated Press article on September 1, 1957, one day prior to Faubus's intervention, used Little Rock as a model of moderation for the South to follow. Tallahassee *Democrat,* September 1, 1957.

18. Bartley, *Rise of Resistance,* pp. 252, 263, 265; Wilhoit, *Politics of Resistance,* p. 181. Eisenhower quote from "Presidential News Conference, September 3, 1957," Branyan and Larsen, eds., *Eisenhower,* vol. II, p. 1120.

19. Governor Orval E. Faubus, Huntsville, Arkansas, to Thomas R. Wagy, July 12, 1977, cited in Wagy, "Governor LeRoy Collins," p. 103.

20. Bartley, *Rise of Resistance,* p. 260; Sherrill, *Gothic Politics,* pp. 75–76, 84–89, 98–99, 107; Wilhoit, *Politics of Resistance,* pp. 177–78.

21. Faubus to Wagy, July 12, 1977, cited in Wagy, "Governor LeRoy Collins," p. 103; Bartley, *Rise of Resistance,* p. 265.

22. Faubus to Eisenhower, September 4, 1957, in Branyan and Larsen, eds., *Eisenhower,* vol. II, p. 1122.

23. Bartley, *Rise of Resistance,* p. 267.

24. Hodges to Coleman, August 28, 1957, Collins Papers.

25. Allen Morris, "Talk to Governors Vital to Collins," St. Petersburg *Times,* September 22, 1957; Tallahassee *Democrat,* September 15, 1957.

26. Faubus to Wagy, July 12, 1977, cited in Wagy, "Governor LeRoy Collins," p. 105; Miami *Daily News,* September 12, 1957.

27. Johnson interview, February 25, 1976.

28. *Diary, 1957,* September 20, 1957, Collins Papers (this diary briefly notes Collins's activities, meetings, and telephone calls); memo from Joe Grotegut, Collins's executive assistant, to Florida's radio stations, September 20, 1957, ibid.

29. Cincinnati *Enquirer,* September 22, 1957; Governor Collins interview, April 10, 1976; Faubus to Wagy, July 12, 1977, cited in Wagy, "Governor LeRoy Collins," p. 106.

30. Governor Collins interview, April 10, 1976; Hodges to Collins, August 28, 1957, Collins Papers; Jacksonville *Florida Times-Union,* September 23, 1957.

31. Bartley, *Rise of Resistance,* pp. 267–68; Wilhoit, *Politics of Resistance,* pp. 179–80.

32. "Remarks by Governor LeRoy Collins at Southern Governors' Conference, Sea Island, Georgia, September 23, 1957," Collins Papers.

33. Atlanta *Constitution,* September 24, 1957; St. Petersburg *Times,* September 24, 1957.

34. Tampa *Morning Tribune,* September 24, 1957; Atlanta *Constitu-*

tion, September 24, 1957; St. Petersburg *Times,* September 24, 1957; Faubus to Wagy, July 12, 1977, cited in Wagy, "Governor LeRoy Collins," p. 109.

35. Eleanor Roosevelt to Collins, October 9, 1957, Collins Papers; Tampa *Morning Tribune,* September 25, 1957; Buffalo, New York, *Evening News,* editorial, September 23, 1957; St. Paul, Minnesota, *Pioneer-Press,* editorial, September 24, 1957; *Newsweek* 50 (September 30, 1957), p. 40.

36. Atlanta *Constitution,* editorial, September 24, 1957; Decatur *Dekalb New Era,* editorial, September 26, 1957.

37. Dr. E. J. J. Kramar, assistant professor of speech, Southwestern Louisiana Institute, Lafayette, to Collins, September 24, 1957, Collins Papers; Lewis P. Jones, professor of history, Wofford College, Spartanburg, South Carolina, to Collins, September 30, 1957, Collins Papers.

38. Telegram from Smathers to Collins, September 24, 1957, Collins Papers. Other politicians congratulating Collins included Commissioner of Agriculture Nathan Mayo, September 26, 1957; U.S. Attorney Harrold Carswell, September 26, 1957; and former U.S. Senator Claude Pepper, September 27, 1957, Collins Papers.

39. Hendrix Chandler, in the Miami *Daily News,* September 25, 1957; Jim Massey, in the Jacksonville *Journal,* September 24, 1957; St. Petersburg *Times,* editorial, September 24, 1957; Directors of the Annual Destin Fishing Tournament to Collins, September 29, 1957, Collins Papers.

40. "Resolution, Introduced and Passed by Martha Reid Chapter, United Daughters of the Confederacy, Jacksonville, Florida, September 27, 1957," Collins Papers.

41. Branyan and Larsen, eds., *Eisenhower,* vol. II, pp. 1129, 1134; Bartley, *Rise of Resistance,* pp. 267–68; Wilhoit, *Politics of Resistance,* pp. 179–80.

42. Charleston, South Carolina, *News and Courier,* September 25, 1957; St. Louis *Post-Dispatch,* September 24, 1957.

43. Tampa *Morning Tribune,* September 26, 1957.

44. "Remarks by Governor Luther H. Hodges in reporting on negotiations between the President of the United States and the Governor of Arkansas with reference to removal of troops from Little Rock: Governor's Press Conference, State Capitol, Raleigh, North Carolina, 10:00 a.m., Thursday, October 3, 1957," p. 1, CGLC, Box 336, File: Race Relations, 1957.

45. Telegram from Eisenhower to Collins, September 26, 1957, ibid.; telegram from Collins to Eisenhower, September 26, 1957, ibid.; tele-

gram from Griffin to Collins, September 30, 1957, ibid.; telegram from Collins to Griffin, September 30, 1957, ibid.

46. "Remarks by Hodges," pp. 1–2, ibid.; *Diary, 1957*, September 30, 1957, Collins Papers.

47. Governor Collins interview, April 10, 1976.

48. Governor Collins interview, April 10, 1976.

49. Governor Collins interview, April 10, 1976.

50. Governor Collins interview, April 10, 1976; "Remarks by Hodges," p. 2, CGLC, Box 336, File: Race Relations, 1957; Sherman Adams, *Firsthand Report: The Story of the Eisenhower Administration* (New York: Harper and Brothers, 1961), p. 357.

51. Governor Collins interview, April 10, 1976; Dwight D. Eisenhower, *The White House Years: Waging Peace, 1956–1961* (Garden City, New York: Doubleday and Company, 1965), p. 173; Adams, *Firsthand Report*, p. 357.

52. Tampa *Morning Tribune*, October 2, 1957; Adams, *Firsthand Report*, p. 357; Governor Collins interview, April 10, 1076.

53. According to Hodges, "After we got it drafted . . . we called Governor Faubus and asked him if he agreed with what we put out, meaning all of it. He approved, in its entirety, the joint communication." Hodges then said: "We have a suggested statement here which ties in with the communication which we propose you release to the press in a few minutes. Would you send a wire or give a press release from Little Rock along these lines and recognizing these particular things." "Remarks by Hodges," p. 2, CGLC, Box 336, File: Race Relations, 1957. Possibly confusion occurred between the "joint communication" to which Faubus agreed "in its entirety" and the "press release" following "along these lines."

54. Adams, *Firsthand Report*, p. 357; Drew Pearson, "Sidelights on White House Meeting," Tallahassee *Democrat*, October 7, 1957; New York *Times*, October 2, 1957.

55. New York *Herald Tribune*, October 2, 1957.

56. *Diary, 1957*, October 1, 1957, Collins Papers; Adams, *Firsthand Report*, p. 358; Governor Collins interview, April 10, 1976; "Remarks by Hodges," p. 3, CGLC, Box 336, File: Race Relations, 1957.

57. Eisenhower, *White House*, p. 174; New York *Times*, October 3, 1957; Faubus to Wagy, July 12, 1977, cited in Wagy, "Governor LeRoy Collins," pp. 112–13.

58. "Statement issued by Governor Collins . . . ," October 1, 1957, CGLC, Box 335, File: News Releases, July–December 1957; Eisenhower, *White House*, p. 174; Governor Collins interview, April 10, 1976.

59. Tallahassee *Democrat*, October 2, 1957.

60. Tallahassee *Democrat*, October 2, 1957; Tampa *Tribune*, September 27, 1957.

61. St. Augustine *Evening Record*, June 7, 1957; Tallahassee *Democrat*, October 2–4, 1957; Jacobstein, *Segregation Factor*, p. 74.

62. *The Presbyterian Outlook* 139 (October 28, 1957), pp. 5–6, Collins Papers.

63. Ibid.

64. Ibid., p. 6; Shofner, "Custom, Law, and History," p. 277; News Release, September 28, 1956, CGLC, Box 327, File: News Releases, July–December 1956.

Chapter 8

1. Allen Morris, "Cracker Politics," Tallahassee *Democrat*, May 7, 1960.

2. "Governor LeRoy Collins: Inaugural Address, January 8, 1957," Collins Papers; "Governor's Message," *Journal of the House*, Thirty-sixth Regular Session, 1957, p. 8; Havard and Beth, *Politics of Mis-Representation*, p. 60.

3. Havard and Beth, *Politics of Mis-Representation*, pp. 58–59; Morris interview, July 13, 1977.

4. Havard and Beth, *Politics of Mis-Representation*, p. 59; St. Petersburg *Times*, April 4, June 1, 1957; Tampa *Morning Tribune*, editorial, June 3, 1957; Miami *Daily News*, editorial, May 26, 1957.

5. St. Petersburg *Times*, April 4, 1957; Tampa *Morning Tribune*, May 26, 1957; Havard and Beth, *Politics of Mis-Representation*, pp. 134–44.

6. Havard and Beth, *Politics of Mis-Representation*, pp. 61–62; Tallahassee *Democrat*, October 6, 1957; Tampa *Morning Tribune*, May 26, June 3, 1957.

7. Tampa *Morning Tribune*, June 3, 1957; Miami *Herald*, June 6, 1957.

8. Tampa *Morning Tribune*, September 8, 9, 23, 1957.

9. Miami *Herald*, October 10, 1957.

10. Editorials in the Tampa *Morning Tribune*, September 23, 1957; Tampa *Daily Times*, October 9, 1957; Daytona Beach *Morning Journal*, October 2, 1957; Orlando *Sentinel*, September 29, 1957.

11. "Statement by Governor Collins," February 26, 1958, CGLC, Box 340, File: Constitutional Revision, 1958; Havard and Beth, *Politics of*

Mis-Representation, p. 62; Tallahassee *Democrat*, editorial, November 2, 1958.

12. Malcolm B. Johnson, "Under the Dome," Tallahassee *Democrat*, April 6, 1959.

13. Ibid.; Havard and Beth, *Politics of Mis-Representation*, p. 200.

14. Durden, "Constitutional Revision," p. 49; "Press Conference, Governor LeRoy Collins," August 14, 1958, CGLC, Box 340, File: Constitutional Advisory Committee, 1958; Tallahassee *Democrat*, April 9, 1959.

15. Malcolm B. Johnson, "Under the Dome," Tallahassee *Democrat*, April 10, 1959.

16. Havard and Beth, *Politics of Mis-Representation*, p. 62; Tallahassee *Democrat*, May 12, 1959.

17. "Excerpts from Remarks by Governor Collins at Southern Governors' Conference, Asheville, North Carolina, October, 1959," in Morris, ed., *Florida Across the Threshold*, p. 53; Governor Collins interview, November 19, 1975; "Reapportionment Article For United Press International, By Governor LeRoy Collins," October 28, 1959, CGLC, Box 357, File: News Releases, 1959.

18. Seventeen papers endorsed the amendment, and ten opposed it. Miami *Herald*, November 1, 1959. Editorials in metropolitan papers supporting the amendment included the Jacksonville *Florida Times-Union*, November 1, 1959; Miami *Herald*, November 2, 1959; and Tampa *Tribune*, November 1, 1959.

19. Miami *Herald*, editorial, November 2, 1959.

20. Miami *Herald*, editorial, November 1, 1959; St. Petersburg *Times*, editorial, November 2, 1959.

21. The vote was 143,668 in favor and 180,089 in opposition. Miami *Herald*, November 4, 1959.

22. *Florida Governor News Conference, 1960*, "Press Conference, Governor LeRoy Collins, March 10, 1960," p. 10. Transcripts of Collins's news conferences from June 30, 1958, to December 29, 1960, are collected and bound in yearly volumes.

23. Leuchtenburg, *Troubled Feast*, p. 102; Governor Collins interview, November 19, 1975.

24. Colburn and Scher, *Florida's Gubernatorial Politics*, pp. 178, 108–14.

25. Havard and Beth, *Politics of Mis-Representation*, pp. 43–47.

26. Johnson, "Under the Dome," Tallahassee *Democrat*, April 6, 1959.

27. J. B. Underhill in the St. Petersburg *Times*, June 1, 1957.

28. Malcolm B. Johnson, "Under the Dome," Tallahassee *Democrat,* May 27, 1957.

29. Ibid.; Orlando *Sentinel,* June 9, 1957.

30. "Governor's Message," *Journal of the House,* Thirty-fifth Regular Session, 1955, p. 12; Tampa *Morning Tribune,* editorial, April 8, 1957.

31. "Governor's Message," *Journal of the House,* Thirty-sixth Regular Session, 1957, p. 15.

32. See, for example, editorials in the Bradenton *Herald,* April 14, 1957; Ft. Lauderdale *Daily News,* April 14, 1957; Ocala *Star Banner,* April 17, 1957; and St. Petersburg *Evening Independent,* April 19, 1957.

33. Miami *Herald,* April 25, 1957; Tallahassee *Democrat,* editorial, May 5, 1957.

34. Howard Jay Friedman, "Summary of 1955 Legislative Action Dealing with Education," *Florida School Bulletin* 18 (September 1955), pp. 10–11; Tallahassee *Democrat,* March 19, April 9, May 1, 10, June 1, 1957.

35. Lowell Brandle, "How to Handle Expected 'Tidal Wave' of Students Is Big Educational Issue," St. Petersburg *Times,* February 7, 1955.

36. "Governor's Message," *Journal of the House,* Thirty-fifth Regular Session, 1955, p. 13; James A. Southerland, "Education," in Morris, ed., *Florida Across the Threshold,* p. 241; "Excerpts from report by Dr. J. Broward Culpepper, executive director of the Board of Control," in ibid., p. 260; St. Petersburg *Evening Independent,* March 17, 1955; Tampa *Morning Tribune,* December 9, 10, 1956, February 5, 1957; St. Petersburg *Times,* October 9, 12, 1956; Colburn and Scher, *Florida's Gubernatorial Politics,* pp. 250–52.

37. Tallahassee *Democrat,* March 18, 1957; Miami *Daily News,* March 17, 1957; Governor Collins interview, April 10, 1976.

38. Tallahassee *Democrat,* March 18, 1957; Governor Collins interview, April 10, 1976.

39. Tallahassee *Democrat,* March 18, 1957; Miami *Daily News,* March 17, 1957.

40. Tallahassee *Democrat,* May 23, 1957.

41. Governor Collins interview, April 10, 1976; Tallahassee *Democrat,* May 24, 1957.

42. "In the matter of the application of the Commonwealth of Massachusetts, for the extradition of Melvin B. Ellis and Frances V. Ellis before the Governor of Florida, May 23, 1957, at the State Capitol, Tallahassee," CGLC, Box 335, File: News Releases, January–June 1957.

43. Bob Delaney, in Miami *Daily News,* May 24, 1957; Martin Waldron, in Tampa *Morning Tribune,* May 24, 1957; William L. Durden,

"Office of the Governor," in Morris, ed., *Florida Across the Threshold*, p. 32.

44. Miami *Herald*, May 22, 1958; Governor Collins interview, September 27, 1979; Collins to Adlai E. Stevenson, May 25, 1959, Collins Papers. The San Juan conference met August 2–5, 1959. *Governor News Conference*, February 19, 1959, p. 8.

45. New York University and the Institute of International Education cohosted the tour. Grants from the Rockefeller Brothers' Fund and the Alfred P. Sloan Foundation financed it. "Report on the Tour of the Soviet Union," *State Government: The Journal of State Affairs* 32 (Autumn 1959), p. 233, CGLC, Box 350, File: Governors' Conference—National, 1959.

46. Governor Collins interview, September 27, 1979; *Governor News Conference*, February 12, 1959, p. 12; July 20, 1959, pp. 1, 5. The most thorough accounts of the trip are "Report on the Tour of the Soviet Union," *State Government: The Journal of State Affairs* 32 (Autumn 1959), pp. 233–39, CGLC, Box 350, File: Governors' Conference—National, 1959; and *A Governor Sees the Soviet: Letters from Governor Luther H. Hodges of North Carolina* (1959), CGLC, Box 351, File: Governors' Conference—Southern, 1959.

47. Governor Collins interview, September 27, 1979. Executive Committee members participating in the tour included Collins, George D. Clyde (Utah), John E. Davis (North Dakota), Stephen L. R. McNichols (Colorado), Robert B. Meyner (New Jersey), William G. Stratton (Illinois), and Cecil H. Underwood (West Virginia). Governors Luther H. Hodges (North Carolina) and Robert E. Smylie (Idaho) replaced James P. Coleman (Mississippi) and William F. Quinn (Hawaii) on the trip. *Governors' Conference: 51st Annual Meeting, August 2–5, 1959*, [p. ii], CGLC, Box 350, File: Governors' Conference—National, 1959; Collins to Members of Governors' Conference Executive Committee, January 23, 1959, CGLC, Box 350, File: Governor's Conference—Executive Committee, 1959.

48. Governor Collins interview, September 27, 1979; *Governor News Conference*, July 20, 1959, p. 1.

49. Governor Collins interview, September 27, 1979. Similar accounts of the incident are detailed in Kenneth Holland, "A Wonderful Morning in Russia," *Presbyterian Life*, September 15, 1959, pp. 22–24, CGLC, Box 370, File: Governors' Conference—National, Executive Committee, Russian Trip, 1960; and *Governor Sees the Soviet*, pp. 27–28, CGLC, Box 351, File: Governors' Conference—Southern, 1959.

50. Governor Collins interview, September 27, 1979.

51. "Interview with Premier Khrushchev at the Kremlin, Moscow, July 7, 1959," pp. 3, 5. This is a photocopy of a transcript of the meeting in Governor Collins's possession. For a thorough discussion of the Khrushchev meeting, see *Governor Sees the Soviet*, pp. 52–63, CGLC, Box 351, File: Governors' Conference—Southern, 1959.

52. *Governor News Conference*, July 20, 1959, p. 10.

53. Ibid., pp. 1, 11.

54. Ibid., pp. 4–5, 7.

55. Tallahassee *Democrat*, October 9, 1957; *Governor News Conference*, March 10, 1960, p. 8; Orlando *Sentinel Star*, September 7, 1975; Perry, "Florida's National Prestige," p. 392.

56. *Governor News Conference*, April 7, 1960, p. 1; May 5, 1960, p. 5.

Chapter 9

1. LeRoy Collins, "How It Looks from the South," *Look* 22 (May 27, 1958), pp. 92, 95–97.

2. Ibid., pp. 98–99.

3. *Governor News Conference*, August 21, 1958, pp. 9–11.

4. Tallahassee *Democrat*, September 22, 1958.

5. Tallahassee *Democrat*, September 28, 1958; St. Petersburg *Times*, September 21, 1958.

6. Tallahassee *Democrat*, September 28, 1958.

7. Frank Trippitt, in St. Petersburg *Times*, September 23, 1958.

8. *Governor News Conference*, February 12, 1959, pp. 5–6, 11; St. Petersburg *Times*, September 28, 1958.

9. Frank Trippitt, in St. Petersburg *Times*, September 27, 1958, may have been the first to use the term "Collins Plan." Perhaps because of charges of personal political promotion, Collins preferred the designation "congressional plan." *Governor News Conference*, October 2, 1958, p. 9; April 20, 1960, p. 2.

10. "Excerpts from Silverman," p. 66.

11. *Governor News Conference*, November 6, 1958, p. 2; October 9, 1958, p. 11; October 2, 1958, p. 5.

12. Ibid., July 29, 1959, pp. 6–7; March 10, 1960, pp. 5–6; April 20, 1960, p. 2; confidential memo to members of the Advisory Council, from Charles Tyroler II, executive director, March 23, 1960, CGLC, Box 366, File: Democratic National Committee, Advisory Council (Collins Plan), 1960.

13. Tomberlin, "The Negro and Education," pp. 189–90; Colburn and Scher, *Florida's Gubernatorial Politics*, p. 227.

14. *Governor News Conference,* October 16, 1958, p. 1; October 9, 1958, p. 1; December 18, 1958, pp. 8–11; Tampa *Tribune,* December 17, 19, 1958; Colburn and Scher, "Race Relations," p. 158; Governor Collins interview, September 27, 1979.

15. Miami *Herald,* October 16, 1958; February 19, September 9, 1959; Governor Collins interview, September 27, 1979; "Transcript from Board Notes," October 15, 1958, CGLC, Box 345, File: Race Relations, 1958; *Governor News Conference,* October 16, 1958, p. 1.

16. Miami *Herald,* October 16, 1958, February 19, 1959; Memorandum from Jess Yarborough, member, Board of Public Instruction of Dade County . . . , October 20, 1958, CGLC, Box 345, File: Race Relations, 1958. Collins was in Miami to receive an Annual Brotherhood Award at a Monday evening dinner. Miami *Herald,* February 15, 17, 1959.

17. *Governor News Conference,* February 19, 1959, pp. 1, 3–4, 6. On February 12, 1959, Collins compared Virginia and North Carolina in some detail (pp. 7–9).

18. The Parent Option Plan, which was advocated by Ervin and Assistant Attorney General Ralph Odum, the state's leading expert on segregation law, would have allowed parents to withdraw their children from integrated schools and provided state aid for private education. Miami *Herald,* February 19, 1959.

19. A United Press International reporter, in Miami *Herald,* February 19, 1959.

20. Tallahassee *Democrat,* April 8, 1959; "Governor's Message," *Journal of the House,* Thirty-seventh Regular Session, 1959, p. 23; Howard Jay Friedman, "1959 Legislative Action Dealing with Education," *Florida School Bulletin* 22 (September 1959), p. 14; Colburn and Scher, "Race Relations," p. 157; *Governor News Conference,* June 6, 1959, p. 2.

21. On the same day, the county-owned-and-operated school at Homestead Air Force Base admitted 20 blacks among its 350 students. Miami *Herald,* September 8, 1959. Presumably because of the school's location, its integration did not attract the attention that was accorded to Orchard Villa.

22. Miami *Herald,* September 9, 17, October 8, 1959; "Excerpts from Silverman," p. 68.

Chapter 10

1. Louis E. Lomax, "The Negro Revolt Against 'The Negro Leaders,' " *Harper's Magazine* 220 (June 1960), pp. 42, 47; Benjamin Muse, *Ten Years of Prelude: The Story of Integration since the Supreme Court's*

1954 Decision (New York: Viking Press, 1964), pp. 204–06; Leuchtenburg, *Troubled Feast*, pp. 98–99; Miami *Herald*, March 9, 1960.

2. St. Petersburg *Times*, March 2, 4, 1960; Tampa *Tribune*, March 14, 1960; Jacksonville *Florida Times-Union*, March 18, 1960; Robert M. White, "The Tallahassee Sit-Ins and CORE: A Nonviolent Revolutionary Submovement" (Ph.D. dissertation, Florida State University, 1964), pp. 102–03, 112, 115–19; Tallahassee *Democrat*, February 14, 21, 1960.

3. White, "Tallahassee Sit-Ins," pp. 122–24; Tallahassee *Democrat*, March 12, 1960.

4. White, "Tallahassee Sit-Ins," pp. 125–28; Tallahassee *Democrat*, March 13, 1960; "Statement by Governor Collins," March 12, 1960, CGLC, Box 328, File: Race Relations—Statements, 1956.

5. *Governor News Conference*, March 3, 1960, pp. 3–4; "Statement by Governor Collins," March 12, 1960, CGLC, Box 328, File: Race Relations—Statements, 1956.

6. Jacksonville *Florida Times-Union*, March 19, 1960; Tallahassee *Democrat*, March 19, 20, 1960.

7. News Release, March 18, 1960, CGLC, Box 377, File: News Releases, 1960.

8. Because he delivered the speech without a text, reports on his precise wording varied. The Miami *Herald*, March 22, 1960, printed a partial transcript. "Excerpts from Silverman," pp. 67–73, included some quotes from the speech. "Remarks by Governor LeRoy Collins," March 20, 1960, CGLC, Box 377, File: News Releases, 1960, was a two-page statement that was distributed to the press before the speech which briefly noted Collins's ideas.

9. Governor Collins interview, April 10, 1976.

10. Miami *Herald*, March 21, 1960; "Excerpts from Silverman," p. 69.

11. "Excerpts from Silverman," p. 70.

12. Sandra L. Fanning, "A Study of Changes in Racial Attitudes as Revealed in Selected Speeches of LeRoy Collins, 1955–1965" (M.A. thesis, University of South Florida, 1968), pp. 39, 53–66, also contends that the "sit-in speech" was an important turning point in Collins's racial views.

13. "Excerpts from Silverman," p. 70. According to the abstract prepared for the press, Collins was to have said, "Any department the management does not wish to make available to all, I think the management should close down," "Remarks by Governor LeRoy Collins," March 20, 1960, CGLC, Box 377, File: News Releases, 1960. He did not make that specific statement in his ad-libbed talk.

14. "Excerpts from Silverman," pp. 71–72.

15. Governor Collins interview, April 10, 1976.

16. Miami *Herald*, March 21, 22, 1960; Frank Trippitt, "Race Tension Worries Capital," St. Petersburg *Times*, March 21, 1960; Tallahassee *Democrat*, March 21, 1960; Tampa *Tribune*, March 22, 1960.

17. St. Petersburg *Evening Independent*, editorial, March 22, 1960. See also editorials in the Ft. Myers *News-Press*, March 22, 1960; and Jacksonville *Florida Times-Union*, March 22, 1960.

18. Charleston, South Carolina, *News and Courier*, editorial, March 22, 1960; Birmingham, Alabama, *News*, editorial, April 6, 1960; St. Louis *Post-Dispatch*, March 21, 1960; Tallahassee *Democrat*, March 21, 1960.

19. Tallahassee *Democrat*, March 21, 1960; Miami *Herald*, March 21, 22, 1960. Lomax, "Negro Revolt," pp. 41–48, analyzes the impact of the sit-in movement on black leadership.

20. St. Louis *Post-Dispatch*, editorial, March 22, 1960; Washington *Post*, editorial, March 23, 1960. See also editorials in the *Christian Science Monitor*, March 23, 1960; Akron, Ohio, *Beacon Journal*, March 24, 1960; Charleston, West Virginia, *Gazette*, April 6, 1960; New York *Post*, March 22, 1960; Philadelphia *Inquirer*, March 22, 1960; and Rochester, New York, *Times-Union*, March 22, 1960.

21. Ed Gunther, quoted in the Miami *Herald*, March 21, 1960, William H. Roundtree, Cocoa, Florida, to Collins, March 22, 1960, Collins Papers.

22. Editorials in the Miami *Daily News*, March 21, 1960; Miami *Herald*, March 22, 1960; Bradenton *Herald*, March 22, 1960; Daytona Beach *Morning Journal*, March 22, 1960. See also editorials in the Sarasota *Herald-Tribune*, March 22, 1960; Orlando *Sentinel*, March 22, 1960; Pensacola *Journal*, March 22, 1960; Ocala *Star-Banner*, March 22, 1960; and Tampa *Tribune*, March 22, 1960.

23. Although Collins had expected a strong reaction from both sides, the conservatives' virulence shocked and perplexed him. Governor Collins interview, April 10, 1976. Seventeen years later, he told a reporter, "I read that speech now and it seems so puny." Tom Fiedler, "Ahead of His Time," Tallahassee *Democrat*, October 9, 1977.

24. For an analysis of mythology's impact on southern society, see Patrick Gerster and Nicholas Cords, eds., *Myth and Southern History* (Chicago: Rand McNally, 1974).

25. Key, *Southern Politics*, pp. 82, 88, 96.

26. Hartsfield and Roady, *Florida Votes*, p. 59; Miami *Herald*, February 21, March 9, May 22, 25, 26, 1960.

27. *Governor News Conference*, January 7, 1960, p. 4; January 28, 1960, p. 1; March 3, 1960, p. 6; March 10, 1960, p. 9; March 17, 1960, pp.

4–5; March 31, 1960, p. 5; April 20, 1960, p. 3; May 5, 1960, p. 1.

28. Caldwell interview; Johnson, "Governors C," Tallahassee *Democrat*, May 22, 1960.

29. Morris interview, July 13, 1977; Tallahassee *Daily Democrat*, May 3, 1950; Johnson, "Governors C," Tallahassee *Daily Democrat*, May 22, 1960; Caldwell interview.

30. *Governor News Conference*, January 22, 1959, p. 7.

31. Johnson, "Governors C," Tallahassee *Democrat*, May 22, 1960; Johnson interview, October 15, 1975.

32. Caldwell interview; Tallahassee *Democrat*, May 22, 1960.

33. *Governor News Conference*, May 20, 1960, p. 2; Key, *Southern Politics*, p. 102. A Miami *Herald*, May 22, 1960, poll showed Bryant leading, with 38.2 percent of the vote; Carlton, 36.5 percent; and 25.3 percent remained undecided.

34. *Governor News Conference*, May 20, 1960, p. 1; Miami *Herald*, May 24, 1960.

35. John Boyles, in Miami *Herald*, May 22, 1960.

36. Steve Trumbull, in Miami *Herald*, May 21, 1960.

37. Bryant received 512,757 votes (55.2 percent) and Carlton 416,052 (44.8 percent). Hartsfield and Roady, *Florida Votes*, p. 59.

38. Miami *Herald*, May 22, 26, 1960.

39. John B. McDermott, in Miami *Herald*, May 26, 1960.

40. Delaney, "Another Political First," Orlando *Sentinel*, Florida Magazine, July 10, 1960.

41. Miami *Herald*, May 26, 1960; Black, *Southern Governors*, p. 96; William Hammack, "Gov. Collins Discusses . . . ," Atlanta *Journal and Constitution Magazine*, July 10, 1960.

42. New York *Times*, editorial, May 26, 1960.

Chapter 11

1. Theodore H. White, *The Making of the President, 1960* (New York: Atheneum House, 1961), pp. 164, 138–42, 284–91; Theodore C. Sorensen, *Kennedy* (New York: Harper and Row, 1965), pp. 80–92, 97–133.

2. White, *Making of the President, 1960*, pp. 34–55, 93–137.

3. Kenneth S. Davis, *The Politics of Honor: A Biography of Adlai E. Stevenson* (New York: G. P. Putnam's Sons, 1967), pp. 400, 409; White, *Making of the President, 1960*, pp. 55–59, 131.

4. Davis, *Politics of Honor*, pp. 402, 425, 434; John Bartlow Martin,

Adlai Stevenson and the World: The Life of Adlai E. Stevenson (Garden City, New York: Doubleday and Company, 1977), pp. 514–15.

5. Crawford Rice, director of news and public affairs, WTVT (CBS), Tampa, Florida, on that station's convention program from Los Angeles, California, which preceded the network telecast each night. Tape 6, Collins Papers.

6. New York *Times*, January 13, 1960; Paul T. David, Ralph M. Goldman, and Richard C. Bain, *The Politics of National Party Conventions* (Washington: Brookings Institution, 1960), p. 66.

7. *Governor News Conference*, January 20, 1960, p. 10.

8. Miami *Herald*, February 29, March 16, 18, April 2, 1960; Arthur Krock, "Butler Still Demos' Angry Man," Miami *Herald*, March 8, 1960; James McCartney, "Outspoken Butler Defies the Rules," Miami *Herald*, March 19, 1960. When interviewing Collins on the July 3, 1960, NBC program "Meet the Press," Frank Vandelinter, of the Nashville *Banner*, mentioned Butler's statement that Johnson could not be nominated because he was a southerner. Tape 70, Collins Papers. A newsperson at a Collins press conference cited Humphrey's evaluation of Butler. *Governor News Conference*, March 17, 1960, p. 2.

9. McCartney, "Outspoken Butler," Miami *Herald*, March 19, 1960; Tallahassee *Democrat*, May 22, 1960; Allen Morris, "Cracker Politics," Tallahassee *Democrat*, May 7, 1960; *Official Report of the Proceedings of the Democratic National Convention and Committee* (Washington: National Document Publishers, 1964), p. xxix; *Governor News Conference*, March 17, 1960, p. 2.

10. Tampa *Tribune*, January 17, 1960; Symington to Collins, January 18, 1960, Collins Papers; Collins to Symington, January 27, 1960, Collins Papers.

11. Truman and Spottswood had been friends since 1946, when they had met during a presidential vacation at Key West. Mrs. Truman, Mrs. Spottswood, Mrs. Collins, Leslie Biffle, secretary of the U.S. Senate during Truman's presidency, and John Perry also attended the luncheon-reception. Miami *Herald*, February 21, 27, 1960; *Governor News Conference*, March 3, 1960, p. 1.

12. Miami *Herald*, February 27, 1960; *Governor News Conference*, March 3, 1960, p. 1; Truman to Collins, March 6, 1960, Collins Papers.

13. Miami *Herald*, May 23, 1960; Harry S. Truman, "How Stevenson Let Me Down," *Look* 24 (June 7, 1960), p. 123; Martin, *Adlai Stevenson*, p. 512.

14. Davidson to Collins, February 8, 1960, CGLC, Box 336, File:

Democratic National Committee, July 16, 1960; Collins to Davidson, February 12, 1960, ibid.

15. Stevenson to Collins, May 25, 1960, Collins Papers; Collins to Stevenson, June 2, 1960, Collins Papers.

16. New York *Times*, January 17, May 21, 1960.

17. New York *Times*, January 17, May 21, 25, 26, 1960.

18. Butler and Governor Brown, of California, the host state for the convention, were also Catholic, which added to the committee's concern. New York *Times*, January 17, May 21, 1960; White, *Making of the President, 1960*, pp. 109–10, 126–30, 288.

19. Jack Bass and Walter DeVries, *The Transformation of Southern Politics: Social Change and Political Consequence since 1945* (New York: New American Library, 1977), pp. 5, 26; *Newsweek* 55 (May 30, 1960), p. 19; David, Goldman, and Bain, *Politics of Conventions,* p. 66.

20. New York *Times*, May 21, 25, 1960. Representatives from the Knights of Columbus, B'nai B'rith, Almas Temple Shrine, and the Order of Ahepa composed the Washington Interfaith Committee. Miami *Herald*, May 22, 1960.

21. Miami *Herald*, February 28, 1960; *Governor News Conference,* March 3, 1960, p. 4; March 10, 1960, p. 8.

22. New York *Times*, May 21, 22, 1960; editorial, May 26, 1960.

23. Jack Anderson, "Washington Merry-Go-Round," Miami *Herald,* June 3, 1960.

24. Hammack, "Gov. Collins," Atlanta *Journal and Constitution Magazine,* July 10, 1960.

25. Collins on the July 3, 1960, NBC program "Meet the Press," Tape 70, Collins Papers.

26. New York *Times*, May 21, 25, 1960; Miami *Herald,* May 25, 1960; Anderson, "Washington Merry-Go-Round," Miami *Herald,* June 3, 1960.

27. Miami *Herald*, June 8, 1960.

28. Charles A. H. Thomson and Frances M. Shattuck, *The 1956 Presidential Campaign* (Washington: Brookings Institution, 1960), pp. 155–63; Sorensen, *Kennedy,* pp. 90–92; Collins to Donald Murray, Brooklyn, New York, May 13, 1964, Collins Papers; Collins on July 3, 1960, NBC program "Meet the Press," Tape 70, Collins Papers.

29. I. Lee Potter, special assistant for southern affairs to Republican National Chairman Thurston B. Morton, in a letter to southern Republican state chairmen. Miami *Herald*, March 19, 1960.

30. *Newsweek* 55 (May 23, 1960), p. 54; (May 2, 1960), p. 17.

31. New York *Times*, July 3, 1960.

32. New York *Times*, July 1, 4, 5, 6, 1960.

33. Telegrams from Collins to Truman, July 1, 1960, and July 2, 1960, CGLC, Box 336, File: Democratic National Committee—Convention Arrangements, 1960; Collins on the July 3, 1960, NBC program "Meet the Press," Tape 70, Collins Papers.

34. Interview with Governor LeRoy Collins, May 22, 1975.

35. Tallahassee *Democrat,* July 4, 1960; New York *Times,* July 8, 1960.

36. "Press release from the office of Governor Collins," July 2, 1959, CGLC, Box 357, File: News Releases, 1959; *Governor News Conference,* January 7, 1960, p. 9; January 20, 1960, p. 5; Smathers to Collins, January 14, 1960, Collins Papers.

37. Tampa *Tribune,* editorial, January 17, 1960.

38. *Governor News Conference,* January 7, 1960, p. 9; John L. Boyles, "Capitol Corner," Miami *Herald,* January 10, 1960.

39. Smathers to Collins, January 14, 1960, Collins Papers; *Governor News Conference,* January 20, 1960, pp. 5–9.

40. New York *Times,* January 25, 1960; Smathers to Collins, January 25, 1960, Collins Papers; "News Release from the Office of the Governor," January 26, 1960, Collins Papers.

41. Miami *Herald,* February 23, 28, 29, March 10, May 15, 1960. According to rumors, Smathers had promised Kennedy ten of the twenty-nine delegates; in return, Kennedy did not enter the Florida primary. Instead, he received only one committed member in the delegation. Grant Stockdale, former Dade County commissioner and Kennedy's chief Florida organizer, was chosen as an alternate. Miami Mayor Robert King High, a strong Kennedy backer, was not selected. John B. McDermott, "Politics in Florida," Miami *Herald,* March 6, 1960.

42. *Governor News Conference,* March 3, 1960, pp. 8, 10; Miami *Herald,* March 10, 1960; John L. Boyles, "Capitol Corner," Miami *Herald,* March 13, 1960.

43. "For the Press," May 14, 1960, CGLC, Box 377, File: News Releases, 1960; *Governor News Conference,* March 31, 1960, pp. 2–4; April 20, 1960, pp. 1–2; Collins to Secretary of State R. A. Gray, June 13, 1960, Collins Papers; Miami *Herald,* May 27, 1960.

Chapter 12

1. Arthur M. Schlesinger, Jr., *Robert Kennedy and His Times* (Boston: Houghton Mifflin, 1978), p. 204.

2. Lakeland *Ledger,* editorial, May 25, 1960.

3. Malcolm B. Johnson, "South Fights Rights Plank," Tallahassee

Democrat, July 13, 1960; New York *Times*, July 12, 13, 1960; *Official Report*, p. 72; WTVT convention program, Tape 3, Collins Papers.

4. Johnson, "South Fights Rights Plank," Tallahassee *Democrat*, July 13, 1960; Miami *Herald*, July 11, 1960; WTVT convention program, Tape 3, Collins Papers.

5. New York *Times*, July 6, 11, 12, 1960; Johnson, "South Fights Rights Plank," Tallahassee *Democrat*, July 13, 1960; WTVT convention program, Tape 6, Collins Papers.

6. Johnson, "South Fights Rights Plank," Tallahassee *Democrat*, July 13, 1960; J. H. Clendinen, "Floridians Ask Truman to Rush to Convention," Tampa *Tribune*, July 13, 1960; Rice on WTVT convention program, Tape 3, Collins Papers.

7. Johnson, "South Fights Rights Plank," Tallahassee *Democrat*, July 13, 1960; WTVT convention program, Tape 3, Collins Papers.

8. WTVT convention program, Tape 3, Collins Papers.

9. Don Shoemaker, "Collins on Rostrum: Match Needs with Deeds," Miami *Herald*, July 13, 1960.

10. Sarasota *Herald-Tribune*, July 14, 1960; *Official Report*, pp. 98–99.

11. Davis, *Politics of Honor*, pp. 400–32.

12. Governor LeRoy Collins, "Demos Never Long-Faced," Jacksonville *Journal*, July 12, 1960. During the convention, Collins wrote a series of columns for United Press International that expressed his views on the proceedings.

13. *Official Report*, pp. 49, 51; Rice on WTVT convention program, Tape 6, Collins Papers; Johnson, "South Fights Rights Plank," Tallahassee *Democrat*, July 13, 1960.

14. *Official Report*, pp. 52–55, 58. A newsperson once asked Collins if he was a "do-gooder." Collins replied, "I hope so." He preferred "do-gooders" to "do-badders." *Governor News Conference*, May 20, 1960, p. 5.

15. Tallahassee *Democrat*, July 13, 1960; George E. Sokolsky, "Deplores Lack of Oratory, Says Collins Best," Tallahassee *Democrat*, July 19, 1960.

16. Daytona Beach *Morning Journal*, editorial, July 13, 1960; Tampa *Times*, editorial, July 16, 1960.

17. Governor LeRoy Collins, "Few Listen: Collins Gives View of Talk," Jacksonville *Journal*, July 13, 1960; Johnson, "South Fights Rights Plank," Tallahassee *Democrat*, July 13, 1960; Richard C. Bain and Judith H. Parris, *Convention Decisions and Voting Records*, 2nd ed. (Washington: Brookings Institution, 1973), p. 304.

18. Jacksonville *Journal*, July 14, 1960; *Official Report*, p. 51; Roosevelt to Collins, July 26, 1960, Collins Papers; Mary Kirwin, Columbus, Ohio, to Collins, July 14, 1960, Collins Papers; Governor Collins interview, May 22, 1975.

19. Governor Collins interview, May 22, 1975; Collins, "Few Listen," Jacksonville *Journal*, July 13, 1960; New York *Times*, July 13, 1960; *Official Report*, p. 61.

20. Governor LeRoy Collins, "Collins' Gavel Holding Up," Jacksonville *Journal*, July 15, 1960; David Laux, New York City, to Collins, July 13, 1960, Collins Papers; Sandra Archer, West Palm Beach, to Collins, July 11, 1960, Collins Papers; Bob Thomas, "Convention Noise Blamed on Politics," Tallahassee *Democrat*, July 15, 1960.

21. Governor Collins interview, May 22, 1975; White, *Making of the President, 1960*, pp. 157–58, 188–91; *Governor News Conference*, July 21, 1960, p. 6.

22. *Official Report*, pp. 75–77, 86; Malcolm B. Johnson, "Florida Group Is Appeased," Tallahassee *Democrat*, July 15, 1960.

23. *Official Report*, p. 103; Russell Baker, "Highlights and Chronology of Nominating Session of the Democratic Convention," New York *Times*, July 14, 1960.

24. Tampa *Tribune*, July 14, 1960; *Official Report*, p. 111; Baker, "Highlights and Chronology," New York *Times*, July 14, 1960.

25. *Official Report*, p. 103.

26. Martin, *Adlai Stevenson*, pp. 525–28; White, *Making of the President, 1960*, pp. 195–201.

27. New York *Times*, July 14, 1960; *Official Report*, pp. 142–43. A constituent later questioned Collins on the propriety of using the term "hoodlums." He admitted that its use had disturbed a number of people. He felt a "stinging rebuke" might bring the overly enthusiastic group back to reality. He did not mean the word to be harsh, and, in fact, explained, "I have often used it at home when my children have been especially unruly." Kurt Arnold, St. Petersburg, to Collins, July 18, 1960, Collins Papers; Collins to Arnold, August 24, 1960, Collins Papers. The governor did not always use the term in this innocuous manner. In January 1960 he called an incident of a swastika being painted on a Jacksonville synagogue an act of "hoodlumism and vandalism." *Governor News Conference*, January 7, 1960, p. 11.

28. Eugene Holloway Roseboom, *A History of Presidential Elections* (New York: Macmillan, 1967), p. 550; White, *Making of the President, 1960*, pp. 198–99.

29. Schlesinger, *Robert Kennedy*, p. 213. With 761 votes needed to

nominate, the final totals were Kennedy, 806; Johnson, 409; Symington, 86; Stevenson, 79½; Mississippi Governor Ross Barnett, 23; Smathers, 30; Humphrey, 41½; and New Jersey Governor Robert B. Meyner, 43. *Official Report*, pp. 168–69.

30. Tampa *Times*, July 14, 1960; Governor LeRoy Collins, "Collins Pleased with Nominating Session," Tampa *Times*, July 14, 1960; *Governor News Conference*, July 21, 1960, pp. 7–8.

31. Richard Wilson, of Coles Publications, and Collins on July 3, 1960, NBC program "Meet the Press," Tape 70, Collins Papers; Donald Murray, Brooklyn, New York, to Collins, December 30, 1963, Collins Papers; Collins to Murray, May 13, 1964, Collins Papers.

32. Governor Collins interview, November 19, 1975. Collins received 1½ votes on the first roll call. Thomson and Shattuck, *1956 Presidential Campaign*, pp. 156–57.

33. Marion T. Gaines, "Southerner's Chances Rise," Pensacola *News*, September 17, 1957; *Newsweek* 50 (September 30, 1957), p. 40; New York *Times*, May 22, 1960; Morris, "Cracker Politics," Tallahassee *Democrat*, May 7, 1960; Governor Collins interview, April 10, 1976; Hammack, "Gov. Collins," Atlanta *Journal and Constitution Magazine*, July 10, 1960. A more humorous suggestion surfaced in a May 1960 news conference. A reporter asked Collins if he could resist the rumored plan that he would run as vice-president on a Republican ticket headed by Richard M. Nixon. Amidst the laughter, Collins stated, "That does not appeal to me any more than I am sure it appeals to Mr. Nixon." *Governor News Conference*, May 20, 1960, p. 4.

34. Collins returned to Florida by car after the convention. At every stop, he was recognized. Governor Collins interview, May 22, 1975.

35. Governor Collins interviews May 22, 1975, November 19, 1975.

36. Schlesinger, *Robert Kennedy*, p. 216.

37. Senator Monroney quoted in Davis, *Politics of Honor*, p. 432.

38. Sorensen, *Kennedy*, p. 164; Schlesinger, *Robert Kennedy*, p. 218; Collins, "Collins' Gavel Holding Up," Jacksonville *Journal*, July 15, 1960.

39. *Official Report*, pp. 236, 243, 246; Governor Collins interview, May 22, 1975.

40. According to an editorial in the Peoria, Illinois, *Journal Star*, July 19, 1960, the only thing gaining "universal agreement" at the convention was the excellent impression made by Collins.

41. Bob Thomas, "Collins Fast with Ad-Libs at the Convention," Tallahassee *Democrat*, July 16, 1960.

42. Malcolm B. Johnson wrote, "Governor Collins is drawing applause from old timers at convention coverage for the way he is handling the

gavel and how he comes through on television," Johnson, "Floridians Unmoved by Bandwagon," Tallahassee *Democrat*, July 14, 1960. At a Collins news conference following the convention, reporters mentioned comments from motion picture and television people complimenting his performance and appearance. One said, "We heard you described variously as a 'political Ronald Coleman' and a 'young Grandpa McCoy.'" *Governor News Conference*, July 21, 1960, p. 9.

43. Bertha Moslin, Clifton, New Jersey, to the editor of the New York *Daily News*, July 21, 1960.

44. Editorials in the New York *Times*, July 15, 1960; Chicago *Tribune*, July 16, 1960; Knoxville *News-Sentinel*, July 15, 1960; Daytona Beach *Evening News*, July 16, 1960; Lakeland *Ledger*, July 20, 1960; Tampa *Times*, July 16, 1960.

45. Cannon to Drew Pearson, a nationally syndicated columnist, July 25, 1960, Collins Papers; Douglas to Collins, July 14, 1960, Collins Papers; Farley to Collins, July 28, 1960, Collins Papers; Pucinski to Collins, July 14, 1960, Collins Papers; Truman to Collins, August 23, 1960, CGLC, Box 365, File: Democratic National Committee, August 16, 1960; Vice-President and Mrs. Nixon to Collins, July 18, 1960, Collins Papers.

46. *Governor News Conference*, July 21, 1960, pp. 6–7.

47. Ibid., p. 6.

48. For example, Collins to Martin Aaronson, Van Nuys, California, August 4, 1960, Collins Papers.

49. Miami, Daytona Beach, West Palm Beach, and Fort Lauderdale peacefully integrated their lunch counters. Tampa *Tribune*, September 4, 1960.

50. Tampa *Tribune*, August 29, September 4, 1960; "The Jacksonville Riot," a special report by the Florida Council on Human Relations, September 1960, p. 2, CGLC, Box 379, File: Race Relations, 1960.

51. According to an unidentified leader, sixty Jacksonville segregationists plus a large number of Ku Klux Klan and Citizens' Council members from neighboring towns and south Georgia made up the group of whites. New York *Times*, August 28, 1960.

52. "The Jacksonville Riot," pp. 3–5, CGLC, Box 379, File: Race Relations, 1960; Tampa *Tribune*, August 28, 29, 31, 1960.

53. New York *Times*, August 29, 1960; Tampa *Tribune*, August 31, 1960; Miami *Herald*, September 1, 1960.

54. Tampa *Tribune*, August 29, 30, 1960. At the Saturday gathering of whites, one man passed out leaflets signed by the "Segregation Forces of Duval County" that said, "We have warned the merchants of Jacksonville

with lunch counters that if they allow our Florida laws to be flounted [*sic*] we will immediately institute a county-wide boycott against any establishment guilty of such acts." New York *Times*, August 28, 1960. Facing such threats, merchants no doubt would have welcomed a "buck-passing" mayoral mandate.

55. Tampa *Tribune*, September 1, 1960; *Governor News Conference*, September 1, 1960, p. 4; Tallahassee *Democrat*, August 31, 1960.

56. New York *Times*, August 28, 1960; *Governor News Conference*, September 1, 1960, pp. 5, 9.

57. *Governor News Conference*, September 1, 1960, pp. 5, 7, 9–10.

58. *Florida Governor Remarks, 1960*, "Remarks by Governor LeRoy Collins to the Executives' Club of Chicago, Chicago, Illinois, September 9, 1960," pp. 1, 3, 7, 8, 10. Selected speeches delivered by Collins in 1960 are bound under this title.

59. St. Petersburg *Times*, September 18, 1960.

60. Collins to Spottswood, Key West, Florida, August 16, 1960, Collins Papers. Collins's assessment proved to be accurate. Richard M. Nixon did win Florida's electoral votes; his total was 795,476 (51.1 percent), compared to Kennedy's 748,700 (48.5 percent). Hartsfield and Roady, *Florida Votes*, p. 33.

61. Jim Hardee, Tallahassee, to Collins, September 1, 1960, CGLC, Box 365, File: Democratic National Committee, September 10, 1960; Collins to Hardee, September 13, 1960, ibid.

62. *Governor News Conference*, September 29, 1960, pp. 10, 11; September 1, 1960, pp. 15–16; August 18, 1960, pp. 1–2; July 21, 1960, p. 3; October 14, 1960, p. 8.

63. St. Petersburg *Times*, October 11, 1960; Tallahassee *Democrat*, October 10, 1960; Julia Sullivan Chapman, "A Southern Moderate Advocates Compliance: A Study of LeRoy Collins as Director of the Community Relations Service" (M.A. thesis, University of South Florida, 1974), p. 19.

64. Frank Trippett, "Florida's Gov. LeRoy Collins: Creative Change Is His Way of Life," St. Petersburg *Times*, October 11, 1960.

65. *Florida Governor Remarks, 1960*, "Remarks by Governor LeRoy Collins to Anti-Defamation League of B'nai B'rith, Hollywood, Florida, December 10, 1960," pp. 3–4.

Chapter 13

1. For a thorough analysis of Collins's NAB presidency, see Manny

Lucoff, "LeRoy Collins and the NAB: Experiment in the Public Interest" (Ph.D. dissertation, University of Iowa, 1971).

2. Interview with Governor LeRoy Collins, November 10, 1977; Ruth F. Espey, "The Anatomy of Defeat: The 1968 United States Senatorial Campaign of LeRoy Collins" (M.A. thesis, University of South Florida, 1974), p. 49; Chapman, "Southern Moderate," pp. 19–20.

3. Chapman, "Southern Moderate," p. 20; Espey, "Anatomy of Defeat," pp. 49–50.

4. Chapman, "Southern Moderate," pp. 20–21; Espey, "Anatomy of Defeat," pp. 50–51; Governor Collins interview, November 10, 1977.

5. For a thorough analysis of Collins and the CRS, see Chapman, "Southern Moderate." Much of the following discussion was published in Thomas R. Wagy, "Governor LeRoy Collins of Florida and the Selma Crisis of 1965," *Florida Historical Quarterly* 57 (April 1979), pp. 403–20.

6. Marquis Childs, "Peacemaker Stands in the Line of Fire," Nashville *Tennessean*, March 16, 1965; *Annual Report of the Community Relations Service, Fiscal Year 1965* (Washington, 1966), p. 1, Collins Papers; Governor Collins interview, November 10, 1977; John Herbers, *The Lost Priority: What Happened to the Civil Rights Movement in America?* (New York: Funk and Wagnalls, 1970), p. 156.

7. Governor Collins interview, November 10, 1977; Espey, "Anatomy of Defeat," p. 52. The Florida newspapers that commented on the appointment concurred with the view of the editors of the Miami *Herald*, July 4, 1964, who believed the nomination "should reassure both friends and foes of the Civil Rights Act." See editorials in the Tampa *Tribune*, July 5, 1964; St. Petersburg *Times*, July 5, 1964; Daytona Beach *Morning Journal*, July 9, 1964; and Miami *News*, July 9, 1964.

8. *Time* 84 (July 17, 1964), pp. 26–27; Sherrill, *Gothic Politics*, pp. 252–53; Lucoff, "LeRoy Collins and the NAB," p. 240.

9. Herbers, *Lost Priority*, p. 156.

10. Espey, "Anatomy of Defeat," pp. 62–63; Governor Collins interview, November 19, 1975; Chapman, "Southern Moderate," p. 64.

11. Chapman, "Southern Moderate," pp. 25, 29, 33.

12. Miami *Herald*, March 11, 1965; Charles E. Fager, *Selma, 1965* (New York: Scribner, 1974), pp. 8–9, 18–20; Oates, *Let the Trumpet Sound*, pp. 325–30; Martin Luther King, "Behind the Selma March," *Saturday Review* 48 (April 3, 1965), p. 16; New York *Times*, February 14, 1965, cited in Chapman, "Southern Moderate," p. 48; New York *Times*, March 14, 1965. For an analysis of King's strategy, see David J. Garrow, *Protest at Selma: Martin Luther King, Jr., and the Voting Rights Act of*

1965 (New Haven, Connecticut: Yale University Press, 1978), pp. 220–36.

13. Fager, *Selma*, pp. 5, 18; *Time* 85 (March 19, 1965), p. 23. The New York *Times*, March 9, 1965, noted that estimates of the size of Clark's posse ranged from one hundred to four hundred.

14. Fager, *Selma*, pp. 47, 86–87; New York *Times*, March 9, 1965.

15. Fager, *Selma*, pp. 81, 93–95; Montgomery *Advertiser*, March 8, 14, 1965; Selma *Times-Journal*, March 8, 1965; *Hosea Williams* v. *George C. Wallace*, 240 F. Supp. 104 (1965); Garrow, *Protest at Selma*, pp. 73–77. The New York *Times*, March 9, 1965, reported these casualty statistics. The Selma *Times-Journal*, March 8, 1965, stated that eighteen of the fifty-six treated were hospitalized, and the Montgomery *Advertiser*, March 8, 1965, noted that only thirty-five were treated.

16. Fager, *Selma*, pp. 98, 102; Garrow, *Protest at Selma*, pp. 78–82, 87–91; Montgomery *Advertiser*, March 9, 1965; Bob Ingram, "Lingo Nearly Got Ax over Selma Debacle," Montgomery *Advertiser*, March 14, 1965; New York *Times*, March 9, 1965.

17. Lyndon B. Johnson, *The Vantage Point: Perspectives of the Presidency, 1963–1968* (New York: Popular Library, 1971), pp. 162–63.

18. Miami *Herald*, March 10, 1956; David L. Lewis, *King: A Critical Biography* (New York: Praeger Publishers, 1970), pp. 277–78; *Time* 85 (March 19, 1965), p. 25; Garrow, *Protest at Selma*, pp. 83–85.

19. Governor Collins interview, November 10, 1977. Agency conciliators had been in Selma since January 1965 seeking to open communications between the conflicting factions. CRS staffmen Max Sechrest, Fred Miller, and James Laue had been intimately involved in the crisis and worked closely with Collins in resolving the dispute. Governor Collins interview, November 10, 1977; Chapman, "Southern Moderate," pp. 49–51.

20. Chapman, "Southern Moderate," p. 54; Governor Collins interview, November 10, 1977.

21. Miami *Herald*, March 10, 12, 1965; Tallahassee *Democrat*, March 11, 1965; King, "Behind the Selma March," p. 57; Chapman, "Southern Moderate," p. 55.

22. Governor Collins interview, November 10, 1977; Tampa *Tribune*, March 11, 1956, cited in Chapman, "Southern Moderate," p. 54.

23. King, "Behind the Selma March," pp. 16, 56. For a discussion of the conflicting interpretations of the meeting, see Lewis, *King*, pp. 278–79. According to Oates, *Let the Trumpet Sound*, p. 350, King decided on a partial march in discussions with his advisers on Monday evening.

24. Selma *Times-Journal*, March 9, 10, 1965; Montgomery *Advertiser*, March 10, 1965; *Time* 85 (March 19, 1965), p. 25.

25. Selma *Times-Journal*, March 10, 1965.

26. Governor Collins interview, November 10, 1977.

27. Governor Collins interview, November 10, 1977.

28. An unidentified informant, New York *Times*, March 10, 1965.

29. Selma *Times-Journal*, March 9, 10, 1965; Lewis, *King*, p. 279; Montgomery *Advertiser*, March 10, 1965; Fager, *Selma*, p. 103; New York *Times*, March 10, 1965.

30. Governor Collins interview, November 10, 1977; Montgomery *Advertiser*, March 12, 1965. King's account in "Behind the Selma March" differed only slightly, but did contend that no deal was made.

31. Governor Collins interview, November 10, 1977; St. Petersburg *Times*, March 10, 1965.

32. Selma *Times-Journal*, March 10, 1965; Montgomery *Advertiser*, March 10, 1965; Fager, *Selma*, p. 103; Governor Collins interview, November 10, 1977. The phrase "human wall" is from King, "Behind the Selma March," p. 57.

33. Credited to an "informed government source" in the Miami *Herald*, March 11, 1965.

34. Fager, *Selma*, pp. 103–05; Selma *Times-Journal*, March 10, 1965; *Time* 85 (March 19, 1965), p. 26.

35. Andrew Kopkind, "Selma," *New Republic* 152 (March 20, 1965), p. 8.

36. Fager, *Selma*, p. 104; *Time* 85 (March 19, 1965), p. 26.

37. Fager, *Selma*, pp. 104–05. *Time* 85 (March 19, 1965), p. 26, and Lewis, *King*, p. 280, also state that Wallace acted to discredit King.

38. *Time* 85 (March 19, 1965), p. 26.

39. Fager, *Selma*, p. 105; New York *Times*, March 10, 1965; Oates, *Let the Trumpet Sound*, p. 352.

40. Miami *Herald*, March 11, 1965; New York *Times*, March 10, 1965; St. Petersburg *Times*, March 10, 1965.

41. Governor Collins interview, November 10, 1977; *Congressional Quarterly Almanac*, 89th Cong., 1st Session (Washington: Congressional Quarterly Service, 1965), vol. 21, p. 563. Garrow, *Protest at Selma*, pp. 133–60, analyzes the impact of the events in Selma on the passage of the voting rights bill.

42. *Williams* v. *Wallace*, pp. 110–11; Johnson, *Vantage Point*, p. 163.

43. Chapman, "Southern Moderate," p. 60.

44. Miami *Herald*, editorial, March 11, 1965; Tallahassee *Democrat*, March 21, 1965.

45. Pensacola *Journal*, March 26, 1965; Miami *Herald*, March 23, 1965; Orlando *Sentinel*, March 23, 1965; Tallahassee *Democrat*, March 23, 1965.

46. John W. Hastings to Collins, March 23, 1965, Collins Papers, cited in Wagy, "Governor LeRoy Collins of Florida and the Selma Crisis of 1965," p. 417.

47. Katherine A. Cunningham to Collins, March 25, 1965, Collins Papers, cited in Wagy, "Governor LeRoy Collins of Florida and the Selma Crisis of 1965," p. 417.

48. Governor Collins interview, November 10, 1977.

49. Chapman, "Southern Moderate," pp. 78, 81–83; Lustig, "He's Tallahassee's Own Statesman," Tallahassee *Democrat*, September 10, 1967.

50. Herbers, *Lost Priority*, p. 86; Leuchtenburg, *Troubled Feast*, pp. 153–54.

Chapter 14

1. Chapman, "Southern Moderate," p. 98. Collins officially declared his candidacy on January 26, 1968. Espey, "Anatomy of Defeat," pp. 66–67, 78. This work provides a good analysis of the 1968 campaign.

2. Dyckman, "LeRoy Collins," St. Petersburg *Times*, The Floridian Magazine, March 15, 1970; Espey, "Anatomy of Defeat," p. 68.

3. McLendon, "The LeRoy Collins Years," St. Petersburg *Times*, The Floridian Magazine, July 7, 1974.

4. Claude Kirk, of West Palm Beach, defeated Miami Mayor Robert King High by a vote of 821,190 to 688,233. Espey, "Anatomy of Defeat," pp. 45–48, 64–66, 70–73, 135, 139; Tallahassee *Democrat*, November 9, 1966.

5. Espey, "Anatomy of Defeat," pp. 73, 75, 134–35.

6. Ibid., pp. 76, 84–91, 94–97, 99–100. Faircloth claimed he actually "steered away from the race issue" and disavowed some of the advertising in his behalf. Collins responded by citing specific incidents in which Faircloth used the race issue. Ibid., pp. 99, 101, 103.

7. Dyckman, "LeRoy Collins," St. Petersburg *Times*, The Floridian Magazine, March 15, 1970.

8. Anonymous letter to the editor of the Tampa *Tribune*, April 2, 1968.

9. Mayo *Free Press*, editorial, May 23, 1968.

10. In the first primary, Collins received 49.1 percent of the votes;

Faircloth, 46 percent; and two minor candidates, the remainder. Espey, "Anatomy of Defeat," p. 91. The results in the runoff election were 410,689 votes for Collins and 407,696 votes for Faircloth. Tom Adams, Secretary of State, comp., *Tabulation of Official Vote, Florida Primary Elections, Democratic and Republican, May 7, 1968 and May 28, 1968*, p. 23.

11. Governor Collins interview, November 10, 1977; Dyckman, "LeRoy Collins," St. Petersburg *Times*, The Floridian Magazine, March 15, 1970.

12. McLendon, "The LeRoy Collins Years," St. Petersburg *Times*, The Floridian Magazine, July 7, 1974.

13. Miami *Herald*, April 23, 1968, cited in Espey, "Anatomy of Defeat," p. 113. See also pp. 73–75, 92, 106, 111–16, 122–26, 134, 142, 145–46.

14. Richard Pettigrew, a state legislator, took over the campaign in July. Espey, "Anatomy of Defeat," pp. 69–70, 116, 118.

15. Gurney spent $714,422 on the campaign, compared to Collins's expenditure of $533,222. Ibid., pp. 129–31, 140; Dyckman, "LeRoy Collins," St. Petersburg *Times*, The Floridian Magazine, March 15, 1970.

16. Espey, "Anatomy of Defeat," pp. 131, 147; Dyckman, "LeRoy Collins," St. Petersburg *Times*, The Floridian Magazine, March 15, 1970.

17. Espey, "Anatomy of Defeat," pp. 131, 147.

18. Ibid., pp. 126–28; Cawthon interview.

19. Gurney received 1,131,499 votes and Collins 892,637. Collins won a majority in Alachua, Dade, Hillsborough, and Monroe counties. He lost Leon County by a vote of 16,537 to 15,187. Tom Adams, Secretary of State, comp., *Tabulation of Official Votes Cast in the General Election, November 5, 1968*, [p. iii].

20. Don Pride, "Collins' Defeat Is Blow to Moderates," St. Petersburg *Times*, November 6, 1968.

21. Dyckman, "LeRoy Collins," St. Petersburg *Times*, The Floridian Magazine, March 15, 1970; Tom Fiedler, "Ahead of His Time," Tallahassee *Democrat*, October 9, 1977.

22. *1980 Census of Population and Housing: Advance Reports, Florida* (Washington: U.S. Department of Commerce, Bureau of the Census, 1981), p. 8.

23. Colburn and Scher, *Florida's Gubernatorial Politics*, pp. 85, 228–30.

24. Mary J. Granger, personal secretary to Governor Collins, to Thomas R. Wagy, June 18, 1980.

25. Moor interview.

26. Dyckman, "LeRoy Collins," St. Petersburg *Times*, The Floridian Magazine, March 15, 1970.

27. Governor Collins interview, July 22, 1982.

28. Dyckman, "LeRoy Collins," St. Petersburg *Times*, The Floridian Magazine, March 15, 1970.

29. Lustig, "He's Tallahassee's Own Statesman," Tallahassee *Democrat,* September 10, 1967.

30. Governor Collins interview, September 17, 1979.

31. Moor interview; McLendon, "The LeRoy Collins Years," St. Petersburg *Times*, The Floridian Magazine, July 7, 1974; Espey, "Anatomy of Defeat," p. 150; Governor Collins interview, May 22, 1975.

32. McLendon, "The LeRoy Collins Years," St. Petersburg *Times*, The Floridian Magazine, July 7, 1974; Dorothy Clifford, "Former Governor Collins is 'Outstanding' Mystery Santa," Tallahassee *Democrat,* December 8, 1976.

33. Tallahassee *Democrat,* December 11, 1979, February 13, 1980.

34. Fiedler, "Ahead of His Time," Tallahassee *Democrat,* October 9, 1977; Tallahassee *Democrat,* March 19, 1979.

35. Wayne Ezell, in Tallahassee *Democrat,* December 8, 1977.

36. Ibid.; Fiedler, "Ahead of His Time," Tallahassee *Democrat,* October 9, 1977.

37. *Governor News Conference,* November 10, 1960, p. 11.

38. Ibid., August 11, 1960, p. 13.

39. Dyckman, "LeRoy Collins," St. Petersburg *Times*, The Floridian Magazine, March 15, 1970.

40. Governor Collins interview, April 10, 1976.

41. William L. Rivers, "The Fine Art of Moderation," *Nation* 175 (December 21, 1957), p. 471, cited in Jacobstein, *Segregation Factor,* p. 76.

42. Jacobstein, *Segregation Factor,* p. 77. See also Colburn and Scher, "Race Relations," p. 168; and Black, *Southern Governors,* p. 93.

43. Morris interview, July 13, 1977.

44. Richard N. Current, *The Lincoln Nobody Knows* (New York: McGraw-Hill, 1958), p. 235.

Bibliography

Primary Sources

Documents

Adams, Tom, Secretary of State, comp. *Tabulation of Official Vote, Florida Primary Election, Democratic and Republican, May 7, 1968 and May 28, 1968.*

———. Secretary of State, comp. *Tabulation of Official Votes Cast in the General Election, November 5, 1968.*

Congressional Quarterly Almanac. 89th Cong., 1st Session. Washington: Congressional Quarterly Service, 1965.

Florida Governor News Conference, 1958, 1959, 1960.

Florida Governor Remarks, 1960.

Journal of the House of Representatives, State of Florida. Twenty-fifth Regular Session, 1935; Twenty-sixth Regular Session, 1937; Twenty-seventh Regular Session, 1939; Thirty-fifth Regular Session, 1955; Extraordinary Session on Reapportionment, 1955; Special Session, 1956; Thirty-sixth Regular Session, 1957; Thirty-seventh Regular Session, 1959.

Journal of the Senate, State of Florida. Twenty-eighth Regular Session, 1941; Twenty-ninth Regular Session, 1943; Thirty-first Regular Session, 1947; Thirty-second Regular Session, 1949; Thirty-third Regular Session, 1951; Thirty-fourth Regular Session, 1953.

1980 Census of Population and Housing: Advance Reports, Florida. Washington: U.S. Department of Commerce, Bureau of the Census, 1981.

Official Report of the Proceedings of the Democratic National Convention and Committee. Washington: National Document Publishers, 1964.

Interviews

Governor Millard Caldwell, July 13, 1977.

Rainey Cawthon, October 14, 1975.

Governor LeRoy Collins, May 22, 1975; November 19, 1975; April 10,

1976; November 10, 1977; September 17, 1979; September 27, 1979; July 22, 1982.
Marvin H. Collins, Jr., October 8, 1975; November 4, 1975.
Mary Call Collins, November 6, 1975.
Jessie Conrad, October 10, 1975.
John Y. Humphress, November 5, 1975.
Malcolm B. Johnson, October 15, 1975; February 25, 1976.
Frank Moor, October 8, 1975.
Allen Morris, July 13, 1977; September 24, 1979.
Hazel Richards, October 6, 1975.
Alice Collins Wadsworth, July 22, 1982.

Manuscripts

Collins family papers. In the possession of Alice Collins Wadsworth, Tallahassee.
Correspondence of Governor LeRoy Collins. Florida State Archives, Tallahassee.
LeRoy Collins Papers. University of South Florida, Tampa.

Newspapers

Included in the Collins Papers are bound collections of newspaper clippings organized chronologically. Clippings also appear randomly in file folders throughout the collection. Newspaper citations from the Collins Papers are not included in the following list of sources.

Atlanta *Constitution,* 1957, 1960.
Birmingham *News,* 1965.
Bradenton *Herald,* 1956, 1957, 1960.
Charleston, South Carolina, *News and Courier,* 1957, 1960.
Chicago *Tribune,* 1960.
Christian Science Monitor, 1960.
Daytona Beach *Evening News,* 1954, 1957, 1960.
Daytona Beach *Morning Journal,* 1953, 1957, 1960, 1964.
Fort Walton Beach *Playground News,* 1957.
Jacksonville *Florida Times-Union,* 1941, 1943, 1947, 1949, 1951, 1953, 1954, 1956, 1957, 1959, 1960.
Lakeland *Ledger,* 1957, 1960.
Leesburg *Commercial-Ledger,* 1952.

Miami *Daily News*, 1957, 1960.
Miami *Herald*, 1953–60, 1964, 1965.
Montgomery *Advertiser*, 1965.
New York *Times*, 1957, 1960, 1965.
Ocala *Star Banner*, 1953, 1957, 1960.
Orlando *Morning Sentinel*, 1951, 1952.
Orlando *Sentinel*, 1953, 1957, 1960.
Orlando *Sentinel Star*, 1975.
Palatka *Daily News*, 1957.
Pensacola *Journal*, 1957, 1965.
Pensacola *News*, 1957.
St. Augustine *Evening Record*, 1957.
St. Louis *Post-Dispatch*, 1957, 1960.
St. Petersburg *Times*, 1953–60, 1964, 1965, 1968, 1970, 1974, 1976, 1978.
Sarasota *Herald Tribune*, 1957, 1960.
Selma *Times-Journal*, 1965.
Tallahassee *Daily Democrat*, 1932, 1934–37, 1940, 1950.
Tallahassee *Democrat*, 1953–60, 1965–67, 1976, 1977, 1979, 1980.
Tallahassee *Weekly True Democrat*, 1909.
Tampa *Daily Times*, 1954, 1955, 1957.
Tampa *Morning Tribune*, 1953, 1954, 1956, 1957.
Tampa *Times*, 1960.
Tampa *Tribune*, 1957–60, 1964, 1968.

Periodicals

Look, 1958, 1960.
New Republic, 1955, 1965.
Newsweek, 1957, 1960.
Saturday Review, 1965.
Time, 1955–57, 1960, 1965.

Secondary Sources

Articles

Abbey, Kathryn T. "Florida versus the Principles of Populism." *Journal of Southern History* 4 (1938), pp. 462–75.
Christie, Terry L. "The Collins-Johns Election, 1954: A Turning Point." *Apalachee* 6 (1967), pp. 5–19.

Colburn, David R., and Scher, Richard K. "Florida Gubernatorial Politics: The Fuller Warren Years." *Florida Historical Quarterly* 53 (April 1975), pp. 389–408.

——. "Race Relations and Florida Gubernatorial Politics Since the *Brown* Decision." *Florida Historical Quarterly* 55 (October 1976), pp. 153–69.

Collier, Bert. "Segregation in Politics." *Current History* 31 (October 1956), pp. 229–33.

Dauer, Manning J., and Kelsay, Robert G. "Unrepresentative States." *National Municipal Review* 46 (December 1955), pp. 571–75.

Doherty, Herbert J., Jr. "Florida and the Presidential Election of 1928." *Florida Historical Quarterly* 26 (October 1947), pp. 174–86.

Friedman, Howard Jay. "1959 Legislative Action Dealing with Education." *Florida School Bulletin* 22 (September 1959), pp. 8–15.

——. "Summary of 1955 Legislative Action Dealing with Education." *Florida School Bulletin* 18 (September 1955), pp. 8–11.

Lomax, Louis E. "The Negro Revolt Against 'The Negro Leaders.'" *Harper's Magazine* 220 (June 1960), pp. 41–48.

McDonnell, Victoria H. "Rise of the 'Businessman's Politician': The 1924 Florida Gubernatorial Race." *Florida Historical Quarterly* 52 (July 1973), pp. 39–50.

Shofner, Jerrell H. "Custom, Law, and History: The Enduring Influence of Florida's 'Black Code.'" *Florida Historical Quarterly* 55 (January 1977), pp. 277–98.

Wagy, Thomas R. "Governor LeRoy Collins of Florida and the Little Rock Crisis of 1957." *Arkansas Historical Quarterly* 38 (Summer 1979), pp. 99–115.

——. "Governor LeRoy Collins of Florida and the Selma Crisis of 1965." *Florida Historical Quarterly* 57 (April 1979), pp. 403–20.

——. "A Tallahassee Lad: The Early Years of Governor LeRoy Collins of Florida." *Apalachee* 8 (1978), pp. 82–94.

Books

Adams, Sherman. *Firsthand Report: The Story of the Eisenhower Administration.* New York: Harper and Brothers, 1961.

Ayers, Brandt, and Naylor, Thomas H., eds. *You Can't Eat Magnolias.* New York: McGraw-Hill, 1972.

Bain, Richard C., and Parris, Judith H. *Convention Decisions and Voting Records,* 2nd ed. Washington: Brookings Institution, 1973.

Bartley, Numan V. *The Rise of Massive Resistance*. Baton Rouge: Louisiana State University Press, 1969.

Bass, Jack, and DeVries, Walter. *The Transformation of Southern Politics: Social Change and Political Consequence since 1945*. New York: New American Library, 1977.

Berman, Daniel M. *It Is So Ordered: The Supreme Court Rules on School Segregation*. New York: W. W. Norton, 1966.

Black, Earl. *Southern Governors and Civil Rights: Racial Segregation as a Campaign Issue in the Second Reconstruction*. Cambridge, Massachusetts: Harvard University Press, 1976.

Branyan, Robert L., and Larsen, Lawrence H., eds. *The Eisenhower Administration, 1953–1961: A Documentary History*, 2 vols. New York: Random House, 1971.

Cash, Wilbur J. *The Mind of the South*. Garden City, New York: Doubleday and Company, 1956.

Colburn, David R., and Scher, Richard K. *Florida's Gubernatorial Politics in the Twentieth Century*. Tallahassee: University Presses of Florida, 1980.

Collins, LeRoy. *Forerunners Courageous: Stories of Frontier Florida*. Tallahassee: Colcade Publishers, 1971.

Current, Richard N. *The Lincoln Nobody Knows*. New York: McGraw-Hill, 1958.

David, Paul T.; Goldman, Ralph M.; and Bain, Richard C. *The Politics of National Party Conventions*. Washington: Brookings Institution, 1960.

Davis, Kenneth S. *The Politics of Honor: A Biography of Adlai E. Stevenson*. New York: C. P. Putnam's Sons, 1967.

Dunn, Hampton. *Yesterday's Tallahassee*. Miami: E. A. Seeman, 1974.

Eisenhower, Dwight D. *The White House Years: Waging Peace, 1956–1961*. Garden City, New York: Doubleday and Company, 1965.

Fager, Charles E. *Selma, 1965*. New York: Scribner, 1974.

Flynt, Wayne. *Cracker Messiah: Governor Sidney J. Catts of Florida*. Baton Rouge: Louisiana State University Press, 1977.

———. *Duncan Upshaw Fletcher: Dixie's Reluctant Progressive*. Tallahassee: Florida State University Press, 1971.

Garrow, David J. *Protest at Selma: Martin Luther King, Jr., and the Voting Rights Act of 1965*. New Haven, Connecticut: Yale University Press, 1978.

Gerster, Patrick, and Cords, Nicholas, eds. *Myth and Southern History*. Chicago: Rand McNally, 1974.

Groene, Bertram H. *Ante-Bellum Tallahassee*. Tallahassee: Florida Heritage Foundation, 1971.

Hartsfield, Annie Mary, and Roady, Elston E. *Florida Votes, 1920–1962: Selected Election Statistics*. Tallahassee: Institute of Governmental Research, Florida State University, 1963.

Havard, William C., and Beth, Loren P. *The Politics of Mis-Representation: Rural-Urban Conflict in the Florida Legislature*. Baton Rouge: Louisiana State University Press, 1962.

Herbers, John. *The Lost Priority: What Happened to the Civil Rights Movement in America?* New York: Funk and Wagnalls, 1970.

Hughes, Emmet John. *The Ordeal of Power: A Political Memoir of the Eisenhower Years*. New York: Atheneum, 1963.

Jacobstein, Helen L. *The Segregation Factor in the Florida Democratic Gubernatorial Primary of 1956*. Gainesville: University of Florida Social Sciences Series, no. 47, 1972.

Johnson, Lyndon B. *The Vantage Point: Perspectives of the Presidency, 1963–1968*. New York: Popular Library, 1971.

Key, V. O., Jr. *Southern Politics in State and Nation*. New York: Alfred A. Knopf, 1950.

Leuchtenburg, William E. *A Troubled Feast: American Society Since 1945*. Boston: Little, Brown, 1973.

Lewis, David L. *King: A Critical Biography*. New York: Praeger Publishers, 1970.

Lion's Tale, The. Tallahassee: Senior Class of Leon High School, 1927.

Martin, John Bartlow. *Adlai Stevenson and the World: The Life of Adlai E. Stevenson*. Garden City, New York: Doubleday and Company, 1977.

Matthews, Donald R., and Prothro, James W. *Negroes and the New South Politics*. New York: Harcourt, Brace, and World, 1966.

Morris, Allen, ed., *Florida Across the Threshold: The Administration of Governor LeRoy Collins, January 4, 1955–January 3, 1961*. Tallahassee, 1961.

———, comp. *The Florida Handbook, 1959–1960*. Tallahassee: Peninsular Publishing Company, 1959.

———, comp. *The Florida Handbook, 1971–1972*. Tallahassee: Peninsular Publishing Company, 1972.

———, comp. *The Florida Handbook, 1975–1976*. Tallahassee: Peninsular Publishing Company, 1975.

Muse, Benjamin. *Ten Years of Prelude: The Story of Integration since the Supreme Court's 1954 Decision*. New York: Viking Press, 1964.

Oates, Stephen B. *Let the Trumpet Sound: The Life of Martin Luther King, Jr*. New York: Harper and Row, 1982.

Paisley, Clifton. *From Cotton to Quail: An Agricultural Chronicle of*

Leon County, Florida, 1860–1967. Gainesville: University of Florida Press, 1968.

Pitts, James E. *Tallahassee Area Statistical Abstract*. Tallahassee: Tallahassee Area Chamber of Commerce, 1971.

Proctor, Samuel. *Napoleon Bonaparte Broward: Florida's Fighting Democrat*. Gainesville: University of Florida Press, 1950.

Roland, Charles P. *The Improbable Era: The South since World War II*. Lexington: University Press of Kentucky, 1975.

Roseboom, Eugene Holloway. *A History of Presidential Elections*. New York: Macmillan, 1967.

Schlesinger, Arthur M., Jr. *Robert Kennedy and His Times*. Boston: Houghton Mifflin, 1978.

Sherrill, Robert. *Gothic Politics in the Deep South: Stars of the New Confederacy*. New York: Grossman, 1968.

Smith, Charles U., and Killian, Lewis M. *The Tallahassee Bus Protest*. New York: Anti-Defamation League of B'nai B'rith, 1958.

Sorensen, Theodore C. *Kennedy*. New York: Harper and Row, 1965.

Thomson, Charles A. H., and Shattuck, Frances M. *The 1956 Presidential Campaign*. Washington: Brookings Institution, 1960.

Tindall, George Brown. *The Disruption of the Solid South*. Athens: University of Georgia Press, 1972.

———. *The Emergence of the New South, 1913–1945*. Baton Rouge: Louisiana State University Press and the Littlefield Fund for Southern History of the University of Texas, 1967.

Tschirgi, Harvey D. *The Florida Merit System: An Investigation of Performance Evaluation in Agencies of the Florida Merit System*. Tallahassee: Florida State University Studies, no. 47, 1966.

Twelve Southerners. *I'll Take My Stand: The South and the Agrarian Tradition*. New York: Harper and Brothers, 1930.

White, Theodore H. *The Making of the President, 1960*. New York: Atheneum House, 1961.

Wilhoit, Francis M. *The Politics of Massive Resistance*. New York: George Braziller, 1973.

Unpublished Materials

Chapman, Julia Sullivan. "A Southern Moderate Advocates Compliance: A Study of LeRoy Collins as Director of the Community Relations Service." M.A. thesis, University of South Florida, 1974.

Espey, Ruth F. "The Anatomy of Defeat: The 1968 United States

Senatorial Campaign of LeRoy Collins." M.A. thesis, University of South Florida, 1974.

Fanning, Sandra L. "A Study of Changes in Racial Attitudes as Revealed in Selected Speeches of LeRoy Collins, 1955–1965." M.A. thesis, University of South Florida, 1968.

Lucoff, Manny. "LeRoy Collins and the NAB: Experiment in the Public Interest." Ph.D. dissertation, University of Iowa, 1971.

Rogers, William Warren. "History of Greenwood Plantation." Manuscript in the author's possession.

Tomberlin, Joseph Aaron. "The Negro and Florida's System of Education: The Aftermath of the *Brown* Case." Ph.D. dissertation, Florida State University, 1967.

White, Robert M. "The Tallahassee Sit-Ins and CORE: A Nonviolent Revolutionary Submovement." Ph.D. dissertation, Florida State University, 1964.

Index

ABOUT THE AUTHOR

Thomas R. Wagy teaches history at East Texas State University at
Texarkana. He received his bachelor of arts degree from Southern
Illinois University and his master's degree and doctorate from
Florida State University. This is his first book.

DATE DUE
